Da Capo Press Music Reprint Series

GENERAL EDITOR

FREDERICK FREEDMAN

VASSAR COLLEGE

CRITICAL

AND

HISTORICAL ESSAYS

EDWARD MACDOWELL

CRITICAL
AND
HISTORICAL ESSAYS

BY
EDWARD MACDOWELL

EDITED BY
W. J. BALTZELL

New Introduction by IRVING LOWENS
Music Critic, *Washington Evening Star*

DA CAPO PRESS • NEW YORK • 1969

A Da Capo Press Reprint Edition

This Da Capo Press edition of Edward MacDowell's *Critical and Historical Essays* is an unabridged republication of the first edition published in Boston in 1912 by Arthur P. Schmidt. It is reprinted by special arrangement with Summy-Birchard Company, Evanston, Illinois.

Library of Congress Catalog Card Number 69-11289

INTRODUCTION

On Monday, October 5, 1896, "the greatest musical genius America has produced"[1] took up his duties as head (and sole member) of the Columbia University Department of Music, newly established that year under the Faculty of Philosophy. The significance of this event was explained in an article by President Seth Low which appeared that day in the New York *Evening Post*:

> By the gift to the university of the endowment known as The Robert Center Fund for instruction in music, another notable educational advance has been made possible. This fund, consisting of the entire estate of the late Robert Center, was presented to the university by his mother, Mrs. E. Mary Ludlow, upon condition that "the net income shall be applied either to the payment of the salary of a professor of music, or to fellowships, or scholarships in music, or be used in any one or more of these, or such ways as shall, in the judgment of the trustees, tend most effectually to elevate the standard of musical instruction in the United States, and to afford the most favorable opportunity for acquiring instruction of the highest order." Upon the receipt of this gift, the trustees immediately established a professorship in music. The gift of this fund has led to much discussion in the public press and elsewhere as to the proper place of music in a university. It is perhaps fair to say that the problem must be solved by experiment rather than by theory; especially because what can be done at a university to improve instruction in music depends to so great an extent upon the situation and surroundings of the university. Mrs. Ludlow has given to Columbia a free hand, and it is reasonable, therefore, to expect, eventually, the best results. Some are of the opinion that a university can do nothing more for music than to give instruction to its students about music as one element in a liberal education. This, no doubt, is the limit of the function of a college in its relation to music. But Columbia, being in a technical sense both a college and a university, I conceive, may hold the same relation to music that it does, for example, to history. In our college history is taught as one

INTRODUCTION

element in a liberal education. In our university, as distinguished from the college, history is taught in such a way as to train historians. Similarly, in the college, and for college students, Columbia ought to provide instruction about music as part of a liberal education. In the university, however, I am of the opinion that Columbia ought to teach the science of music in such a way as to train composers. If it be objected that this is the business of a conservatory rather than a university, it remains to be said that music, though an art, has its scientific basis on the side of composition, which brings it as normally within the scope of the university as, for instance, its sister art of architecture.... The musician needs practical instruction in the use of musical instruments which he also must obtain, for the time being at any rate, outside the university; but it is not impossible to imagine in the case of Columbia that the time will come when the scientific instruction in the university on the theory and history of music shall be supplemented, as occasion may arise, by practical instruction either within or without the university, as may prove most advantageous. In the meanwhile, as the first and most essential step towards a wise solution of the various problems involved, the trustees have selected as the first incumbent of the musical chair the American musician who, by common consent, is unsurpassed both in the thoroughness of his musical training and as a composer of music, Mr. Edward Alexander MacDowell. It ought to be a matter of congratulation to New York that Mr. MacDowell is a native of this city. Apart from his natural gifts, he has had a most thorough musical education abroad. He is, therefore, well equipped for the scientific instruction in music that it is distinctly the aim of Columbia to give; and, for the same reason, he is competent to guide our development with reference to the collegiate side of musical instruction, that is to say, the teaching about music as one element in a liberal education. I hope that the people of New York who are interested in music will cooperate with Columbia in its efforts thus to place musical instruction in this country upon the highest possible plane....

Although no announcement by Columbia's Department of Music seems to have been issued for the 1896–97 school year, it is not necessary merely to assume that Low's ideas about music education and those of the thirty-four-year-old MacDowell were similar. The two men had been in touch with each other for some time before MacDowell's appointment was made public on May 4, 1896, and their correspondence demonstrates the closeness of their ideas. Perhaps the most polished expression of MacDowell's philosophy may be found in a brief article entitled "Music at Columbia" which was published in the December, 1896, issue of the *Columbia University Bulletin*. [2] This important essay, which has been overlooked by music historians for some reason, is quoted in its entirety below:

> In formulating the courses of music at Columbia, the great difficulty seemed to be to decide between theory and practice; an ideal being one thing, and attainment quite another. The generally accepted idea of a university's sphere of work is that it should represent the highest attainable instruction, leaving to minor institutions the matter of preparatory training. To apply this theory to music is possible only to a limited extent, owing to the fact that there is little or no substratum of musical culture for what should be university work to build upon. Until the minor institutions include some preparatory musical training in their curricula, university work in the art must be something of a compromise, if it is to appeal to more than a very few.

> Music occupies a peculiar position in our culture. Without having been generally recognized as an element of school or university training, it has succeeded in slipping into our lives without official recognition. The result is that it is studied seriously only by specialists. In other words, our doctors, lawyers, literary, and scientific men generally, know but little of the art except that which comes to them through the medium of social intercourse. The most painful ignorance is often displayed by novelists and poets when they write of music, and but few learned men, even among the very greatest, have grasped the fact that in ignoring music they have deprived themselves of one of the most precious boons granted mankind. A man of great attainments once remarked to a friend of mine that he "understood music was pleasing to women and children, but to him it was not only a bore, but positively offensive." Now, it is shameful to our civilization that a university-bred man could display such ignorance. With painting, and perhaps sculpture, it is somewhat better, and a remark such as the above would hardly be ventured upon with a reference to these arts; still, before a picture is bought nowadays an expert is generally consulted to determine its artistic value. This state of things is all the more humiliating, inasmuch as it is entirely unnecessary.

In university work proper instrumental and vocal instruction seems out of place as tending toward specialism. The
proper place for this is a school of musical technology.
If such a school could be under the control of a university,
and have the influence of a university behind it, thus re-
moving it from all business or personal considerations, it
would be a powerful factor in the advancement of art in
America; in fact, it would give art an advantage not
enjoyed elsewhere in the world. A university has a wider
and more generally cultured public to draw from than any
conservatory can have, the latter attracting, as it does,
only specialists. Beside those who would include music as
an element of liberal culture, there are surely many among
university students who would gladly specialize in music
if the calling were presented to them and their advisers
as one of dignity, and commanding serious and universal
consideration. The same student now has to choose between
the many outside conservatories if he wishes to specialize
in music. This immediately takes him out of the pale of
university work, thus prejudicing the minds of parents and
guardians, who probably already have strong opinions on
the subject of a calling that to them seems vague in everything, except general good-for-nothingism. Such opinions
are very excusable, considering the fact that music has
never been recognized in our schools as an indispensable
element of liberal culture.

In my opinion, our universities should establish schools of
technology for the arts as well as for the sciences: the
university work proper to consist mainly of original work
in composition, of consideration of the higher art principles,
history, and of the study of literature and the sister arts.
In my opinion, music, painting, history, and literature,
including languages, should be elements of liberal culture,
elements that are also indispensable to the specialist in art.
Architecture was once dubbed "frozen music;" poetry has
melody; music has color; and all the arts possess in common what is vaguely called "feeling." This certainly sounds
trite enough; still, I am firmly convinced that one art can
learn more from another in a year than in a decade of
delving into hidden causes and abstruse technic that belong
in the domain of science. No music lover can appreciate or
understand music to its full without a corresponding appreciation of the other arts. To the specialist an additional
scientific training is indispensable and a school of technology is its proper sphere.

This is an ideal; attainment being, as I have said, a very
different matter. At present, in Courses I and II the gen-

eralization of music will be attempted. In them I shall endeavor to explain, as far as is possible, its principles, history, and aesthetic potence, thus giving the student, for the most part, a non-technical survey of the subject. As a matter of fact, university work should commence (with certain reservations) at Course II, but until the minor institutions add the study of music to their regular curricula our courses must include much that is comparatively elementary. This also holds good in regard to Course III, which treats of simple harmony. As an auxiliary help to Course I, I trust the broadening influence of the independent series of lectures, forming Course VI, will be of great benefit.

Courses III, IV, and V, which include harmony, counterpoint, and composition, are designed for the specialist in music. Course V is specially directed to those who compose already. The work, aside from the technic of orchestration and symphonic forms, will consist mainly of original composition, aided by criticism and discussion from both technical and aesthetic standpoints. Courses I, III, and IV, I hope, may be the germ from which a school of technology may spring. As for a union of the arts in university work, it seems to need time before such a radical departure from all precedent were feasible. In the meanwhile, however, New York, with its wonderful art treasures, offers a substitute that it is difficult to overestimate. Our American nature is averse to pessimism, and undaunted hope, combined with a wonderful capacity for hard work, have made us what we are. It seems to fall to us by right of birth, as the youngest nation, to aspire to the highest and to break new roads. That this national characteristic must extend into our music is to me a for[e]gone conclusion, and I trust the time is not far off when my opinion will be verified.

The *Bulletin* article happened to catch the eye of A.E. Keet, managing editor of *The Forum,* and he was so impressed with it that on January 20, 1897, he wrote to MacDowell and solicited a four thousand or five thousand word piece on "Music as an Element of Liberal Culture" for the April issue, giving February 25 as the deadline. MacDowell apparently accepted the invitation, since Keet wrote to him again on March 9, brushing aside the excuse that illness had prevented him from preparing the article. "It will be just as timely in the May *Forum,*" said Keet. "If, however, this [a March 27 deadline] should be impossible, pray take your own time and send it to me when you are able. I would just like to know a week or so in advance of sending the article so that I may be able to make provision for it." [3] If MacDowell actually wrote the article, it does not appear to have survived in manuscript or typescript; certainly, it never was published in the pages of *The Forum*. By the spring of 1897, MacDowell, who was teaching all five courses offered during the Department's first year (Course VI was never offered by Columbia as MacDowell described it in the *Bulletin*), in addition to composing, teaching piano privately, and carrying on a career as a piano virtuoso, was a very, very busy young man.

MacDowell did write the announcement for the 1897–98 school year, apparently the first to be issued by the Department of Music, and in the context of his *Critical and Historical Essays*, certain portions of it turn out to be very interesting, for reasons which will quickly become clear. Especially pertinent were his descriptions of Courses I and II:

> Course I—General Musical Course. Lectures and Private Reading, with illustrations. Two hours weekly. Professor MacDowell.
> Saturdays, 9.30 to 10.30. Wednesdays, 1.30 to 2.30.
> This course, while outlining the purely technical side of music, aims at giving a general idea of music from its historical and aesthetic side. Courses I and II give together a complete survey of the subject.
> Course I treats of the beginnings of music, the Greek modes and their evolution, systems of notation, the Troubadours and Minnesingers, counterpoint and fugue, beginnings of opera, the clavecinists, beginnings of programme music, harmony, beginnings of the modern orchestra, evolution of forms, the symphony and opera up to Beethoven. Analysis.

> Course II—General Music Course.
> Wednesdays, at 2.30. Saturdays, at 10.30.
> Course II treats of the development of forms, the song, romanticism, instrumental development and the composers for piano-forte, revolutionary influences, the virtuoso, modern orchestration and symphonic forms, the music drama, impressionism versus absolute music, and color versus form, the relationship of music to the other arts, musical criticism.

According to the 1897–98 announcement, Courses I and II were "open to properly qualified Seniors in Columbia College as electives and also to all properly qualified university students; and, with the consent of the Dean of the College, to all properly qualified students of the College." Furthermore, they were "open to the public, special students and auditors being admitted under the usual regulations provided they are able to demonstrate to the Professor of Music that they are competent to profit by the instruction. . . . Degrees are not conferred upon special students, and additional courses of study are not required of them. Auditors are not examined upon their work, neither are they counted as students. . . . Auditors may be admitted to Courses I and II without examination."

MacDowell taught Columbia's music courses I and II for seven of the eight academic years during which he served as the department head—he was on sabbatical leave for 1902–03, and during his absence the courses were not given, even though he had an assistant, Leonard B. McWhood, by that time—and the perceptive reader will have already gathered that the *Critical and Historical Essays*, published posthumously in 1912 by Arthur P. Schmidt as edited by W. J. Baltzell, were, in fact, MacDowell's lectures (or some of them) for those courses. To call these lectures "essays" may seem a bit grand. "I think my husband would have felt that just such a title implies a more finished product than one finds," Marian MacDowell wrote about the *Critical and Historical Essays* some years after their appearance. "Mr. MacDowell had an extraordinary memory, and seldom had more than mere notes in delivering his lectures. Occasionally in preparing the lectures, without quite realizing it, he dictated far more than he had intended, not always using this material in his class room. These Essays represent the result of what he dictated to me as he walked up and down his music room trying to crystallize his ideas; they were printed unedited." [4] Just what Mrs. MacDowell meant by "unedited" will be discussed a bit later.

What kind of lecturer was MacDowell? According to his wife (writing many years afterward), "when he started at Columbia he almost immediately made a surprising success of what he was doing. Personality had something to do with this; also his ability as a pianist where he could illustrate clearly and by examples show what he was trying to teach. But it was more than that. It was his clearly receptive mind which grasped almost immediately whatever he read or felt. His classrooms were crowded in those very early years." [5] But by Mrs. MacDowell's own admission, her ideas were not based on first-hand observation. "I myself never heard him lecture as I had a strong conviction that wives might occasionally be seen but rarely known, so never once did I go to Columbia," she candidly confessed. "One of the most illuminating ways in which I have been able to judge of his power as a teacher came from articles written by two men who were his students: one was John Erskine, who gave many pages to MacDowell in his autobiography, and the other was Upton Sinclair." [6]

MacDowell became Professor of Music at Columbia at the same time that John Erskine entered the college as a freshman resolved to pursue a career in music, and he had a profound influence on the youngster. "Not only my early months at Columbia College, but all my years, were colored by knowing MacDowell," he wrote half a century later. "Had I begun to study English literature in the usual approach, I should have tried to admire, simply because my teachers and even more famous critics told me to do so, a number of authors who were not really first rate. But after a few hours in MacDowell's classroom I saw that literature is an art, like music, and every art should be studied in its master-pieces, from the standpoint of an apprentice who hopes some day to practice what he has learned, not simply to collect opinions about it." [7]

After an amusing interview, MacDowell gave Erskine permission to enroll for Course III (general theory, dictation, harmony, modulation, imitation, analysis, and the commencement of composition in the smaller forms) and Course IV (strict and free counterpoint, canon, choral figuration, fugue, analysis, and the commencement of composition in the larger forms). On Wednesday, October 7, 1896, at 3:30 P.M.—exactly two days after his seventeenth birthday—Erskine attended his first class with Mac-Dowell. He wrote:

> MacDowell was one of the most stimulating geniuses I ever met. But in the sense here defined he was a good teacher only for those who were already well grounded. I had the impression always that his point of departure was not the precise frontier of his students' knowledge or ignorance,

but some musical problem which at the moment engaged his own attention. He would begin the hour standing up, often leaning comfortably against the piano, but in a moment, finding words inadequate, he would sit down and begin to play. Apparently because our inactivity bothered him, he'd ask one of us to write a theme on a blackboard and to do something or other with it, but it wasn't always clear what the theme and its development would illustrate, and as soon as we began asking for information about it, our questions were likely to suggest new directions of thought, which however brilliant left us somewhat breathless.[8]

Erskine does not appear to have registered for either Course I or Course II, and this may help to explain some of the discrepancies between his account of college days with MacDowell (his viewpoint being that of a professional musician) and that of Upton Sinclair, who registered in 1897 (shortly after his graduation from the College of the City of New York) "as a special student, with the intention of acquiring all the culture there was in sight." [9] Sinclair, who was nineteen at the time, wrote in 1926:

There were two courses in general music, one elementary and the other advanced; ... I took them both in successive years, so during those two years I spent one or two hours each week in the presence of the composer. There were, I think, not more than a dozen students in the class. I remember times when there were only six or eight present — which gives you an idea of how much Columbia University valued genius in those days.

Edward MacDowell was the first man of genius I had ever met. I was going in for that business myself, or thought I was, so I lost nothing about him; I watched his appearance, his mannerisms, his every gesture. I listened to every word he said and thought it over and pondered it.

He differed from most musicians whom I have since met in being a man of wide general culture. He had read good literature and talked wisely about books. I got the impression that he was something of a rebel in his political thinking, but I cannot recall a single specific saying upon this subject. But he was certainly a friend of every freedom, and of every beautiful and generous impulse. He hated pretense and formalism, and all things which repress the free creative spirit.

I would not say that Edward MacDowell was a successful

teacher after the university pattern. He was lacking in that
subtle pedagogical technique which can now be acquired
through correspondence courses. I think he was quite new
at the game, and didn't know quite how to set about it.
We began obediently with primitive music and ancient
music, and we got down to Palestrina, and it was all
entirely dull and respectable. Then MacDowell would find
himself trying to tell us about music, and what it meant,
and he would grope around for words, and find very
jumbled and inadequate ones, and conclude with a gesture
of despair. I had developed a habit of staying after the
class, and talking with him, and one day I said, "You are
not a man of words. Why do you try to lecture in words?
You ought to play us the music and talk about it before
and afterward."

Being a really great man, he was willing to take advice,
even from a boy. He began hesitatingly to try it, and in a
very short time his class in general musical culture was
spending its time listening to MacDowell play some music,
and then asking him questions about it.[10]

But perhaps the most graphic description of MacDowell as
lecturer was written by a student Mrs. MacDowell did not mention
—Jo Shipley Watson. Miss Watson appears to have attended Mac-
Dowell's lectures after the turn of the century, and her recollections of Course I were published in September, 1907, some five
months before MacDowell's death:

The first lectures, treating of the archaic beginnings of
music, might have easily fallen into a business-like recital
of dates, but Professor MacDowell never sank into the
passionless routine of lecture giving. His were not the
pedantic discourses students link most often to university
chairs. They were beautifully illuminated talks, delivered
with so much freedom and such a rush of enthusiasm that
one felt the hour never held all that wanted to be said, and
in its longing to get out, the abundant knowledge kept
spilling over into the to-morrows. His ideas were not tied
up in a manuscript, nor doled out from notes. They came
untrammeled from a wonderfully versatile mind, and they
were illustrated with countless musical quotations and in-
terlined with a wealth of literary and historical references.
There was no regular textbook; some students carried a
Rockstro or a Hunt, but the majority depended upon the
references made during the lectures.

These were numerous, and gave a broad view of this speculative period in musical history. In connection with Egyptian music, we were asked to read Wilkinson, Petri, and Fappius, also Miss Edwards' *Thousand Miles up the Nile*, Ambros on Chinese music, LeVega on Mexican music, Monro's book on Greek music, and Westphal and Bellamore upon the same subject; also Plato for the state of music in Pythagoras' time. In Homer we were asked to read of the first finding of the lyre. Gibbon's *Rome* and *The Arabian Nights* were referred to as giving an idea of the magnificence and splendor of court life when Arabia was the centre of civilization. We read Spencer on aroused emotion, Blaserna and Helmholtz on vibration and sound, Hagen's great work on Minnesinging [*sic*], and looked in the encyclopedias, Chambers' and Britannica, under Troubadours and Poetry. There were many quotations from the poets, oftenest from Tennyson.

Music was brought from behind the centuries and spread before us like a huge map. Whatever meaning lay hidden under the musical theories of the ancients was brought out and explained in a clear and conscientious way. Short decisive sentences swept into every obscure corner, and from all sides we saw reflected Professor MacDowell's resolute spirit and sincerity of purpose.

At the end of the first semester we had left the legendary period of music history. Besides a clear exposition of Greek dancing metres and Greek modes, Ambrosian chants and Authentic modes, and the Plagal modes of Gregory, Hucbald's Organum and Guido d'Arezzo's scale, we had two lectures in acoustics, upon vibration and sound, several lectures upon the development of clefs, neumae, and time measurements.

From Hucbald, who originated harmony, and d'Arezzo, the originator of counterpoint, we came to the music of the Troubadours, who added the flourishes. But it was through the Minnesingers, Walter von der Vogelweide, Heinrich von Miessen, Nitkhard [*sic*], and Heinrich von Ofterdingen, who sang of death and life, of pathos and purity, that we came first to know MacDowell, the poet.

The lectures that followed were on the rise of the Belgian School and the development of Canon, Counterpoint, and Fugue. Professor MacDowell took the keenest pleasure in tossing off these old musical puzzles, following the voices, as they chased after each other with a series of exclamations: "The dryest stuff!" "Tricks!" "Want of tonality!"

The lectures on musical form were distinguished by many brilliant demonstrations of MacDowell's genius. The ease and rapidity with which he flashed his thoughts upon the blackboard were both inspiring and bewildering to the student who must grope his way through notes before he can reach an idea. If any were unwise enough to stop even for a moment, to catch these spontaneous thoughts as they flew along the staff, they were very apt upon looking up to see them vanishing like phantoms in a cloud of white chalk.

The closing lectures were in reality delightfully informal concerts, for which the class began to assemble as early as 8:30 o'clock. By 9:30 every student would be in his chair, which he had dragged as near to the piano as the early suburbanite would let him. Some one at the window would say, "Here he comes!" and, entering the room with a huge bundle of music under one arm and his hat in his hand, MacDowell would deposit them on the piano and turn to us with his gracious smile.

Then, instead of sitting down, he would continue to walk up and down the room, the pace set by his energetic steps. He had an abundant word supply and his short, terse sentences were easy to follow. . . .[11]

Lawrence Gilman, author of the first—and still the best—biography of MacDowell, summed up the situation admirably in a single paragraph:

The impression has gone abroad that he had little didactic capacity, that he was disinclined toward and disqualified for methodical work. It cannot, of course, be said that his inclinations tended irresistibly toward pedagogy, or that he loved routine. Yet that he had uncommon gifts as a teacher, that he was singularly methodical in his manner of work, are facts beyond question. His students have testified to the strikingly suggestive and illuminating manner in which his instruction was imparted. His lectures, which he wrote out in full, are remarkable for the amount of sheer "brain-stuff" that was expended upon them. They are erudite, accurate, and scholarly; they are original in thought, they are lucid and stimulating in their presentation and interpretation of fact, and they are often admirable in expression. They would reflect uncommon credit upon a writer who had given his life to the critical, historical, and philosophical study of music; as the work of a man who had been primarily absorbed in making music, rather than in discussing it, they are extraordinary.[12]

Reading through the lectures in the *Critical and Historical Essays*, the nagging question inevitably arises: Was Gilman, writing in 1908 after the death of MacDowell, referring to the lectures as they appeared in 1912, as edited by Baltzell? There would appear to be some reason to doubt it. As Baltzell himself points out in his Preface, the twenty-one lectures he edited do not represent MacDowell's most advanced thought. "It is a matter for sincere regret that Mr. MacDowell put in permanent form only a portion of the lectures prepared for the two courses just mentioned," Baltzell notes. "While some were read from manuscript, others were given from notes and illustrated with musical quotations. This was the case, very largely, with the lectures prepared for the advanced course, which included extremely valuable and individual treatment of the subject of the piano, its literature and composers, modern music, etc." [13] And as Philip Hale, one of MacDowell's closest friends, pointed out in a brief notice of the book, the lectures that "were the most interesting as a revelation of the composer's mind and an expression of his opinions, were for the most part notes, not always connected, serving as a cue to extemporaneous elaboration of a thought. To prepare many of the lectures for the press would be a task of unusual difficulty." [14] Thus, the Baltzell volume contains only lectures of a fairly rudimentary character, and it is not wholly characteristic of MacDowell's thought.

We are now in a position to retrace our steps and to examine Mrs. MacDowell's statement that the lectures were "printed unedited." This is clearly not the case, and the culpability can be laid squarely at the door of Baltzell. It will be remembered that, according to Mrs. MacDowell, the essays "represent the result of what he [MacDowell] dictated to me as he walked up and down his music room trying to crystallize his ideas." She did not mention that she went one step further and had this dictation typed up for her husband's use at Columbia—she did not type them herself since she never learned to master the machine. To this typescript, MacDowell added handwritten emendations and corrections. Shortly before MacDowell's death, Mrs. MacDowell invited his pupil and close friend, W. H. Humiston, to Peterborough to go through "his sketch-books and manuscripts to see if there was completed work of any kind which had not yet been published, and which could be used." [15] Humiston accomplished this labor of love during the summer of 1907 and added some emendations and corrections to the typescript of the lectures.

After MacDowell's death in January, 1908, Lawrence Gilman decided to revise the monograph he had contributed in 1905 to the "Living Masters of Music" series published by John Lane. "That book could not, of course, remain in the series after the death of MacDowell three years later," he wrote in the Preface to the later study. "It was therefore taken from its place and used as a foundation for the present volume, which supercedes it in every respect." [16] The revised version was sent to the printer in September, 1908, and copyrighted by the John Lane Company on December 31, 1908. For the revision, Gilman was given access to MacDowell's papers, among them being the typescript to which Humiston had added his corrections, and Gilman quoted copiously from the typescript in his book—a fortunate circumstance.

Just why Baltzell was selected to prepare MacDowell's lectures for posthumous publication is something of a mystery. Among MacDowell's close friends were some of the foremost music critics of the day—Gilman, Hale, Huneker, and Finck, to name but a few —and there were still around quite a few of his students, many of whom had attended the Columbia lectures, including Humiston. In 1912, Baltzell was a forty-eight-year-old Pennsylvania (oddly enough, his December 18 birthdate was the same as MacDowell's, although he was three years younger) who had never been in contact with MacDowell while the composer was at Columbia. From 1897 to 1907, Baltzell served successively as assistant editor and editor of *The Etude* (Philadelphia) ; he then moved to Boston and took over as editor of *The Musician,* a magazine which devoted quite a bit of space to MacDowell under his aegis. He was active in a 1910 pageant put on by the MacDowell Colony in Peterborough, and it was at that time that he apparently made the acquaintance of Mrs. MacDowell for the first time. Whether it was Mrs. MacDowell or Arthur P. Schmidt, MacDowell's publisher, who arranged for him to edit the lectures is not known. In any event, the typescript was placed in his charge, and he added his editorial work to that of Humiston.

Was Baltzell a good editor? Since the typescript on which he labored seems to have disappeared—at least a portion of it was still extant in 1938, when Arthur P. Schmidt loaned nine leaves, containing emendations in the hands of MacDowell, Humiston, and Baltzell, to the Columbia University Library for its spectacular exhibition illustrating the life and work of the composer [17]— to determine Baltzell's competence would appear to be an impossible task. But providentially, there are Gilman's 1908 quotations from the typescript on which Humiston had worked. A comparison between Gilman's version and Baltzell's is most illuminating:

Gilman (1908)

..."Thus Spake Zarathustra" may be considered the apotheosis of this power of suggestion in tonal colour, and in it I believe we can see the tendency I allude to. It stuns by its glorious magnificence of tonal texture. The suggestion, at the beginning, of the rising sun, is a mighty example of the overwhelming power of tone-colour. The upward sweep of the music to the highest regions of light has something splendrous about it; and yet I remember once hearing in London a song sung in the street at night that seemed to me to contain a truer germ of music. (pp. 74–75)

... [Bach . . . accomplished his work as] one of the world's mightiest tone-poets not by means of the contrapuntal methods of his day, but in spite of them. The laws of canon and fugue are based upon as prosaic a foundation as those of the Rondo and Sonata Form, and I find it impossible to imagine their ever having been a spur, an incentive, to poetic musical speech. (p. 76)

Baltzell (1912)

..."Thus Spake Zarathustra" may be considered the apotheosis of this power of suggestion in tonal colour, and in it I believe we can see the tendency I allude to. This work stuns by its glorious magnificence of tonal texture; the suggestion, in the opening measures, of the rising sun is a mighty example of the overwhelming power of tone colour. The upward sweep of the music to the highest regions of light has much of splendour about it; and yet I remember once hearing in London, sung in the street at night, a song that seemed to me to contain a truer germ of music. (p. 272)

... Bach, one of the world's mightiest tone poets, accomplished his mission, not by means of the contrapuntal fashion of his age, but in spite of it. The laws of canon and fugue are based upon as prosaic a foundation as those of the rondo and sonata form; I find it impossible to imagine their ever having been a spur or an incentive to poetic musical speech. (p. 265)

[Of Mozart he wrote:] It is impossible to forget the fact that in his piano works he was first and foremost a piano virtuoso, a child prodigy: of whom filigree work (we cannot call this Orientalism, for it was more or less of German pattern, traced from the *fioriture* of the Italian opera singer) was expected by the public for which his sonatas were written. (p. 76)

... If we read on one page of some history (every history of music has such a page) that Mozart's sonatas are sublime; that they far transcend anything written for the harpsichord or clavichord by Haydn or his contemporaries, we are apt to echo the saying. ... (pp. 76–77)

... But let us look the thing straight in the face: Mozart's sonatas are compositions entirely unworthy of the author of "The Magic Flute" and "Don Giovanni," or of any composer with pretensions to more than mediocre talent. They are written in a style of flashy harpsichord virtuosity such as Liszt in his most despised moments never descended to. Yet I am well aware that this statement would be dismissed as either absurd or heretical, according to the point of view of the particular objector. (p. 77)

[Of Schumann he said happily:] His music is not avowed programme-music; neither is it,

When we consider Mozart, it is impossible to forget the fact that in his piano works he was first and foremost a piano virtuoso, a child prodigy, of whom filigree work was expected by the public for which he wrote his sonatas. (We cannot call this orientalism, for it was more or less of German pattern, traced from the fioriture of the Italian opera singer.) (p. 200)

...if we read on one page of some history (every history of music has such a page) that Mozart's sonatas are sublime, that they do not contain one note of mere filigree work, and that they far transcend anything written for the harpsichord or clavichord by Haydn or his contemporaries, we echo the saying. ... (p. 193)

... It is time to ... look the thing itself straight in the face. It is a fact that Mozart's sonatas are compositions entirely unworthy of the author of the "Magic Flute," or of any composer with pretensions to anything beyond mediocrity. They are written in a style of flashy harpsichord virtuosity such as Liszt never descended to, even in those of his works at which so many persons are accustomed to sneer.

Such a statement as I have just made may be cried down as rank heresy, first by the book readers and then by the general public. ... (p. 194)

... His music is not avowed programme music; neither is it, as is much of Schubert's, pure delight as was much of Schubert's, pure delight in beautiful sound. It did not break through formalism by sheer violence of emotion, as did Beethoven's: it represents the rhapsodical revery of an inspired poet to whom no imaginative vagary seems strange or alien, and who has the faculty of relating his visions, never attempting to give them coherence, and unaware of their character until perhaps when, awakened from his dream, he naively wonders what they may have meant—you remember that he added titles to his music after it was composed. He put his dreams in music and guessed their meaning afterward. (p. 78)

To all of this new, strange music Liszt and Chopin added the wonderful tracery of Orientalism. The difference between these two is, that with Chopin this tracery developed poetic thought as with a thin gauze; whereas with Liszt the embellishment itself made the starting-point for almost a new art in tonal combination, the effects of which one sees on every hand to-day. To realise its influence one need only compare the easy mastery of the arabesque displayed in the simplest piano piece of to-day with the awkward and gargoyle-like figuration of Beethoven and his predecessors. We may justly attribute this to Liszt rather than to Chopin, whose nocturne embellishments are but first cousins to those of the Englishman, John Field. (pp. 78–79)

[Of Wagner:] His music-dramas, shorn of the fetters of the actual

in beautiful melodies and sounds. It did not break through formalism by sheer violence of emotion, as did Beethoven's; least of all has it Mendelssohn's orthodox dress. It represents, as well as I can put it, the rhapsodical reverie of a great poet to whom nothing seems strange, and who has the faculty of relating his visions, never attempting to give them coherence, until, perhaps, when awakened from his dream, he naively wonders what they may have meant. It will be remembered that Schumann added titles to his music after it was composed. (pp. 203–04)

To all of this new, strange music, Liszt and Chopin added the wonderful tracery of orientalism. As I have said before, the difference between these two is that with Chopin this tracery enveloped poetic thought as with a gauze; whereas with Liszt, the embellishment itself made the starting point for almost a new art in tonal combination, the effects of which are seen on every hand to-day. To realize its influence, one need only compare the graceful arabesques of the most simple piano piece of to-day with the awkward and gargoyle-like figuration of Beethoven and his predecessors. We may justly attribute this to Liszt rather than to Chopin, whose nocturne embellishments are but first cousins to those of the Englishman, John Field. . . . (p. 204)

. . . Thus, the music dramas of Wagner, shorn of the fetters of spoken word, emancipated from the materialism of acting, painting, and furniture, must be considered the greatest achievement in our art. (p. 79)

... If by the word "form" our purists meant the most poignant expression of poetic thought in music, if they meant by this term the art of arranging musical sounds so that they constituted the most telling presentation of a musical idea, I should have nothing to say. But as it is, the word in almost its invariable use by theorists stands for what are called "stoutly-built periods," "subsidiary themes" and the like, a happy combination of which in certain prescribed keys is supposed to constitute good form. Such a principle, inherited from the necessities and fashions of the dance, and changing from time to time, is surely not worthy of the strange worship it has received. In their eagerness to press this great revolutionist [Beethoven] into their own ranks in the fight of narrow theory against expansion and progress, the most amusing mistakes are constantly occurring. For example, the first movement of this sonata [the so-called "Moonlight"]—which, as we know, is a poem of profound sorrow and the most poignant resignation alternating with despair—has, by some strange torturing, been cited as being in strict sonata-form by one theorist (Harding: Novello's primer), is dubbed a free fantasy by another (Matthews), and is described as being in song-form by

the actual spoken word, emancipated from the materialism of acting, painting, and furniture, may be considered as the greatest achievement in our art. . . . (p. 260)

... If by the word "form" our theorists meant the most poignant expression of poetic thought in music, if they meant by this word the art of arranging musical sounds into the most telling presentation of a musical idea, I should have nothing to say: for if this were admitted instead of the recognized forms of modern theorists for the proper utterance, we should possess a study of the power of musical sounds which might truly justify the title of musical intellectuality. As it is, the word "form" stands for what have been called "stoutly built periods," "subsidiary themes," and the like, a happy combination of which in certain prescribed keys was supposed to constitute good form. Such a device, originally based upon the necessities and fashions of the dance, and changing from time to time, is surely not worthy of the strange worship it has received. A form of so doubtful an identity that the first movement of a certain Beethoven sonata can be dubbed by one authority "sonata-form," and by another "free fantasia," certainly cannot lay claim to serious intellectual value. (pp. 263–264)

another: all of which is somewhat weakened by the dictum of
still another theorist that the
music is absolutely formless! A
form of so doubtful an identity
can surely lay small claim to
any serious intellectual value.
(pp. 79–80)

. . . In our modern days we too
often, Procrustes-like, make our
ideas to fit the forms. We put
our guest, the poetic thought,
that comes to us like a homing
bird from out of the mystery of
the blue sky—we put this confiding stranger straightway into
that iron bed: the "sonata-
form"—or perhaps even the
"third-rondo form," for we have
quite an assortment; and should
the idea survive, and grow, and
become too large for the bed,
and if we have grown to love it
too much to cut off its feet and
thus *make* it fit (as did that old
robber of Attica), why then we
run the risk of having some wise-
acre say, as is said of Chopin:
"Yes—but he is weak in sonata-
form!" (pp. 80–81)

. . . In our modern days, we too
often, Procrustes-like, make our
ideas to fit the forms. We put
our guest, the poetic thought,
that comes to us like a homing
bird from out the mystery of the
blue sky—we put this confiding
stranger straightway into that
iron bed, the "sonata form," or
perhaps even the third rondo
form, for we have quite an assortment. Should the idea survive and grow too large for the
bed, and if we have learned to
love it too much to cut off its
feet and thus *make* it fit (as did
that old robber of Attica), why
we run the risk of having some
critic wise in his theoretical
knowledge, say, as was and is
said of Chopin, "He is weak in
sonata form!" (p. 27)

. . . Form should be nothing more
than a synonym for *coherence.*
No idea, whether great or small,
can find utterance without form;
but that form will be inherent in
the idea, and there will be as
many forms as there are adequately expressed ideas in the
world. (p. 81)

. . . Form should be a synonym
for *coherence.* No idea, whether
great or small, can find utterance
without form, but that form will
be inherent to the idea, and there
will be as many forms as there
are adequately expressed ideas.
(p. 264)

The reader may draw his own conclusions.

Baltzell was guilty of sins of omission as well as of commission.
In 1912, Dvořák's reputation was at its zenith in America, and
his viewpoint in regard to the sources of our national music was

very popular. MacDowell's ideas on the subject, always individ-
ualistic, must have appeared quite eccentric to Baltzell when he
came across them in the lecture on "Folk-Song and its Relation
to Nationalism in Music." Perhaps this is why he excised the following extraordinary passage, which is quoted in full by Gilman:

> A man is generally something different from the clothes he
> wears or the business he is occupied with; but when we do
> see a man identified with his clothes we think little of him.
> And so it is with music. So-called Russian, Bohemian, or
> any other purely national music has no place in art, for
> its characteristics may be duplicated by anyone who takes
> the fancy to do so. On the other hand, with the vital ele-
> ment of music—personality—stands alone. We have seen
> the Viennese Strauss family adopting the cross rhythms
> of the Spanish—or, to be more accurate, the Moorish or
> Arab—school of art. Moszkowski the Pole writes Spanish
> dances. Cowen in England writes a Scandinavian Sym-
> phony. Grieg the Norwegian writes Arabian music; and,
> to cap the climax, we have here in America been offered a
> pattern for an "American" national musical costume by
> the Bohemian Dvořák—though what the Negro melodies
> have to do with Americanism in art still remains a mystery.
> Music that can be made by "recipe" is not music, but
> "tailoring." To be sure, this tailoring may serve to cover a
> beautiful thought; but—why cover it? and, worst of all,
> why cover it (if covered it must be: if the trademark of
> nationality is indispensable, which I deny)—why cover it
> with the badge of whilom slavery rather than with the
> stern but at least manly and free rudeness of the North
> American Indian? If what is called local tone colour is
> necessary to music (which it most emphatically is not),
> why not adopt some of the Hindoo *Ragas* and modes—
> each one of which (and the modes number over 72) will
> give an individual tonal character to the music written
> according to its rules? But the means of "creating" a
> national music to which I have alluded are childish. No:
> before a people can find a musical writer to echo its genius
> it must first possess men who truly represent it—that is to
> say, men who, being part of the people, love the country
> for itself: men who put into their music what the nation
> has put into its life; and in the case of America it needs
> above all, both on the part of the public and on the part
> of the writer, absolute freedom from the restraint that
> an almost unlimited deference to European thought and
> prejudice has imposed upon us. Masquerading in the so-
> called nationalism of Negro clothes cut in Bohemia will not

> help us. What we must arrive at is the youthful optimistic
> vitality and the undaunted tenacity of spirit that charac-
> terizes the American man. This is what I hope to see
> echoed in American music.[18]

It does not take much imagination to see in this paragraph an
uncanny prediction of Charles Ives.

The *Critical and Historical Essays* were widely reviewed in
the newspapers and magazines of the day, but only Hale, of all
MacDowell's coterie, seems to have taken open public notice of its
appearance. Hale expressed his disappointment with the book
mildly but quite clearly, and here may be found perhaps the reason
for its strange neglect by Gilman and Huneker—perhaps they
too were disappointed, knowing the man himself, and they found
it more politic to remain silent than to risk offending Mrs. Mac-
Dowell, who had allowed the lectures to be published as edited by
Baltzell. Perhaps the most cogent notice was one which appeared
(without author attribution) in the August 29, 1912, issue of *The
Nation*: [19]

> One cannot but regret that MacDowell ever accepted the
> Columbia professorship. There was little understanding
> of or sympathy with his aims and ideals on the part of the
> faculty, and while some of his pupils have since made
> names for themselves, most of those who had the privi-
> lege of attending his lectures were little more than
> "barbarians," as he characterized the university students
> collectively, speaking from the aesthetic point of view.
> It was not like teaching at a conservatory, where all the
> students have a practical knowledge of music. Doubtless the
> very fact that not a few of his hearers at the University
> had no such training impelled him to strive for that lucidity
> of explanation which will agreeably impress every reader
> of his book. What one regrets is that he should have ever
> taken the time to prepare these lectures. They are on the
> whole not much better than a similar set of lectures that
> might have been prepared by half a dozen musical journal-
> ists in the country. But no one in the country can give to
> the world the inspired songs or piano or orchestral pieces
> which he might have composed during the months it must
> have taken him to collect and digest the material for these
> lectures. Another set of "Eight Songs" or of "Woodland
> Sketches" would have been of infinitely greater value to
> the world than this volume of Columbia lectures.

Yet it is in itself a good book, and interesting; a book which may be cordially commended to the attention of those who are enamored of MacDowell's music. For, beside much that is almost inevitably conventional in the discussion of ancient, mediaeval, and modern music, of scales, counterpoint, folksongs, Troubadours, sonatas, operas, and so on, there is also a good deal of the precious individuality of MacDowell's mind.

Frankness is what MacDowell missed in most of the books on musical history and criticism, as in the attitude towards art in general. People do not dare, he says, to admire the London Law Courts; all things must be measured by the straight lines of Grecian architecture. "Let us have frankness, and if we have no feelings on a subject, let us remain silent rather than echo that drone in the hive of modern thought, the '*authority* in art.'" He is indignant with the musical historians for perpetually parroting the ridiculous assertion that the increasing and decreasing of a tone in loudness as an element of musical expression was first *discovered* at Mannheim, about 1760, whereas Plutarch already referred to this thing. . . . He does not join in the admiration of the Mastersingers; they were mainly valuable, in his opinion, for having furnished Wagner a subject for his wonderful opera. Hans Sachs was perhaps the only one of them whose melodies show anything but the flattest mediocrity.

In all these "heresies" one cannot but agree with MacDowell as against the historians. . . .[20]

The modern-day reader of the *Critical and Historical Essays* will easily discover more astounding "heresies" in MacDowell's thought than did Henry T. Finck in 1912, and it is in these "heresies," which pop up in the most unexpected places, that the permanent value of the volume resides. One must go quickly past the conventionalities, until one comes across (in a lecture on "The Merging of the Suite into the Sonata," of all places) sentences such as these:

In art our opinions must, in all cases, rest directly on the thing under consideration and not on what is written about it. In my beliefs I am no respecter of the written word, that is to say, the mere fact that a statement is made by a well-known man, is printed in a well-known work, or is endorsed by many prominent names, means nothing to me if the thing itself is available for examination. Without a thorough knowledge of music, including its history and development, and, above all, musical "sympathy," individual criticism is, of course, valueless; at the same time the acquirement of this knowledge and sympathy is not difficult, and I hope that we may yet have a public in America that shall be capable of forming its own ideas, and not to be influenced by tradition, criticism, or fashion.

We need to open our eyes and see for ourselves instead of trusting the direction of our steps to the guidance of others. Even an opinion based on ignorance, frankly given, is of more value to art than a platitude gathered from some outside source. If it is not a platitude but the echo of some fine thought, it only makes it worse, for it is not sincere, unless of course it is quoted understandingly. We need freshness and sincerity in forming our judgments in art, for it is upon these that art lives. . . .

Every person with even the very smallest love and sympathy for art possesses ideas which are valuable to that art. From the tiniest seeds sometimes the greatest trees are grown. Why, therefore, allow these tender germs of individualism to be smothered by that flourishing, arrogant bay tree of tradition — fashion, authority, convention?[21]

Contrary to the legend that has grown up around him, which portrays MacDowell as a pale aesthete with a Wildean rose in his hand, the composer was cantankerous, testy, argumentative, and very much of a maverick. One does not have to read between the lines—although one must choose one's way carefully—to discover that he was also a man of considerable intellect and a man of such eloquence that even his prejudices have the semblance of truth. He is a man who does not deserve his current obscurity.

Washington, D. C.   Irving Lowens
September 1, 1968

Footnotes

[1]This phrase, frequently found in contemporaneous references to MacDowell, has never been traced to its original source. It seems to have been used for the first time (set within quotation marks) in a press release announcing MacDowell's appointment to the Columbia University faculty.

[2]Pp. 13–16.

[3]Both Keet letters are in the collection of MacDowell materials located in the Music Division of the Library of Congress.

[4]In an undated letter to John F. Porte printed, in part, in his *Edward MacDowell* (New York, 1922), p. 10.

[5]From Marian MacDowell's unpublished memoirs, apparently dictated to her amanuensis, Nina Maud Richardson, in the 1940's or 1950's. In the collection of MacDowell materials located in the Music Division of the Library of Congress.

[6]*Ibid.*

[7]*The Memory of Certain Persons* (Philadelphia, 1947), pp. 73–74.

[8]John Erskine, "MacDowell at Columbia: Some Recollections," *The Musical Quarterly*, XXVIII (1942), pp. 397–398.

[9]Upton Sinclair, "MacDowell, "*The American Mercury*, VII (1926), p. 50. A slightly different version of this article appeared in an English periodical, *The Sackbut*, in December, 1925.

[10]*Ibid.*, pp. 50–51.

[11]"At Edward MacDowell's Lectures," *The Musician*, XII (1907), pp. 426–427.

[12]Lawrence Gilman, *Edward MacDowell: A Study* (New York, 1908; reprinted New York, 1969, by Da Capo Press, with an introduction by Margery L. Morgan), pp. 43–44.

[13]*Infra*, p. iv.

[14]"Dramatic and Musical Review," *Boston Herald*, April 29, 1912.

[15]W. H. Humiston, "Personal Recollections of Edward MacDowell," *The Musician*, XIII (1908), p. 161.

[16]Gilman, *op. cit.*, p. vii.

[17]According to Richard Angell's working notebook pertaining to the exhibition. (The notebook is now located in the Music Library, Columbia University.) The Schmidt catalogue was subsequently purchased by Summy-Birchard, and the old records and papers of the firm, including thousands of manuscripts, were donated to the Music Division of the Library of Congress by Mr. David Sengstack. The typescript of the MacDowell lectures apparently was not included in the donation; its present whereabouts is unknown.

[18]Gilman, *op. cit.*, pp. 83–85.

[19]Pp. 197–198.

[20]The unsigned review was written by Henry T. Finck, according to Daniel C. Haskell, comp., *The Nation...*, *Indexes of Titles and Contributors* (New York, 1953), II, p. 155.

[21]*Infra*, pp. 191–193.

CRITICAL
AND
HISTORICAL ESSAYS

is proof of his power of expression in verse and lyric forms. Above these and animating them were what Mr. Lawrence Gilman terms "his uncommon faculties of vision and imagination." What he thought, what he said, what he wrote, was determined by the poet's point of view, and this is evident on nearly every page of these lectures.

He was a wide reader, one who, from natural bent, dipped into the curious and out-of-the-way corners of literature, as will be noticed in his references to other works in the course of the lectures, particularly to Row-botham's picturesque and fascinating story of the formative period of music. Withal he was always in touch with contemporary affairs. With the true outlook of the poet he was fearless, individual, and even radical in his views. This spirit, as indicated before, he carried into his lectures, for he demanded of his pupils that above all they should be prepared to do their own thinking and reach their own conclusions. He was accustomed to say that we need in the United States, a public that shall be independent in its judgment on art and art products, that shall not be tied down to verdicts based on tradition and convention, but shall be prepared to reach conclusions through knowledge and sincerity.

That these lectures may aid in this splendid educational purpose is the wish of those who are responsible for placing them before the public.

W. J. BALTZELL.

CONTENTS

CRITICAL AND HISTORICAL ESSAYS

I

THE ORIGIN OF MUSIC

DARWIN'S theory that music had its origin "in the sounds made by the half-human progenitors of man during the season of courtship" seems for many reasons to be inadequate and untenable. A much more plausible explanation, it seems to me, is to be found in the theory of Theophrastus, in which the origin of music is attributed to the whole range of human emotion.

When an animal utters a cry of joy or pain it expresses its emotions in more or less definite tones; and at some remote period of the earth's history all primeval mankind must have expressed its emotions in much the same manner. When this inarticulate speech developed into the use of certain sounds as symbols for emotions — emotions that otherwise would have been expressed by the natural sounds occasioned by them — then we have the beginnings of speech as distinguished from music, which is still the universal language. In other words, intellectual development begins with articulate speech, leaving music for the expression of the emotions.

To symbolize the sounds used to express emotion, if I may so put it, is to weaken that expression, and it would naturally be the strongest emotion that would first feel the inadequacy of the new-found speech. Now what is mankind's strongest emotion? Even in the nineteenth century Goethe could say, "'Tis fear that constitutes the god-like in man." Certainly before the Christian era the soul of mankind had its roots in fear. In our superstition we were like children beneath a great tree of which the upper part was as a vague and fascinating mystery, but the roots holding it firmly to the ground were tangible, palpable facts. We feared — we knew not what. Love was human, all the other emotions were human; fear alone was indefinable.

The primeval savage, looking at the world subjectively, was merely part of it. He might love, hate, threaten, kill, if he willed; every other creature could do the same. But the wind was a great spirit to him; lightning and thunder threatened him as they did the rest of the world; the flood would destroy him as ruthlessly as it tore the trees asunder. The elements were animate powers that had nothing in common with him; for what the intellect cannot explain the imagination magnifies.

Fear, then, was the strongest emotion. Therefore auxiliary aids to express and cause fear were necessary when the speech symbols for fear, drifting further and further away from expressing the actual thing, became words, and words were inadequate to express and cause fear. In that vague groping for sound symbols which would cause and express fear far better than mere words, we have the beginning of what is gradually to develop into music.

We all know that savage nations accompany their dances by striking one object with another, sometimes by a clanking of stones, the pounding of wood, or perhaps the clashing of stone spearheads against wooden shields (a custom which extended until the time when shields and spears were discarded), meaning thus to express something that words cannot. This meaning changed naturally from its original one of being the simple expression of fear to that of welcoming a chieftain; and, if one wishes to push the theory to excess, we may still see a shadowy reminiscence of it in the manner in which the violinists of an orchestra applaud an honoured guest — perchance some famous virtuoso — at one of our symphony concerts by striking the backs of their violins with their bows.

To go back to the savages. While this clashing of one object against another could not be called the beginning of music, and while it could not be said to originate a musical instrument, it did, nevertheless, bring into existence music's greatest prop, rhythm, an ally without which music would seem to be impossible. It is hardly necessary to go into this point in detail. Suffice it to say that the sense of rhythm is highly developed even among those savage tribes which stand the lowest in the scale of civilization to-day, for instance, the Andaman Islanders, of whom I shall speak later; the same may be said of the Tierra del Fuegians and the now extinct aborigines of Tasmania; it is the same with the Semangs of the Malay Peninsula, the Ajitas of the Philippines, and the savages inhabiting the interior of Borneo.

As I have said, this more or less rhythmic clanking of stones together, the striking of wooden paddles against the side of a canoe, or the clashing of stone spearheads against wooden shields, could not constitute the first musical instrument. But when some savage first struck a hollow tree and found that it gave forth a sound peculiar to itself, when he found a hollow log and filled up the open ends, first with wood, and then — possibly getting the idea from his hide-covered shield — stretched skins across the two open ends, then he had completed the first musical instrument known to man, namely, the drum. And such as it was then, so is it now, with but few modifications.

Up to this point it is reasonable to assume that primeval man looked upon the world purely subjectively. He considered himself merely a unit in the world, and felt on a plane with the other creatures inhabiting it. But from the moment he had invented the first musical instrument, the drum, he had created something outside of nature, a voice that to himself and to all other living creatures was intangible, an idol that spoke when it was touched, something that he could call into life, something that shared the supernatural in common with the elements. A God had come to live with man, and thus was unfolded the first leaf in that noble tree of life which we call religion. Man now began to feel himself something apart from the world, and to look at it objectively instead of subjectively.

To treat primitive mankind as a type, to put it under one head, to make one theorem cover all mankind, as it were, seems almost an unwarranted boldness. But I think it is warranted when we consider that, aside from language, music is the very first sign of the dawn of civilization. There is even the most convincingly direct testimony in its favour. For instance:

In the Bay of Bengal, about six hundred miles from the Hoogly mouth of the Ganges, lie the Andaman Islands. The savages inhabiting these islands have the unenviable reputation of being, in common with several other tribes, the nearest approach to primeval man in existence. These islands and their inhabitants have been known and feared since time immemorial; our old friend Sinbad the Sailor, of "Arabian Nights" fame, undoubtedly touched there on one of his voyages. These savages have no religion whatever, except the vaguest superstition, in other words, fear, and they have no musical instruments of any kind. They have reached only the *rhythm* stage, and accompany such dances as they have by clapping their hands or by stamping on the ground. Let us now look to Patagonia, some thousands of miles distant. The Tierra del Fuegians have precisely the same characteristics, no religion, and no musical instruments of any kind. Retracing our steps to the Antipodes we find among the Weddahs or "wild hunters" of Ceylon exactly the same state of things. The same description applies without distinction equally well to the natives in the interior of Borneo, to the Semangs of the Malay Peninsula, and to the now extinct aborigines of Tasmania. According to Virchow their dance is demon worship of a purely anthropomorphic character; no musical instrument of any kind was known to them. Even the simple expression of emotions by the voice, which we have seen is its most primitive medium, has not been replaced to any extent among these races since their discovery of speech, for the Tierra del Fuegians, Andamans, and Weddahs have but one sound to represent emotion, namely, a cry to express joy; having no other means for the expression of sorrow, they paint themselves when mourning.

It is granted that all this, in itself, is not conclusive; but it will be found that no matter in what wilderness one may hear of a savage beating a drum, there also will be a well-defined religion.

Proofs of the theory that the drum antedates all other musical instruments are to be found on every hand. For wherever in the anthropological history of the world we hear of the trumpet, horn, flute, or other instrument of the pipe species, it will be found that the drum and its derivatives were already well known. The same may be said of the lyre species of instrument, the forerunner of our guitar (*kithara*), *tebuni* or Egyptian harp, and generally all stringed instruments, with this difference, namely, that wherever the lyre species was known, both pipe and drum had preceded it. We never find the lyre without the drum, or the pipe without the drum; neither do we find the lyre and the drum without the pipe. On the other hand, we often find the drum alone, or the drum and pipe without the lyre. This certainly proves the antiquity of the drum and its derivatives.

I have spoken of the purely rhythmical nature of the pre-drum period, and pointed out, in contrast, the musical quality of the drum. This may seem somewhat strange, accustomed as we are to think of the drum as a purely rhythmical instrument. The sounds given out by it seem at best vague in tone and more or less uniform in quality. We forget that all instruments of percussion, as they are called, are direct descendants of the drum. The bells that hang in our church towers are but modifications of the drum; for what is a bell but a metal drum with one end left open and the drum stick hung inside?

Strange to say, as showing the marvellous potency of primeval instincts, bells placed in church towers were supposed to have much of the supernatural power that the savage in his wilderness ascribed to the drum. We all know something of the bell legends of the Middle Ages, how the tolling of a bell was supposed to clear the air of the plague, to calm the storm, and to shed a blessing on all who heard it. And this superstition was to a certain extent ratified by the religious ceremonies attending the casting of church bells and the inscriptions moulded in them. For instance, the mid-day bell of Strasburg, taken down during the French Revolution, bore the motto

"I am the voice of life."

Another one in Strasburg:

"I ring out the bad, ring in the good."

Others read

"My voice on high dispels the storm."

"I am called Ave Maria
I drive away storms."

"I who call to thee am the Rose of the World and am called Ave Maria."

The Egyptian *sistrum*, which in Roman times played an important rôle in the worship of Isis, was shaped somewhat like a tennis racquet, with four wire strings on which rattles were strung. The sound of it must have been akin to that of our modern tambourine, and it served much the same purpose as the primitive drum, namely, to drive away Typhon or Set, the god of evil. Dead kings were called "Osiris" when placed in their tombs, and *sistri* put with them in order to drive away Set.

Beside bells and rattles we must include all instruments of the tambourine and gong species in the drum category. While there are many different forms of the same instrument, there are evidences of their all having at some time served the same purpose, even down to that strange instrument about which Du Chaillu tells us in his "Equatorial Africa", a bell of leopard skin, with a clapper of fur, which was rung by the wizard doctor when entering a hut where someone was ill or dying. The leopard skin and fur clapper seem to have been devised to make no noise, so as not to anger the demon that was to be cast out. This reminds us strangely of the custom of ringing a bell as the priest goes to administer the last rites.

It is said that first impressions are the strongest and most lasting; certain it is that humanity, through all its social and racial evolutions, has retained remnants of certain primitive ideas to the present day. The army death reveille, the minute gun, the tolling of bells for the dead, the tocsin, etc., all have their roots in the attributes assigned to the primitive drum; for, as I have already pointed out, the more civilized a people becomes, the more the word-symbols degenerate. It is this continual drifting away of the word-symbols from the natural sounds which are occasioned by emotions that creates the necessity for auxiliary means of expression, and thus gives us instrumental music.

Since the advent of the drum a great stride toward civilization had been made. Mankind no longer lived in caves but built huts and even temples, and the conditions under which he lived must have been similar to those of the natives of Central Africa before travellers opened up the Dark Continent to the caravan of the European trader. If we look up the subject in the narratives of Livingstone or Stanley we find that these people lived in groups of coarsely-thatched huts, the village being almost invariably surrounded by a kind of stockade. Now this manner of living is identically the same as that of all savage tribes which have not passed beyond the drum state of civilization, namely, a few huts huddled together and surrounded by a palisade of bamboo or cane. Since the pith would decompose in a short time, we should probably find that the wind, whirling across such a palisade of pipes — for that is what our bamboos would have turned to — would produce musical sounds, in fact, exactly the sounds that a large set of Pan's pipes would produce. For after all what we call Pan's pipes are simply pieces of bamboo or cane of different lengths tied together and made to sound by blowing across the open tops.

The theory may be objected to on the ground that it scarcely proves the antiquity of the pipe to be less than that of the drum; but the objection is hardly of importance when we consider that the drum was known long before mankind had reached the "hut" stage of civilization. Under the head of pipe, the trumpet and all its derivatives must be accepted. On this point there has been much controversy. But it seems reasonable to believe that once it was found that sound could be produced by blowing across the top of a hollow pipe, the most natural thing to do would be to try the same effect on all hollow things differing in shape and material from the original bamboo. This would account for the conch shells of the Amazons which, according to travellers' tales, were used to proclaim an attack in war; in Africa the tusks of elephants were used; in North America the instrument did not rise above the whistle made from the small bones of a deer or of a turkey's leg.

That the Pan's pipes are the originals of all these species seems hardly open to doubt. Even among the Greeks and Romans we see traces of them in the double trumpet and the double pipe. These trumpets became larger and larger in form, and the force required to play them was such that the player had to adopt a kind of leather harness to strengthen his cheeks. Before this development had been reached, however, I have no doubt that all wind instruments were of the Pan's pipes variety; that is to say, the instruments consisted of a hollow tube shut at one end, the sound being produced by the breath catching on the open edge of the tube.

Direct blowing into the tube doubtless came later. In this case the tube was open at both ends, and the sound was determined by its length and by the force given to the breath in playing. There is good reason for admitting this new instrument to be a descendant of the Pan's pipes, for it was evidently played by the nose at first. This would preclude its being considered as an originally forcible instrument, such as the trumpet.

Now that we have traced the history of the pipe and considered the different types of the instrument, we can see immediately that it brought no great new truth home to man as did the drum.

The savage who first climbed secretly to the top of the stockade around his village to investigate the cause of the mysterious sounds would naturally say that the Great Spirit had revealed a mystery to him; and he would also claim to be a wonder worker. But while his pipe would be accepted to a certain degree, it was nevertheless second in the field and could hardly replace the drum. Besides, mankind had already commenced to think on a higher plane, and the pipe was reduced to filling what gaps it could in the language of the emotions.

The second strongest emotion of the race is love. All over the world, wherever we find the pipe in its softer, earlier form, we find it connected with love songs. In time it degenerated into a synonym for something contemptibly slothful and worthless, so much so that Plato wished to banish it from his "Republic," saying that the Lydian pipe should not have a place in a decent community.

On the other hand, the trumpet branch of the family developed into something quite different. At the very beginning it was used for war, and as its object was to frighten, it became larger and larger in form, and more formidable in sound. In this respect it only kept pace with the drum, for we read of Assyrian and Thibetan trumpets two or three yards long, and of the Aztec war drum which reached the enormous height of ten feet, and could be heard for miles.

Now this, the trumpet species of pipe, we find also used as an auxiliary "spiritual" help to the drum. We are told by M. Huc, in his "Travels in Thibet," that the llamas of Thibet have a custom of assembling on the roofs of Lhassa at a stated period and blowing enormous trumpets, making the most hideous midnight din imaginable. The reason given for this was that in former days the city was terrorized by demons who rose from a deep ravine and crept through all the houses, working evil everywhere. After the priests had exorcised them by blowing these trumpets, the town was troubled no more. In Africa the same demonstration of trumpet blowing occurs at an eclipse of the moon; and, to draw the theory out to a thin thread, anyone who has lived in a small German Protestant town will remember the chorals which are so often played before sunrise by a band of trumpets, horns, and trombones from the belfry of some church tower. Almost up to the end of the last century trombones were intimately connected with the church service; and if we look back to Zoroaster we find the sacerdotal character of this species of instrument very plainly indicated.

Now let us turn back to the Pan's pipes and its direct descendants, the flute, the clarinet, and the oboe. We shall find that they had no connection whatever with religious observances. Even in the nineteenth century novel we are familiar with the kind of hero who played the flute — a very sentimental gentleman always in love. If he had played the clarinet he would have been very sorrowful and discouraged; and if it had been the oboe (which, to the best of my knowledge, has never been attempted in fiction) he would have needed to be a very ill man indeed.

Now we never hear of these latter kinds of pipes being considered fit for anything but the dance, love songs, or love charms. In the beginning of the seventeenth century Garcilaso de la Vega, the historian of Peru, tells of the astonishing power of a love song played on a flute. We find so-called "courting" flutes in Formosa and Peru, and Catlin tells of the Winnebago courting flute. The same instrument was known in Java, as the old Dutch settlers have told us. But we never hear of it as creating awe, or as being thought a fit instrument to use with the drum or trumpet in connection with religious rites. Leonardo da Vinci had a flute player make music while he painted his picture of Mona Lisa, thinking that it gave her the expression he wished to catch — that strange smile reproduced in the Louvre painting. The flute member of the pipe species, therefore, was more or less an emblem of eroticism, and, as I have already said, has never been even remotely identified with religious mysticism, with perhaps the one exception of Indra's flute, which, however, never seems to have been able to retain a place among religious symbols. The trumpet, on the other hand, has retained something of a mystical character even to our day. The most powerful illustration of this known to me is in the "Requiem" by Berlioz. The effect of those tremendous trumpet calls from the four corners of the orchestra is an overwhelming one, of crushing power and majesty, much of which is due to the rhythm.

To sum up. We may regard rhythm as the intellectual side of music, melody as its sensuous side. The pipe is the one instrument that seems to affect animals — hooded cobras, lizards, fish, etc. Animals' natures are purely sensuous, therefore the pipe, or to put it more broadly, melody, affects them. To rhythm, on the other hand, they are indifferent; it appeals to the intellect, and therefore only to man.

This theory would certainly account for much of the potency of what we moderns call music. All that aims to be dramatic, tragic, supernatural in our modern music, derives its impressiveness directly from rhythm.* What would that shudder of horror in Weber's "Freischütz" be without that throb of the basses ? Merely a diminished chord of the seventh. Add the pizzicato in the basses and the chord sinks into something fearsome; one has a sudden choking sensation, as if one were listening in fear, or as if the heart had almost stopped beating. All through Wagner's music dramas this powerful effect is employed,

---

* The strength of the "Fate" motive in Beethoven's fifth symphony undoubtedly lies in the succession of the four notes at equal intervals of time. Beethoven himself marked it *So pocht das Schicksal an die Pforte.*

from "The Flying Dutchman" to "Parsifal." Every composer from Beethoven to Nicodé has used the same means to express the same emotions; it is the medium that pre-historic man first knew; it produced the same sensation of fear in him that it does in us at the present day.

Rhythm denotes a thought; it is the expression of a purpose. There is will behind it; its vital part is intention, power; it is an act. Melody, on the other hand, is an almost unconscious expression of the senses; it translates feeling into sound. It is the natural outlet for sensation. In anger we raise the voice; in sadness we lower it. In talking we give expression to the emotions in sound. In a sentence in which fury alternates with sorrow, we have the limits of the melody of speech. Add to this rhythm, and the very height of expression is reached; for by it the intellect will dominate the sensuous.

II

ORIGIN OF SONG *vs.* ORIGIN OF INSTRUMENTAL MUSIC

EMERSON characterized language as "fossil poetry," but "fossil music" would have described it even better; for as Darwin says, man *sang* before he became human.

Gerber, in his "Sprache als Kunst," describing the degeneration of sound symbols, says "the saving point of language is that the original material meanings of words have become forgotten or lost in their acquired ideal meaning." This applies with special force to the languages of China, Egypt, and India. Up to the last two centuries our written music was held in bondage, was "fossil music," so to speak. Only certain progressions of sounds were allowed, for religion controlled music. In the Middle Ages folk song was used by the Church, and a certain amount of control was exercised over it; even up to the fifteenth and sixteenth centuries the use of sharps and flats was frowned upon in church music. But gradually music began to break loose from its old chains, and in our own century we see Beethoven snap the last thread of that powerful restraint which had held it so long.

The vital germ of music, as we know it, lay in the fact that it had always found a home in the hearts of the common people of all nations. While from time immemorial theory, mostly in the form of mathematical problems, was being fought over, and while laws were being laid down by religions and governments of all nations as to what music must be and what music was forbidden to be, the vital spark of the divine art was being kept alive deep beneath the ashes of life in the hearts of the oppressed common folk.   They still sang as they felt; when the mood was sad the song mirrored the sorrow; if it were gay the song echoed it, despite the disputes of philosophers and the commands of governments and religion.   Montaigne, in speaking of language, said with truth, "'Tis folly to attempt to fight custom with theories."   This folk song, to use a Germanism, we can hardly take into account at the present moment, though later we shall see that spark fanned into fire by Beethoven, and carried by Richard Wagner as a flaming torch through the very home of the gods, "Walhalla."

Let us go back to our dust heap.   Words have been called "decayed sentences," that is to say, every word was once a small sentence complete in itself.   This theory seems true enough when we remember that mankind has three languages, each complementing the other.   For even now we say many words in one, when that word is reinforced and completed by our vocabulary of sounds and expression, which, in turn, has its shadow, gesture. These shadow languages, which accompany all our words, give to the latter vitality and raise them from mere abstract symbols to living representatives of the idea.   Indeed, in certain languages, this auxiliary expression even overshadows the spoken word.   For instance, in Chinese, the *theng* or intonation of words is much more important than the actual words themselves. Thus the third intonation or *theng*, as it is called in the Pekin dialect, is an upward inflection of the voice. A word with this upward inflection would be unintelligible if given the fourth *theng* or downward inflection. For instance, the word "kwai" with a downward inflection means "honourable," but give it an upward inflection "kwai" and it means "devil."

Just as a word was originally a sentence, so was a tone in music something of a melody. One of the first things that impresses us in studying examples of savage music is the monotonic nature of the melodies; indeed some of the music consists almost entirely of one oft-repeated sound. Those who have heard this music say that the actual effect is not one of a steady repetition of a single tone, but rather that there seems to be an almost imperceptible rising and falling of the voice. The primitive savage is unable to sing a tone clearly and cleanly, the pitch invariably wavering. From this almost imperceptible rising and falling of the voice above and below one tone we are able to gauge more or less the state of civilization of the nation to which the song belongs. This phrase-tone corresponds, therefore, to the sentence-word, and like it, gradually loses its meaning as a phrase and fades into a tone which, in turn, will be used in new phrases as mankind mounts the ladder of civilization.

At last then we have a single tone clearly uttered, and recognizable as a musical tone. We can even make a plausible guess as to what that tone was. Gardiner, in his "Music of Nature," tells of experiments he made in order to determine the normal pitch of the human voice. By going often to the gallery of the London Stock Exchange he found that the roar of voices invariably amalgamated into one long note, which was always F. If we look over the various examples of monotonic savage music quoted by Fletcher, Fillmore, Baker, Wilkes, Catlin, and others, we find additional corroboration of the statement; song after song, it will be noticed, is composed entirely of F, G, and even F alone or G alone. Such songs are generally ancient ones, and have been crystallized and held intact by religion, in much the same way that the chanting heard in the Roman Catholic service has been preserved.

Let us assume then that the normal tone of the human voice in speaking is F or G for men, and for women the octave higher. This tone does very well for our everyday life; perhaps a pleasant impression may raise it somewhat, *ennui* may depress it slightly; but the average tone of our "commonplace" talk, if I may call it that, will be about F. But let some sudden emotion come, and we find monotone speech abandoned for impassioned speech, as it has been called. Instead of keeping the voice evenly on one or two notes, we speak much higher or lower than our normal pitch.

And these sounds may be measured and classified to a certain extent according to the emotions which cause them, although it must be borne in mind that we are looking at the matter collectively; that is to say, without reckoning on individual idiosyncrasies of expression in speech. Of course we know that joy is apt to make us raise the voice and sadness to lower it. For instance, we have all heard gruesome stories, and have noticed how naturally the voice sinks in the telling. A ghost story told with an upward inflection might easily become humourous, so instinctively do we associate the upward inflection with a non-pessimistic trend of thought. Under stress of emotion we emphasize words strongly, and with this emphasis we almost invariably raise the voice a fifth or depress it a fifth; with yet stronger emotion the interval of change will be an octave. We raise the voice almost to a scream or drop it to a whisper. Strangely enough these primitive notes of music correspond to the first two of those harmonics which are part and parcel of every musical sound. Generally speaking, we may say that the ascending inflection carries something of joy or hope with it, while the downward inflection has something of the sinister and fearful. To be sure, we raise our voices in anger and in pain, but even then the inflection is almost always downward; in other words, we pitch our voices higher and let them fall slightly. For instance, if we heard a person cry "Ah/" we might doubt its being a cry of pain, but if it were "Ah\" we should at once know that it was caused by pain, either mental or physical.

The declamation at the end of Schubert's "Erlking" would have been absolutely false if the penultimate note had ascended to the tonic instead of descending a fifth. "The child lay dead."

How fatally hopeless would be the opening measures of "Tristan and Isolde" without that upward inflection which comes like a sunbeam through a rift in the cloud; with a downward inflection the effect would be that of unrelieved gloom. In the Prelude to " Lohengrin," Wagner pictures his angels in dazzling white. He uses the highest vibrating sounds at his command. But for the dwarfs who live in the gloom of Niebelheim he chooses deep shades of red, the lowest vibrating colour of the solar spectrum. For it is in the nature of the spiritual part of mankind to shrink from the earth, to aspire to something higher; a bird soaring in the blue above us has something of the ethereal; we give wings to our angels. On the other hand, a serpent impresses us as something sinister. Trees, with their strange fight against all the laws of gravity, striving upward unceasingly, bring us something of hope and faith; the sight of them cheers us. A land without trees is depressing and gloomy. As Ruskin says, "The sea wave, with all its beneficence, is yet devouring and terrible; but the silent wave of the blue mountain is lifted towards Heaven in a stillness of perpetual mercy; and while the one surges unfathomable in its darkness, the other is unshaken in its faithfulness."

And yet so strange is human nature that that which we call civilization strives unceasingly to nullify emotion. The almost childlike faith which made our church spires point heavenward also gave us Gothic architecture, that emblem of frail humanity striving towards the ideal. It is a long leap from that childlike faith to the present day of skyscrapers. For so is the world constituted.

A great truth too often becomes gradually a truism, then a merely tolerated and uninteresting theory; gradually it becomes obsolete and sometimes even degenerates into a symbol of sarcasm or a servant of utilitarianism. This we are illustrating every day of our lives. We speak of a person's being "silly," and yet the word comes from "sælig," old English for "blessed"; to act "sheepishly" once had reference to divine resignation, "even as a sheep led to the slaughter," and so on *ad infinitum*. We build but few great cathedrals now. Our tall buildings generally point to utilitarianism and the almighty dollar.

But in the new art, music, we have found a new domain in which impulses have retained their freshness and warmth, in which, to quote Goethe, "first comes the act, then the word"; first the expression of emotion, then the theory that classifies it; a domain in which words cannot lose their original meanings entirely, as in speech. For in spite of the strange twistings of ultra modern music, a simple melody still embodies the same pathos for us that it did for our grandparents. To be sure the poignancy of harmony in our day has been heightened to an incredible degree. We deal in gorgeous colouring and mighty sound masses which would have been amazing in the last century; but still through it all we find in Händel, Beethoven, and Schubert, up to Wagner, the same great truths of declamation that I have tried to explain to you.

Herbert Spencer, in an essay on "The Origin and Functions of Music," speaks of speech as the parent of music. He says, "utterance, which when languaged is speech, gave rise to music." The definition is incomplete, for "languaged utterance," as he calls it, which is speech, is a duality, is either an expression of emotion or a mere symbol of emotion, and as such has gradually sunk to the level of the commonplace. As Rowbotham points out, impassioned speech is the parent of music, while unimpassioned speech has remained the vehicle for the smaller emotions of life, the everyday expression of everyday emotions.

In studying the music of different nations we are confronted by one fact which seems to be part and parcel of almost every nationality, namely, the constant recurrence of what is called the five tone (pentatonic) scale. We find it in primitive forms of music all the world over, in China and in Scotland, among the Burmese, and again in North America. Why it is so seems almost doomed to remain a mystery. The following theory may nevertheless be advanced as being at least plausible:

Vocal music, as we understand it, and as I have already explained, began when the first tone could be given clearly; that is to say, when the sound sentence had amalgamated into the single musical tone. The pitch being sometimes F, sometimes G, sudden emotion gives us the fifth, C or D, and the strongest emotion the octave, F or G. Thus we have already the following sounds in our first musical scale.

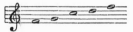

We know how singers slur from one tone to another. It is a fault that caused the fathers of harmony to prohibit what are called hidden fifths in vocal music. The jump from G to C in the above scale fragment would be slurred, for we must remember that the intoning of clear individual sounds was still a novelty to the savage. Now the distance from G to C is too small to admit two tones such as the savage knew; consequently, for the sake of uniformity, he would try to put but one tone between, singing a mixture of A and B♭, which sound in time fell definitely to A, leaving the mystery of the half-tone unsolved. This addition of the third would thus fall in with the law of harmonics again. First we have the keynote; next in importance comes the fifth; and last of all the third. Thus again is the absence of the major seventh in our primitive scale perfectly logical; we may search in vain in our list of harmonics for the tone which forms that interval.

Now that we have traced the influence of passionate utterance on music, it still remains for us to consider the influence of something very different. The dance played an important rôle in the shaping of the art of music; for to it music owes periodicity, form, the shaping of phrases into measures, even its rests. And in this music is not the only debtor, for poetry owes its very "feet" to the dance.

Now the dance was, and is, an irresponsible thing. It had no *raison d'être* except purely physical enjoyment. This rhythmic swaying of the body and light tapping of the feet have always had a mysterious attraction and fascination for mankind, and music and poetry were caught in its swaying measures early in the dawn of art.

instruments. The relative antiquity of the lyre and the lute as compared with the harp has been much discussed, the main contention against the lyre being that it is a more artificial instrument than the harp; the harp was played with the fingers alone, while the lyre was played with a plectrum (a small piece of metal, wood, or ivory). Perhaps it would be safer to take the lute as the earliest form of the stringed instrument, for, from the very first, we find two species of instruments with strings, one played with the fingers, the prototype of our modern harps, banjos, guitars, etc., the other played with the plectrum, the ancestor of all our modern stringed instruments played by means of bows and hammers, such as violins, pianos, etc.

However this may be, one thing is certain, the possession of these instruments implies already a considerable measure of culture, for they were not haphazard things. They were made for a purpose, were invented to fill a gap in the ever-increasing needs of expression. In Homer we find a description of the making of a lyre by Hermes, how this making of a lyre from the shell of a tortoise that happened to pass before the entrance to the grotto of his mother, Maïa, was his first exploit; and that he made it to accompany his song in praise of his father Zeus. We must accept this explanation of the origin of the lyre, namely, that it was deliberately invented to accompany the voice. For the lyre in its primitive state was never a solo instrument; the tone was weak and its powers of expression were exceedingly limited. On the other hand, it furnished an excellent background for the voice and, which was still more to the point, the singer could accompany himself. The drum had too vague a pitch, and the flute or pipe necessitated another performer, besides having too much similarity of tone to the voice to give sufficient contrast. Granted then that the lyre was invented to accompany the voice, and without wasting time with surmises as to whether the first idea of stringed instruments was received from the twanging of a bow-string or the finding of a tortoise shell with the half-dessicated tendons of the animal still stretching across it, let us find when the instrument was seemingly first used.

That the lyre and lute are of Asiatic origin is generally conceded, and even in comparatively modern times, Asia seems to be the home of its descendants. The Tartars have been called the troubadours of Asia — and of Asia in the widest sense of the word — penetrating into the heart of the Caucasus on the west and reaching through the country eastward to the shores of the Yellow Sea. Marco Polo, the celebrated Venetian traveller, and M. Huc, a French missionary to China and Thibet, as well as Spencer, Atkinson, and many others, speak of the wandering bards of Asia. Marco Polo's account of how Jenghiz Kahn, the great Mongol conqueror, sent an expedition composed entirely of minstrels against Mien, a city of 30,000 inhabitants, has often been quoted to show what an abundance — or perhaps superfluity would be the better word — of musicians he had at his court.

That the lyre could not be of Greek origin is proved by the fact that no root has been discovered in the language for *lyra*, although there are many special names for varieties of the instrument. Leaving aside the question of the geographical origin of the instrument, we may say, broadly, that wherever we find a nation with even the smallest approach to a history, there we shall find bards singing of the exploits of heroes, and always to the accompaniment of the lyre or the lute. For at last, by means of these instruments, impassioned speech was able to lift itself permanently above the level of everyday life, and its lofty song could dispense with the soft, sensuous lull of the flute. And we shall see later how these bards became seers, and how even our very angels received harps, so closely did the instrument become associated with what I have called impassioned speech, which, in other words, is the highest expression of what we consider godlike in man.

III

THE MUSIC OF THE HEBREWS AND THE HINDUS

THE music of the Hebrews presents one of the most interesting subjects in musical history, although it has an unfortunate defect in common with so many kindred subjects, namely, that the most learned dissertation must invariably end with a question mark. When we read in Josephus that Solomon had 200,000 singers, 40,000 harpers, 40,000 sistrum players, and 200,000 trumpeters, we simply do not believe it. Then too there is lack of unanimity in the matter of the essential facts. One authority, describing the *machol*, says it is a stringed instrument resembling a modern viola; another describes it as a wind instrument somewhat like a bagpipe; still another says it is a metal ring with a bell attachment like an Egyptian sistrum; and finally an equally respected authority claims that the *machol* was not an instrument at all, but a dance. Similarly the *maanim* has been described as a trumpet, a kind of rattle box with metal clappers, and we even have a full account in which it figures as a violin.

The temple songs which we know have evidently been much changed by surrounding influences, just as in modern synagogues the architecture has not held fast to ancient Hebrew models but has been greatly influenced by different countries and peoples. David may be considered the founder of Hebrew music, and his reign has been well called an "idyllic episode in the otherwise rather grim history of Israel."

Of the instruments named in the Scriptures, that called the harp in our English translation was probably the *kinnor*, a kind of lyre played by means of a plectrum, which was a small piece of metal, wood, or bone. The psaltery or *nebel* (which was of course derived from the Egyptian *nabla*, just as the *kinnor* probably was in some mysterious manner derived from the Chinese *kin*) was a kind of dulcimer or zither, an oblong box with strings which were struck by small hammers. The timbrel corresponds to our modern tambourine. The *schofar* and *keren* were horns. The former was the well-known ram's horn which is still blown on the occasion of the Jewish New Year.

In the Talmud mention is made of an organ consisting of ten pipes which could give one hundred different sounds, each pipe being able to produce ten tones. This mysterious instrument was called *magrepha*, and although but one Levite (the Levites were the professional musicians among the Hebrews) was required to play it, and although it was only about three feet in length, its sound was so tremendous that it could be heard ten miles away. Hieronymus speaks of having heard it on the Mount of Olives when it was played in the Temple at Jerusalem. To add to the mystery surrounding this instrument, it has been proved by several learned authorities that it was merely a large drum; and, to cap the climax, other equally respected writers have declared that this instrument was simply a large shovel which, after being used for the sacrificial fire in the temple, was thrown to the ground with a great noise, to inform the people that the sacrifice was consummated.

It is reasonably certain that the seemingly incongruous titles to the Psalms were merely given to denote the tune to which they were to be sung, just as in our modern hymns we use the words *Canterbury*, *Old Hundredth*, *China*, etc.

The word *selah* has never been satisfactorily explained, some readings giving as its meaning "forever," "hallelujah," etc., while others say that it means repeat, an inflection of the voice, a modulation to another key, an instrumental interlude, a rest, and so on without end.

Of one thing we may be certain regarding the ancient Hebrews, namely, that their religion brought something into the world that can never again be lost. It fostered idealism, and gave mankind something pure and noble to live for, a religion over which Christianity shed the sunshine of divine mercy and hope. That the change which was to be wrought in life was sharply defined may be seen by comparing the great songs of the different nations. For up to that time a song of praise meant praise of a *King*. He was the sun that warmed men's hearts, the being from whom all wisdom came, and to whom men looked for mercy. If we compare the Egyptian hymns with those of the Hebrews, the difference is very striking. On the walls of the great temples of Luxor and the Ramesseum at Thebes, as well as on the wall of the temple of Abydos and in the main hall of the great rock-hewn temple of Abu-Simbel, in Nubia, is carved the "Epic of Pentaur," the royal Egyptian scribe of Rameses II:

My king, his arms are mighty, his heart is firm. He bends his bow and none can resist him. Mightier than a hundred thousand men he marches forward. His counsel is wise and when he wears the royal crown, Alef, and declares his will, he is the protector of his people. His heart is like a mountain of iron. Such is King Rameses.

If we turn to the Hebrew prophets, this is their song:

The mountains melted from before the Lord and before Him went the pestilence; burning coals went forth at His feet. Hell is naked before Him and destruction hath no covering. He hangeth the earth upon nothing and the pillars of heaven tremble and are astonished at His reproof. Though He slay me, yet will I trust in Him. For I know that my Redeemer liveth, and at the last day He shall stand upon the earth.

As with the Hebrews, music among the Hindus was closely bound to religion. When, 3000 years before the Christian era, that wonderful, tall, white Aryan race of men descended upon India from the north, its poets already sang of the gods, and the Aryan gods were of a different order from those known to that part of the world; for they were beautiful in shape, and friendly to man, in great contrast to the gods of the Davidians, the pre-Aryan race and stock of the Deccan. These songs formed the *Rig-Veda*, and are the nucleus from which all Hindu religion and art emanate.

We already know that when the auxiliary speech which we call music was first discovered, or, to use the language of all primitive nations, when it was first bestowed on man by the gods, it retained much of the supernatura potency that its origin would suggest. In India, music was invested with divine power, and certain hymns — especially the prayer or chant of Vashishtha — were, according to the *Rig-Veda*, all powerful in battle. Such a magic song, or chant, was called a *brahma*, and he who sang it a *brahmin*. Thus the very foundation of Brahminism, from which rose Buddhism in the sixth century B.C., can be traced back to the music of the sacred songs of the *Rig-Veda* of India. The priestly or Brahmin caste grew therefore from the singers of the Vedic hymns. The Brahmins were not merely the keepers of the sacred books, or Vedas, the philosophy, science, and laws of the ancient Hindus (for that is how the power of the caste developed), but they were also the creators and custodians of its secular literature and art. Two and a half thousand years later Prince Gautama or Buddha died, after a life of self-sacrifice and sanctity. On his death five hundred of his disciples met in a cave near Rajagriha to gather together his sayings, and chanted the lessons of their great master. These songs became the bible of Buddhism, just as the *Vedas* are the bible of Brahminism, for the Hindu word for a Buddhist council means literally "a singing together."

Besides the sacred songs of the Brahmins and Buddhists, the Hindus had many others, some of which partook of the occult powers of the hymns, occult powers that were as strongly marked as those of Hebrew music. For while the latter are revealed in the playing of David before Saul, in the influence of music on prophecy, the falling of the walls of Jericho at the sound of the trumpets of Joshua, etc., in India the same supernatural power was ascribed to certain songs. For instance, there were songs that could be sung only by the gods, and one of them, so the legend runs, if sung by a mortal, would envelop the singer in flames. The last instance of the singing of this song was during the reign of Akbar, the great Mogul emperor (about 1575 A.D.). At his command the singer sang it standing up to his neck in the river Djaumna, which, however, did not save him, for, according to the account, the water around him boiled, and he was finally consumed by a flame of fire. Another of Akbar's singers caused the palace to be wrapped in darkness by means of one of these magic songs, and another averted a famine by causing rain to fall when the country was threatened by drought. Animals were also tamed by means of certain songs, the only relic of which is found in the serpent charmers' melodies, which, played on a kind of pipe, seem to possess the power of controlling cobras and the other snakes exhibited by the Indian fakirs.

Many years before Gautama's time, the brahmas or singers of sacred songs of ancient India formed themselves into a caste or priesthood; and the word "Brahma," from meaning a sacred singer, became the name of the supreme deity; in time, as the nation grew, other gods were taken into the religion. Thus we find in pre-Buddha times the trinity of gods: Brahma, Vishnu, and Siva, with their wives, Sarasvati or learning, Lakshmi or beauty, and

Paravati, who was also called Kali, Durga, and Mahadevi, and was practically the goddess of evil. Of these gods Brahma's consort, Sarasvati, the goddess of speech and learning, brought to earth the art of music, and gave to mankind the *Vina*.

This instrument is still in use and may be called the national instrument of India. It is composed of a cylindrical pipe, often bamboo, about three and a half feet long, at each end of which is fixed a hollow gourd to increase the tone. It is strung lengthwise with seven metal wires held up by nineteen wooden bridges, just as the violin strings are supported by a bridge. The scale of the instrument proceeds in half tones from
The tones are produced by plucking the strings with the fingers (which are covered with a kind of metal thimble), and the instrument is held so that one of the gourds hangs over the left shoulder, just as one would hold a very long-necked banjo.

It is to the Krishna incarnation of Vishnu that the Hindu scale is ascribed. According to the legend, Krishna or Vishnu came to earth and took the form of a shepherd, and the nymphs sang to him in many thousand different keys, of which from twenty-four to thirty-six are known and form the basis of Hindu music. To be sure these keys, being formed by different successions of quartertones, are practically inexhaustible, and the 16,000 keys of Krishna are quite practicable. The differences in tone, however, were so very slight that only a few of them have been retained to the present time.

The Hindus get their flute from the god Indra, who, from being originally the all-powerful deity, was relegated by Brahminism to the chief place among the minor gods — from being the god of light and air he came to be the god of music. His retinue consisted of the *gandharvas*, and *apsaras*, or celestial musicians and nymphs, who sang magic songs. After the rise and downfall of Buddhism in India the term *raga* degenerated to a name for a merely improvised chant to which no occult power was ascribed.

The principal characteristics in modern Hindu music are a seemingly instinctive sense of harmony; and although the actual chords are absent, the melodic formation of the songs plainly indicates a feeling for modern harmony, and even form. The actual scale resembles our European scale of twelve semitones (twenty-two *s'rutis*, quarter-tones), but the modal development of these sounds has been extraordinary. Now a "mode" is the manner in which the notes of a scale are arranged. For instance, in our major mode the scale is arranged as follows: tone, tone, semitone, tone, tone, tone, semitone. In India there are at present seventy-two modes in use which are produced by making seventy-two different arrangements of the scale by means of sharps and flats, the only rule being that each degree of the scale must be represented; for instance, one of the modes *Dehrâsan-Karabhárna* corresponds to our major scale. Our minor (harmonic) scale figures as *Kyravâni*. *Tânarupi* corresponds to the following succession of notes,

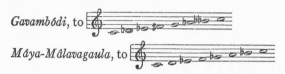

Gavambódi, to

Máya-Málavagaula, to

It can thus easily be seen how the seventy-two modes are possible and practicable. Observe that the seven degrees of the scale are all represented in these modes, the difference between them being in the placing of half-tones by means of sharps or flats. Not content with the complexity that this modal system brought into their music, the Hindus have increased it still more by inventing a number of formulæ called *ragas* (not to be confounded with those rhapsodical songs, the modern descendant of the magic chants, previously mentioned).

In making a Hindu melody (which of course must be in one of the seventy-two modes, just as in English we should say that a melody must be in one of our two modes, either major or minor) one would have to conform to one of the *ragas*, that is to say, the melodic outline would have to conform to certain rules, both in ascending and descending. These rules consist of omitting notes of the modes, in one manner when the melody ascends, and in another when it descends. Thus, in the *raga* called *Mohànna*, in ascending the notes must be arranged in the following order: 1, 2, 3, 5, 6, 8; in descending it is 8, 7, 5, 4, 2, 1. Thus if we wished to write a melody in the mode *Tânarupi — raga Mohànna —* we could never use the fourth, F, or the seventh, B, if our melody ascended; if our melody descended we should have to avoid the sixth, A♯, and the third, E♭♭. As one can easily perceive, many strange melodic effects are produced by these means. For instance, in the *raga Mohànna*, in which the fourth and seventh degrees of the scale are avoided in ascending, if it were employed in the mode *Dehrásin-Karabhárna*, which corresponds to our own major scale, it would have a pronounced Scotch tinge so long as the melody ascended; but let it *descend* and the Scotch element is deserted for a decided North American Indian, notably Sioux tinge. The Hindus are an imaginative race, and invest all these *ragas* and modes with mysterious attributes, such as anger, love, fear, and so on. They were even personified as supernatural beings; each had his or her special name and history. It was proper to use some of them only at midday, some in the morning, and some at night. If the mode or *raga* is changed during a piece, it is expressed in words, by saying, for instance, that "*Mohànna*" (the new "*raga*") is here introduced to the family of *Tânarupi*. The melodies formed from these modes and *ragas* are divided into four classes, *Rektah, Teranah, Tuppah,* and *Ragni.* The *Rektah* is in character light and flowing. It falls naturally into regular periods, and resembles the *Teranah*, with the exception that the latter is only sung by men. The character of the *Tuppah* is not very clear, but the *Ragni* is a direct descendant of the old magic songs and incantations; in character it is rhapsodical and spasmodic.

IV

THE MUSIC OF THE EGYPTIANS, ASSYRIANS, AND CHINESE

In speaking of the music of antiquity we are seriously hampered by the fact that there is practically no actual music in existence which dates back farther than the eighth or tenth century of the present era. Even those well-known specimens of Greek music, as they are claimed to be, the hymns to Apollo, Nemesis, and Calliope, do not date farther back than the third or fourth century, and even these are by no means generally considered authentic. Therefore, so far as actual sounds go, all music of which we have any practical knowledge dates from about the twelfth century.

Theoretically, we have the most minute knowledge of the scientific aspect of music, dating from more than five hundred years before the Christian era. This knowledge, however, is worse than valueless, for it is misleading. For instance, it would be a very difficult thing for posterity to form any idea as to what our music was like if all the actual music in the world at the present time were destroyed, and only certain scientific works such as that of Helmholtz on acoustics and a few theoretical treatises on harmony, form, counterpoint and fugue were saved.

From Helmholtz's analysis of sounds one would get the idea that the so-called tempered scale of our pianos caused thirds and sixths to sound discordantly.

From the books on harmony one would gather that consecutive fifths and octaves and a number of other things were never indulged in by composers, and to cap the climax one would naturally accept the harmony exercises contained in the books as being the very acme of what we loved best in music. Thus we see that any investigation into the music of antiquity must be more or less conjectural.

Let us begin with the music of the Egyptians. The oldest existing musical instrument of which we have any knowledge is an Egyptian lyre to be found in the Berlin Royal Museum. It is about four thousand years old, dating from the period just before the expulsion of the Hyksos or "Shepherd" kings.

At that time (the beginning of the eighteenth dynasty, 1500-2000 B. C.) Egypt was just recovering from her five hundred years of bondage, and music must already have reached a wonderful state of development. In wall paintings of the eighteenth dynasty we see flutes, double flutes, and harps of all sizes, from the small one carried in the hand, to the great harps, almost seven feet high, with twenty-one strings; the never-failing sistrum (a kind of rattle); kitharas, the ancestors of our modern guitars; lutes and lyres, the very first in the line of instruments culminating in the modern piano.

One hesitates to class the trumpets of the Egyptians in the same category, for they were war instruments, the

tone of which was probably always forced, for Herodotus
says that they sounded like the braying of a donkey.
The fact that the cheeks of the trumpeter were reinforced
with leather straps would further indicate that the instruments were used only for loud signalling.

According to the mural paintings and sculptures in
the tombs of the Egyptians, all these instruments were
played together, and accompanied the voice. It has long
been maintained that harmony was unknown to the
ancients because of the mathematical measurement of
sounds. This might be plausible for strings, but pipes
could be cut to any size. The positions of the hands of
the executants on the harps and lyres, as well as the use of
short and long pipes, make it appear probable that something of what we call harmony was known to the Egyptians.

We must also consider that their paintings and sculptures were eminently symbolic. When one carves an
explanation in hard granite it is apt to be done in shorthand, as it were. Thus, a tree meant a forest, a prisoner
meant a whole army; therefore, two sculptured harpists
or flute players may stand for twenty or two hundred.
Athenæus, who lived at the end of the second and beginning of the third century, A. D., speaks of orchestras of
six hundred in Ptolemy Philadelphus's time (300 B. C.),
and says that three hundred of the players were harpers,
in which number he probably includes players on other
stringed instruments, such as lutes and lyres. It is therefore to be inferred that the other three hundred played wind
and percussion instruments. This is an additional reason
for conjecturing that they used chords in their music; for

six hundred players, not to count the singers, would hardly play entirely in unison or in octaves. The very nature of the harp is chordal, and the sculptures always depict the performer playing with both hands, the fingers being more or less outstretched. That the music must have been of a deep, sonorous character, we may gather from the great size of the harps and the thickness of their strings. As for the flutes, they also are pictured as being very long; therefore they must have been low in pitch. The reed pipes, judging from the pictures and sculptures, were no higher in pitch than our oboes, of which the highest note is D and E above the treble staff.

It is claimed that so far as the harps were concerned, the music must have been strictly diatonic in character. To quote Rowbotham, "the harp, which was the foundation of the Egyptian orchestra, is an essentially non-chromatic instrument, and could therefore only play a straight up and down diatonic scale." Continuing he says, "It is plain therefore that the Egyptian harmony was purely diatonic; such a thing as modern modulation was unknown, and every piece from beginning to end was played in the same key." That this position is utterly untenable is very evident, for there was nothing to prevent the Egyptians from tuning their harps in the same order of tones and half tones as is used for our modern pianos. That this is even probable may be assumed from the scale of a flute dating back to the eighteenth or nineteenth century B. C. (1700 or 1600 B. C.), which was found in the royal tombs at Thebes, and which is now in the Florence Museum.

Its scale was

The only thing about which we may be reasonably certain in regard to Egyptian music is that, like Egyptian architecture, it must have been very massive, on account of the preponderance in the orchestra of the low tones of the stringed instruments.

The sistrum was, properly speaking, not considered a musical instrument at all. It was used only in religious ceremonies, and may be considered as the ancestor of the bell that is rung at the elevation of the Host in Roman Catholic churches. Herodotus (born 485 B. C.) tells us much about Egyptian music, how the great festival at Bubastis in honour of the Egyptian Diana (*Bast* or *Pascht*), to whom the cat was sacred, was attended yearly by 700,000 people who came by water, the boats resounding with the clatter of castanets, the clapping of hands, and the soft tones of thousands of flutes. Again he tells us of music played during banquets, and speaks of a mournful song called *Maneros*. This, the oldest song of the Egyptians (dating back to the first dynasty), was symbolical of the passing away of life, and was sung in connection with that gruesome custom of bringing in, towards the end of a banquet, an effigy of a corpse to remind the guests that death is the birthright of all mankind, a custom which was adopted later by the Romans.

Herodotus also gives us a vague but very suggestive glimpse of what may have been the genesis of Greek tragedy, for he was permitted to see a kind of nocturnal Egyptian passion play, in which evidently the tragedy of Osiris was enacted with ghastly realism. Osiris, who represents the light, is hunted by Set or Typhon, the god of darkness, and finally torn to pieces by the followers of Set, and buried beneath the waters of the lake; Horus, the son of Osiris, avenges his death by subduing Set, and Osiris appears again as the ruler of the shadowland of death.

This strange tragedy took place at night, on the shore of the lake behind the great temple at Saïs. Osiris was dressed royally, in white, and after the horrible pursuit and his murder by Set and his sinister band, Horus, the rising sun, dispels the gloom, and a glorious new god of light appears. Set and his followers are driven back to the gloomy temple where, perhaps, there was another scene showing the shade of Osiris, enthroned and ruling the dead. We have no means of knowing the character of the music which accompanied this mystery play; but certainly the deep tones of the harps and the flutes, together with the chanting of men's voices, must have been appropriate. Add to these the almost silent rattle of the sistrum, which, for the Egyptians, possessed something of the supernatural, and we have an orchestral colouring which is suggestive, to say the least.

With this we will leave Egyptian music, simply calling attention to the works of Resellini, Lepsius, Wilkinson, and Petri, which contain copies of mural paintings and temple and tomb sculptures relating to music. For instance, pages 103, 106, and 111 of Lepsius's third book, "Die Denkmäler aus Ægypten und Æthiopen," will be found very interesting, particularly page 106, which shows some of the rooms of the palace of Amenotep IV, of the eighteenth dynasty (about 1500 or 1600 B. C.), in which dancing and music is being taught. In the same work, second book, on pages 52 and 53, are pictures taken from a tomb near Gizeh, showing harp and flute players and singers. The position of the hands of the singers — they hold them behind their ears — is a manner of illustrating the act of hearing, and arises from the hieroglyphic *double* way of putting things; for instance, in writing hieroglyphics the word is often first spelled out, then comes another sign for the pronunciation, then sometimes even two other signs to emphasize its meaning.

The music of the Assyrians may be summed up very briefly. All that can be gathered from the bas-relief sculptures is that shrill tones and acute pitch must have characterized their music. As Rowbotham says, alluding to the Sardanapalus wall sculpture now in the British Museum in London, "What can one think of the musical delicacy of a nation the King of which, dining alone with his queen, chooses to be regaled with the sounds of a lyre and a big drum close at his elbow?" The instruments represented in these bas-reliefs, aside from the drum, are high-pitched: flutes, pipes, trumpets, cymbals, and the smaller stringed instruments. These were all portable, and some, such as drums and dulcimers, were strapped to the body, all of which points to the eminently warlike character of the people. Instead of clapping the hands to mark the time as did the Egyptians, they stamped their feet. The dulcimer was somewhat like a modern zither, and may be said to contain the germ of our piano; for it was in the form of a flat case, strapped to the body and held horizontally in front of the player. The strings were struck with a kind of plectrum, held in the right hand, and were touched with the left hand immediately afterwards to stop the vibration, just as the dampers in the pianoforte fall on the string the moment the key is released. There existed among the Chaldeans a science of music, which, of course, is a very different thing from practical music, but it was so imbued with astronomical symbolism that it seems hardly worth while to consider it here. The art of Babylonia and Assyria culminated in architecture and bas-relief sculpture, and it is chiefly valuable as being the germ from which Greek art was developed.

In considering Chinese music one has somewhat the same feeling as one would have in looking across a flat plain. There are no mountains in Chinese music, and there is nothing in its history to make us think that it was ever anything but a more or less puerile playing with sound; therefore there is no separating modern Chinese music from that of antiquity. To be sure, Confucius (about 500 B. C.) said that to be well governed a nation must possess good music. Pythagoras, Aristotle, and Plato, in Greece, said the same thing, and their maxims proved a very important factor in the music of ancient times, for the simple reason that an art controlled by government can have nothing very vital about it. Hebrew music was utterly annihilated by laws, and the poetic imagination thus pent up found its vent in poetry, the result being some of the most wonderful works the world has ever known. In Egypt, this current of inspiration from the very beginning was turned toward architecture. In Greece, music became a mere stage accessory or a subject for the dissecting table of mathematics; in China, we have the dead level of an obstinate adherence to tradition, thus proving Sir Thomas Browne's saying, "The mortallest enemy unto knowledge, and that which hath done the greatest execution upon truth, hath been a peremptory adhesion unto tradition, and more especially the establishing of our own belief upon the dictates of antiquity."

The Chinese theory is that there are eight different musical sounds in nature, namely:

1. The sound of skin.
2. The sound of stone.
3. The sound of metal.
4. The sound of clay.
5. The sound of silk.
6. The sound of wood.
7. The sound of bamboo.
8. The sound of gourd.

The sound of skin has a number of varieties, all different kinds of drums.

The sound of stone is held by the Chinese to be the most beautiful among sounds, one between that of metal and of wood. The principal instrument in this category is the *king*, and in mythology it is the chosen instrument of Kouei, the Chinese Orpheus. This instrument has a large framework on which are hung sixteen stones of different sizes, which are struck, like drums, with a kind of hammer. According to Amiot, only a certain kind of stone found near the banks of the river Tee will serve for the making of these instruments, and in the year 2200 B.C. the Emperor Yu assessed the different provinces so many stones each for the palace instruments, in place of tribute.

The sound of metal is embodied in the various kinds of bells, which are arranged in many different series, sometimes after the patterns of the *king*, while sometimes they are played separately.

The sound of clay, or baked earth, is given by a kind of round egg made of porcelain — for that is what it amounts to — pierced with five holes and a mouthpiece, upon blowing through which the sound is produced — an instrument somewhat suggestive of our ocarina.

The sound of silk is given by two instruments: one a kind of flat harp with seven strings, called *che*, the other with twenty-five strings, called *kin*, in size from seven to nine feet long. The ancient form of this instrument is said to have had fifty strings.

The sound of wood is a strange element in a Chinese orchestra, for it is produced in three different ways: first, by an instrument in the form of a square wooden box with a hole in one of its sides through which the hand, holding a small mallet, is inserted, the sound of wood being produced by hammering with the mallet on the inside walls of the box, just as the clapper strikes a bell. This box is placed at the northeast corner of the orchestra, and begins every piece. Second, by a set of strips of wood strung on a strap or cord, the sound of which is obtained by beating the palm of the hand with them. The third is the strangest of all, for the instrument consists of a life-size wooden tiger. It has a number of teeth or pegs along the ridge of its back, and it is "played" by stroking these pegs rapidly with a wooden staff, and then striking the tiger on the head. This is the prescribed end of every Chinese orchestral composition, and is supposed to be a symbol of man's supremacy over brute creation. The tiger has its place in the northwest corner of the orchestra.

The sound of bamboo is represented in the familiar form of Pan's pipes, and various forms of flutes which hardly need further description.

And finally the sound of the gourd. The gourd is a kind of squash, hollowed out, in which from thirteen to twenty-four pipes of bamboo or metal are inserted; each one of these pipes contains a metal reed, the vibration of which causes the sound. Below the reed are cut small holes in the pipes, and there is a pipe with a mouthpiece to keep the gourd, which is practically an air reservoir, full of air. The air rushing out through the bamboo pipes will naturally escape through the holes cut below the reeds, making no sound, but if the finger stops one or more of these holes, the air is forced up through the reeds, thus giving a musical sound, the pitch of which will be dependent on the length of the pipes and the force with which the air passes through the reed.

Other instruments of the Chinese are gongs of all sizes, trumpets, and several stringed instruments somewhat akin to our guitars and mandolins. Neither the Chinese nor the Japanese have ever seemed to consider the voice as partaking of the nature of music. This is strange, for the language of the Chinese depends on flexibility of the voice to make it even intelligible. As a matter of fact, singing, in our sense of the word, is unknown to them.

V

THE MUSIC OF THE CHINESE (*Continued*)

HAVING described the musical instruments in use in China we still have for consideration the music itself, and the conditions which led up to it.

Among the Chinese instruments mentioned in the preceding chapter, the preponderance of instruments of percussion, such as drums, gongs, bells, etc., has probably been noticed. In connection with the last named we meet with one of the two cases in Chinese art in which we see the same undercurrent of feeling, or rather superstition, as that found among western nations. We read in the writings of Mencius, the Chinese philosopher (350 B. C.), the following bit of gossip about the king Senen of Tse.

"The king," said he, "was sitting aloft in the hall, when a man appeared, leading an ox past the lower part of it. The king saw him, and asked, 'Where is the ox going?'

"The man replied, 'We are going to consecrate a bell with its blood.'

"The king said, 'Let it go. I cannot bear its frightened appearance as if it were an innocent person going to the place of death.'

"The man answered, 'Shall we then omit the consecration of the bell?'

"The king said, 'How can that be omitted?   Change the ox for a sheep.'"

As stated before, this is one of the few cases in which Chinese superstition coincides with that of the West; for our own church bells were once consecrated in very much the same manner, a survival of that ancient universal custom of sacrifice.   With the exception of this resemblance, which, however, has nothing to do with actual music, everything in Chinese art is exactly the opposite of our western ideas on the subject.

The Chinese orchestra is composed of about sixteen different types of percussion instruments and four kinds of wind and stringed instruments, whereas in our European orchestras the ratio is exactly reversed.   Their orchestras are placed at the back of the stage, ours in front of it. The human voice is not even mentioned in their list of musical sounds (sound of metal, baked clay, wood, skin, bamboo, etc)., whereas we consider it the most nearly perfect instrument existing.   This strange perversity once caused much discussion in days when we knew less of China than we do at present, as to whether the Chinese organs of hearing were not entirely different from those of western nations.   We now know that this contradiction runs through all their habits of life.   With them white is the colour indicative of mourning;   the place of honour is on the left hand;   the seat of intellect is in the stomach;   to take off one's hat is considered an insolent gesture;   the magnetic needle of the Chinese compass is reckoned as pointing south, instead of north;   even up to the middle of the nineteenth century the chief weapon

in war was the bow and arrow, although they were long before acquainted with gunpowder — and so on, *ad infinitum*.

We are aware that the drum is the most primitive instrument known to man. If all our knowledge of the Chinese
were included in a simple list of their orchestral instruments, we should recognize at once that the possession
of the gourd, mouth-organ, and lute indicates a nation
which has reached a high state of civilization; on the
other hand, the great preponderance of bells, gongs, drums,
etc., points unmistakably to the fact that veneration of
the laws and traditions of the past (a past of savage bar-
barism), and a blind acquiescence in them, must constitute
the principal factor in that civilization. The writings
of Chinese philosophers are full of wise sayings about
music, but in practice the music itself becomes almost
unbearable. For instance, in the Confucian *Analects* we
read, "The Master (Confucius)* said: 'How to play music
may be known. At the commencement of the piece, all
the parts should sound together. As it proceeds, they
should be in harmony, severally distinct, and flowing
without a break, and thus on to the conclusion.'" The
definition is certainly remarkable when one considers
that it was given about five hundred years before our
era. In practice, however, the Chinese do not distinguish
between musical *combinations* of sound and *noise;* therefore
the above definition must be taken in a very different
sense from that which ordinarily would be the case. By
harmony, Confucius evidently means similarity of noises,

* *Kong.* His disciples called him *Fu Tsee,* or " the master "; Jesuit
missionaries Latinized this to Confucius.

and by "melody flowing without a break" he means absolute monotony of rhythm. We know this from the hymns to the ancestors which, with the hymns to the Deity, are the sacred songs of China, songs which have come down from time immemorial.

According to Amiot one of the great court functions is the singing of the "Hymn to the Ancestors," which is conducted by the Emperor. Outside the hall where this ceremony takes place are stationed a number of bell and gong players who may not enter, but who, from time to time, according to fixed laws, join in the music played and sung inside. In the hall the orchestra is arranged in the order prescribed by law: the *ou*, or wooden tiger, which ends every piece, is placed at the northwest end of the orchestra, and the *tschou*, or wooden box-drum, which begins the music, at the northeast; in the middle are placed the singers who accompany the hymn by posturing as well as by chanting. At the back of the hall are pictures of the ancestors, or merely tablets inscribed with their names, before which is a kind of altar, bearing flowers and offerings. The first verse of the hymn consists of eight lines in praise of the godlike virtues of the ancestors, whose spirits are supposed to descend from Heaven and enter the hall during the singing of this verse by the chorus. Then the Emperor prostrates himself three times before the altar, touching his head to the earth each time. As he offers the libations and burns the perfumes on the altar, the chorus sings the second verse of eight lines, in which the spirits are thanked for answering the prayer and entreated to accept the offerings. The

Emperor then prostrates himself nine times, after which he resumes his position before the altar, while the last verse of eight lines, eulogistic of the ancestors, is being chanted; during this the spirits are supposed to ascend again to Heaven. The hymn ends with the scraping of the tiger's back and striking it on the head.

We can imagine the partial gloom of this species of chapel, lighted by many burning, smoky joss-sticks, with its glint of many-coloured silks, and gold embroidery; the whining, nasal, half-spoken, monotonous drone of the singers with their writhing figures bespangled with gold and vivid colour; the incessant stream of shrill tones from the wind instruments; the wavering, light clatter of the musical stones broken by the steady crash of gongs and the deep booming of large drums; while from outside, the most monstrous bell-like noises vaguely penetrate the smoke-laden atmosphere. The ceremony must be barbarously impressive; the strange magnificence of it all, together with the belief in the actual presence of the spirits, which the vague white wreaths of joss-stick smoke help to suggest, seem to lend it dignity. From the point of view of what we call music, the hymn is childish enough; but we must keep in mind the definition of Confucius. According to the Chinese, music includes that phase of sound which we call mere noise, and the harmonizing of this noise is Chinese art. We must admit, therefore, that from this point of view their orchestra is well balanced, for what will rhyme better with noise than more noise? The gong is best answered by the drum, and the tomtom by the great bell.

China also has its folk song, which seems to be an irrepressible flower of the field in all countries. This also follows the precepts of the sages in using only the five-note or pentatonic scale found among so many other nationalities. It differs, however, from the official or religious music, inasmuch as that unrhythmic perfection of monotony, so loved by Confucius, Mencius, and their followers, is discarded in favour of a style more naturally in touch with human emotion. These folk songs have a strong similarity to Scotch and Irish songs, owing to the absence of the fourth and seventh degrees of the scale. If they were really sung to the accompaniment of chords, the resemblance would be very striking. The Chinese singing voice, however, is not sonorous, the quality commonly used being a kind of high, nasal whine, very far removed from what we call music. The accompaniment of the songs is of a character most discordant to European ears, consisting as it does mainly of constant drum or gong beats interspersed with the shrill notes of the *kin*, the principal Chinese stringed instrument. Ambros, the historian, quotes a number of these melodies, but falls into a strange mistake, for his version of a folk song called " *Tsin-fa* " is as follows:

Now this is exactly as if a Chinaman, wishing to give his
countrymen an idea of a Beethoven sonata, were to eliminate all the harmony and leave only the bare melody
accompanied by indiscriminate beats on the gong and a
steady banging on two or three drums of different sizes.
This is certainly the manner in which the little melody
just quoted would be accompanied, and not by European
chords and rhythms.

If we could eliminate from our minds all thoughts of
music and bring ourselves to listen only to the *texture*
of sounds, we could better understand the Chinese ideal
of musical art. For instance, if in listening to the deep,
slow vibrations of a large gong we ignore completely all
thought of pitch, fixing our attention only upon the
roundness and fullness of the sound and the way it gradually diminishes in volume without losing any of its pulsating colour, we should then realize what the Chinese
call music. Confucius said, "When the music master

Che first entered on his office, the finish with the *Kwan-Ts'eu* (Pan's-pipes) was magnificent — how it filled the ears!" And that is just what Chinese music aims to do, it "fills the ears" and therefore is "magnificent."*

With their views as to what constitutes the beautiful in music it is not strange that the Chinese find our music detestable. It goes too fast for them. They ask, "Why play another entirely different kind of sound until one has already enjoyed to the full what has gone before?" As they told Père Amiot many years ago: "Our music penetrates through the ear to the heart, and from the heart to the soul; that your music cannot do." Amiot had played on a harpsichord some pieces by Rameau ("*Les Cyclopes*," "*Les Charmes*," etc.) and much flute music, but they could make nothing of it.

According to their conception of music, sounds must follow one another slowly, in order to pass through the

* The Chinese theatre has been called an unconscious parody of our old-fashioned Italian opera, and there are certainly many resemblances. In a Chinese play, when the situation becomes tragic, or when one of the characters is seized with some strong emotion, it finds vent in a kind of aria. The dialogue is generally given in the most monotonous manner possible — using only high throat and head tones, occasionally lowering or raising the voice on a word, to express emotion. This monotonous, and to European ears, strangely nonchalant, nasal recitative, is being continually interrupted by gong pounding and the shrill, high sound of discordant reed instruments. When one or more of the characters commits suicide (which as we know is an honoured custom in China) he sings — or rather whines — a long chant before he dies, just as his western operatic colleagues do, as, for instance, Edgar in "Lucia di Lammermoor" and even, to come nearer home, Siegfried in "Götterdämmerung."

ears to the heart and thence to the soul; therefore they went back with renewed satisfaction to their long, monotonous chant accompanied by a pulsating fog of clangour.

Some years ago, at the time of that sudden desire of China, or more particularly of Li Hung Chang, to know more of occidental civilization, some Chinese students were sent by their government to Berlin to study music. After about a month's residence in Berlin these students wrote to the Chinese government asking to be recalled, as they said it would be folly to remain in a barbarous country where even the most elementary principles of music had not yet been grasped.

To go deeply into the more technical side of Chinese music would be a thankless task, for in the Chinese character the practical is entirely overshadowed by the speculative. All kinds of fanciful names are given to the different tones, and many strange ideas associated with them. Although our modern chromatic scale (all but the last half-tone) is familiar to them, they have never risen to a practical use of it even to this day. The Chinese scale is now, as it always has been, one of five notes to the octave, that is to say, our modern major scale with the fourth and seventh omitted.

From a technical point of view, the instruments of bamboo attain an importance above all other Chinese instruments. According to the legend, the Pan's-pipes of bamboo regulated the tuning of all other instruments, and as a matter of fact the pipe giving the note F, the universal tonic, is the origin of all measures also. For this pipe, which in China is called the "musical foot," is at the same time a standard measure, holding exactly twelve hundred millet seeds, and long enough for one hundred millet seeds to stand end on end within it.

In concluding this consideration of the music of the Chinese, I would draw attention to the unceasing repetition which constitutes a prominent feature in all barbarous or semi-barbarous music. In the "Hymn of the Ancestors" this endless play on three or four notes is very marked.

I Verse

In other songs it is equally apparent.

This characteristic is met with in the music of the American Indians, also in American street songs, in fact in all music of a primitive nature, just as our school children draw caricatures similar to those made by great chiefs and medicine men in the heart of Africa, and, similarly, the celebrated "graffiti" of the Roman soldiers were precisely of the same nature as the beginnings of Egyptian art. In art, the child is always a barbarian more or less, and all strong emotion acting on a naturally weak organism or a primitive nature brings the same result, namely, that of stubborn repetition of one idea. An example of this is Macbeth, who, in the very height of his passion, stops to juggle with the word "sleep," and in spite of the efforts of his wife, who is by far the more civilized of the two, again and again recurs to it, even though he is in mortal danger. When Lady Macbeth at last breaks down, she also shows the same trait in regard to her bloodstained hands. It is not so far from Scotland to the Polar regions, and there we find that when Kane captured a young Eskimo and kept him on his ship, the only sign of life the prisoner gave was to sing over and over to himself the following:

Coming back again to civilization, we find Tennyson's Elaine, in her grief, repeating incessantly the words, "Must I then die."

The music of the Siamese, Burmese, Javanese, and Japanese has much in common with that of the Chinese, the difference between the first two and the last named being mainly in the absence of the *king*, or musical stones, or rather the substitution of sets of drums in place of it. For instance, the Burmese drum-organ, as it is called, consists of twenty-one drums of various sizes hung inside a great hoop. Their gong-organ consists of fifteen or more gongs of different sizes strung inside a hoop in the same manner. The player takes his place in the middle of the hoop and strikes the drums or gongs with a kind of stick. These instruments are largely used in processions, being carried by two men, just as a sedan chair is borne; the player, in order to strike all the gongs and bells, must often walk backwards, or strike them behind his back.

In Javanese and Burmese music these sets of gongs and drums are used incessantly, and form a kind of high-pitched, sustained tone beneath which the music is played or sung.

In Siamese music the wind instruments have a prominent place. After having heard the Siamese Royal Orchestra a number of times in London, I came to the conclusion that the players on the different instruments *improvise* their parts, the only rule being the general character of the melodies to be played, and the finishing together. The effect of the music was that of a contrapuntal nightmare, hideous to a degree which one who has not heard it cannot conceive. Berlioz, in his "Soirées de l'orchestre," well described its effect when he said:

"After the first sensation of horror which one cannot repress, one feels impelled to laugh, and this hilarity can only be controlled by leaving the hall. So long as these impossible sounds continue, the fact of their being gravely produced, and in all sincerity *admired* by the players, makes the 'concert' appear inexpressibly 'comic.'"

The Japanese had the same Buddhistic disregard for euphony, but they have adopted European ideas in music and are rapidly becoming occidentalized from a musical point of view. Their principal instruments are the *koto* and the *samisen*. The former is similar to the Chinese *che*, and is a kind of large zither with thirteen strings, each having a movable bridge by means of which the pitch of the string may be raised or lowered. The *samisen* is a kind of small banjo, and probably originated in the Chinese *kin*.

From Buddhism to sun worship, from China to Peru and Mexico, is a marked change, but we find strange resemblances in the music of these peoples, seeming almost to corroborate the theory that the southern American races may be traced back to the extreme Orient. We remember that in the Chinese sacred chants — "official" music as one may call it — all the notes were of exactly the same length. Now Garcilaso de la Vega (1550), in his "Commentarios Reales," tells us that unequal time was unknown in Peru, that all the notes in a song were of exactly the same length. He further tells us that in his time the voice was but seldom heard in singing, and that all the songs were played on the flute, the words being so well known that the melody of the flute immediately suggested them. The Peruvians were essentially a pipe race, while, on the other hand, the instruments of the Mexicans were of the other extreme, all kinds of drums, copper gongs, rattles, musical stones, cymbals, bells, etc., thus completing the resemblance to Chinese art. In Prescott's "Conquest of Peru" we may

read of the beautiful festival of Raymi, or adoration of
the sun, held at the period of the summer solstice. It
describes how the Inca and his court, followed by the
whole population of the city, assembled at early dawn
in the great square of Cuzco, and how, at the appearance
of the first rays of the sun, a great shout would go up, and
thousands of wind instruments would break forth into a
majestic song of adoration. That the Peruvians were a
gentler nation than the Mexicans can be seen from their
principal instrument, the pipe.

While it has been strenuously denied that on such occa-
sions human sacrifices were offered in Peru, the Mexicans,
that race whose principal instruments were drums and
brass trumpets, not only held such sacrifices, but, strange
to say, held them in honour of a kind of god of music,
Tezcatlipoca. This festival was the most important in
Mexico, and took place at the temple or "teocalli," a
gigantic, pyramid-like mass of stone, rising in terraces to
a height of eighty-six feet above the city, and culminating
in a small summit platform upon which the long procession of priests and victims could be seen from all parts of
the city. Once a year the sacrifice was given additional
importance, for then the most beautiful youth in Mexico
was chosen to represent the god himself. For a year
before the sacrifice he was dressed as Tezcatlipoca, in
royal robes and white linen, with a helmet-like crown of
sea shells with white cocks' plumes, and with an anklet
hung with twenty gold bells as a symbol of his power,
and he was married to the most beautiful maiden in
Mexico. The priests taught him to play the flute, and

whenever the people heard the sound of it they fell down and worshipped him.

The account may be found in Bancroft's great work on the "Native Races of the Pacific," also Sahagun's "Nueva España and Bernal Diaz," but perhaps the most dramatic description is that by Rowbotham:

And when the morning of the day of sacrifice arrived, he was taken by water to the Pyramid Temple where he was to be sacrificed, and crowds lined the banks of the river to see him in the barge, sitting in the midst of his beautiful companions. When the barge touched the shore, he was taken away from those companions of his forever, and was delivered over to a band of priests, exchanging the company of beautiful women for men clothed in black mantles, with long hair matted with blood — their ears also were mangled. These conducted him to the steps of the pyramid, and he was driven up amidst a crowd of priests, with drums beating and trumpets blowing. As he went up he broke an earthen flute on every step to show that his love, and his delights were over. And when he reached the top, he was sacrificed on an altar of jasper, and the signal that the sacrifice was completed was given to the multitudes below by the rolling of the great sacrificial drum.*

* This drum was made of serpents' skins, and the sound of it was so loud that it could be heard eight miles away.

VI

THE MUSIC OF GREECE

THE first name of significance in Greek music is that of Homer. The hexameters of "The Iliad" and "The Odyssey" were quite probably chanted, but the four-stringed lyre which we associate with the ancient Greek singers was only used for a few preluding notes — possibly to pitch the voice of the bard — and not during the chant itself. For whatever melody this chant possessed, it depended entirely upon the raising and lowering of the voice according to the accent of the words and the dramatic feeling of the narrative. For its rhythm it depended upon that of the hexameter, which consists of a line of six dactyls and spondees, the line always ending with a spondee. Really the line should end with a dactyl ($-\smile\smile$) and a spondee ($--$). If a line ends with two spondees it is a spondaic hexameter.

From this it would seem that while the pitch of the chant would be very difficult to gauge, owing to the diversity of opinion as to how to measure in actual sounds the effect of emotions upon the human voice, at least the *rhythm* of the chants would be well defined, owing to the hexameter in which the latter were written. Here again, however, we are cast adrift by theory, for in practice nothing could be more misleading than such a deduction. For instance, the following lines from Longfellow's

"Evangeline" are both in this metre, although the rhythm of one differs greatly from that of the other.

Wearing her Norman cap, and her kirtle of blue, and the earrings

and

Shielding the house from storms, on the north were the barns and the farm-yard.

Now if we think that these lines can be sung to the same musical rhythm we are very far from the truth, although both are hexameters, namely,

$$- \smile\smile \; - \smile \; - \; \smile\smile \; - \; \smile\smile \; - \; \smile\smile \; - \; \smile\smile \; - -$$
$$- \smile\smile \; - \smile \; - \; \smile\smile \; - \; \smile\smile \; - \; \smile\smile \; - -$$

dactyls, ending with spondee.

Thus we see that metre in verse and rhythm in music are two different things, although of course they both had the same origin.

After all has been said, it is perhaps best to admit that, so far as Greek music is concerned, its better part certainly lay in poetry. In ancient times all poetry was sung or chanted; it was what I have called impassioned speech. The declamation of "The Iliad" and "The Odyssey" constituted what was really the "vocal" music of the poems. With the Greeks the word "music" (*mousikê*) included all the æsthetic culture that formed part of the education of youth; in the same general way a poet was called a singer, and even in Roman times we find Terence, in his "Phormio," alluding to poets as musicians. That Æschylus and Sophocles were not musicians, as we understand the term, is very evident in spite of the controversies on the subject.

Impassioned speech, then, was all that existed of vocal music, and as such was in every way merely the audible expression of poetry. I have no doubt that this is the explanation of the statement that Æschylus and Sophocles wrote what has been termed the *music* to their tragedies. What they really did was to teach the chorus the proper declamation and stage action. It is well known that at the Dionysian Festival it was to the poet as "chorus master" that the prize was awarded, so entirely were the arts identified one with the other. That declamation may often reach the power of music, it is hardly necessary to say. Among modern poets, let any one, for instance, look at Tennyson's "Passing of Arthur" for an example of this kind of music; the mere sound of the words completes the picture. For instance, when Arthur is dying and gives his sword, Excalibur, to Sir Bedivere with the command to throw it into the mere, the latter twice fails to do so, and returns to Arthur telling him that all he saw was

> "The water lapping on the crag
> And the long ripple washing in the reeds."

But when at last he throws it, the magic sword

> "Made lightnings in the splendour of the moon
> And flashing round and round, and whirl'd in an arch
> Shot like a streamer of the northern morn.
> So flashed and fell the brand Excalibur."

Again, when Sir Bedivere, carrying the dying king, stumbles up over the icy rocks to the shore, his armour clashing and clanking, the verse uses all the clangour of cr — ck, the slipping s's too, and the vowel *a* is used in all its changes; when the shore is finally reached, the verse suddenly turns into smoothness, the long *o*'s giving the same feeling of breadth and calm that modern music would attempt if it treated the same subject.

Here are the lines:

> Dry clash'd his harness in the icy caves
> And barren chasms, and all to left and right
> The bare, black cliff clang'd round him as he based
> His feet on juts of slippery crag that rang
> Sharp-smitten with the dint of arméd heels.
> And on a sudden, lo! the level lake
> And the long glories of the winter moon.

When we think of the earlier Greek plays, we must imagine the music of the words themselves, the cadenced voices of the protagonist or solitary performer, and the chorus, the latter keeping up a rhythmic motion with the words. This, I am convinced, was the extent of Greek music, so far as that which was ascribed to the older poets is concerned.

Instrumental music was another thing, and although we possess no authentic examples of it, we know what its scales consisted of and what instruments were in use. It would be interesting to pass in review the tragedies of Æschylus and Sophocles, the odes of Sappho and Pindar, those of the latter having a novel periodicity of form which gives force to the suggestion that these choric dances were the forerunners of our modern instrumental forms.

Such matters, however, take us from our actual subject, and we will therefore turn to Pythagoras, at Crotona, in Italy (about 500 B. C.), whom we find already laying down the rules forming a mathematical and scientific basis for the Greek musical scale.

More than three centuries had passed since Homer had chanted his "Iliad" and "Odyssey," and in the course of the succeeding fifty years some of the master spirits of the world were to appear. When we think of Pythagoras, Gautama, Buddha, Confucius, Æschylus, Sophocles, Sappho, Pindar, Phidias, and Herodotus as contemporaries — and this list might be vastly extended — it seems as if some strange wave of ideality had poured over mankind. In Greece, however, Pythagoras's theory of metempsychosis (doctrine of the supposed transmigration of the soul from one body to another) was not strong enough to make permanent headway, and his scientific theories unhappily turned music from its natural course into the workshop of science, from which Aristoxenus in vain attempted to rescue it.

At that time Homer's hexameter had begun to experience many changes, and from the art of rhythm developed that of rhyme and form. The old lyre, from having four strings, was developed by Terpander, victor in the first musical contest at the feast of Apollo Carneius, into an instrument of seven strings, to which Pythagoras *

* The fundamental doctrine of the Pythagorean philosophy was that the essence of all things rests upon musical relations, that numbers are the principle of all that exists, and that the world subsists by the rhythmical order of its elements. The doctrine of the "Harmony of the spheres" was based on the idea that the celestial spheres were separated from each other by intervals corresponding with the relative length of strings arranged so as to produce harmonious tones.

added an eighth, Theophrastus a ninth, and so on until the number of eighteen was reached.

Flute and lyre playing had attained a high state of excellence, for we hear that Lasus, the teacher of the poet Pindar (himself the son of a Theban flute player), introduced into lyre playing the runs and light passages which, until that time, it had been thought possible to produce only on the flute.

The dance also had undergone a wonderful development rhythmically; for even in Homer's time we read in "The Odyssey" of the court of Alcinoüs at Phocæa, how two princes danced before Ulysses and played with a scarlet ball, one throwing it high in the air, the other always catching it with his feet off the ground; and then changing, they flung the ball from one to the other with such rapidity that it made the onlookers dizzy. During the play, Demidocus chanted a song, and accompanied the dance with his lyre, the players never losing a step. As Aristides (died 468 B. C.), speaking of Greek music many centuries later said: "Metre is not a thing which concerns the ear alone, for in the dance it is to be *seen*." Even a statue was said to have silent rhythm, and pictures were spoken of as being musical or unmusical.

Already in Homer's time, the Cretans had six varieties of $\frac{5}{4}$ time to which they danced:

The first was known as the Cretic foot, being in a way the model or type from which the others were made; but the others were called pæons. The "Hymn to Apollo" was called a pæon or pæan, for the singers danced in Cretic rhythms as they chanted it.

There were many other dances in Greece, each having its characteristic rhythm. For instance, the Molossian dance consisted of three long steps, $- - - \left(\frac{3}{2}\right)$; that of the Laconians was the dactyl, $- \smile \smile \left(\frac{4}{4}\right)$, which was sometimes reversed $\smile \smile - \left(\frac{4}{4}\right)$. In the latter form it was also the chief dance of the Locrians, the step being called anapæst. From Ionia came the two long and two short steps, $- - \smile \smile$, $\left(\frac{3}{4} \, \mathord{\text{♩}} \, \mathord{\text{♩}} \, \mathord{\text{♫}}\right)$, or $\smile \smile - - \left(\frac{3}{4} \, \mathord{\text{♫}} \, \mathord{\text{♩}} \, \mathord{\text{♩}}\right)$, which were called Ionic feet. The Doric steps consisted primarily of a trochee and a spondee, $- \smile - -$ or $\frac{7}{8}$ time. These values, however, were arranged in three other different orders, namely, $\smile - - - \, | \, - - \smile - \, | \, - - - \smile \, |$ and were called the first, second, third, or fourth epitrite, according to the positions of the short step. The second epitrite was considered the most distinctly Doric.

The advent of the Dionysian * festivals in Greece threatened to destroy art, for those wild Bacchic dances, which are to be traced back to that frenzied worship of Bel and Astarte in Babylon, wild dances amenable only to the impulse of the moment, seemed to carry everything before them. Instead of that, however, the hymns to Bacchus, who was called in Phœnicia the flute god, from which the characteristics of his worship are indicated,

* Dionysus, the same as the Roman Bacchus.

were the germs from which tragedy and comedy developed, and the mad bacchanalian dances were tamed into dithyrambs. For the Corybantes, priests of the goddess Cybele, brought from Phrygia, in Asia Minor, the darker form of this worship; they mourned for the death of Bacchus, who was supposed to die in winter and to come to life again in the spring. When these mournful hymns were sung, a goat was sacrificed on the altar; thus the origin of the word "tragedy" or "goat song" (*tragos*, goat, and *odos*, singer). As the rite developed, the leader of the chorus would chant the praises of Dionysus, and sing of his adventures, to which the chorus would make response. In time it became the custom for the leader, or coryphæus, to be answered by one single member of the chorus, the latter being thus used merely for the chanting of commentaries on the narrative. The answerer was called "hypocrite," afterward the term for actor.

This was the material from which Æschylus created the first tragedy, as we understand the term. Sophocles (495–406 B. C.) followed, increasing the number of actors, as did also Euripides (480–406 B. C.).

Comedy (*komos*, revel, and *odos*, singer) arose from the spring and summer worship of Bacchus, when everything was a jest and Nature smiled again.

The dithyramb (*dithyrambos* or Bacchic step, | — ‿ ‿ — |) brought a new step to the dance and therefore a new element into poetry, for all dances were choric, that is to say they were sung as well as danced.

Arion was the first to attempt to bring the dithyramb into poetry, by teaching the dancers to use a slower movement and to observe greater regularity in their various steps. The Lydian flute, as may be supposed, was the instrument which accompanied the dithyramb, associated with all kinds of harsh, clashing instruments, such as cymbals, tambourines, castanets. These Arion tried to replace by the more dignified Grecian lyre; but it was long before this mad dance sobered down to regular rhythm and form. From Corinth, where Arion first laboured, we pass to Sicyon, where the taming of the dithyramb into an art form was accomplished by Praxilla, a poetess who added a new charm to the lilt of this Bacchic metre, namely, rhyme.

And this newly acquired poetic wealth was in keeping with the increasing luxury and magnificence of the cities, for we read in Athenæus and Diodorus that Agrigentum sent to the Olympic games three hundred chariots, drawn by white horses. The citizens wore garments of cloth of gold, and even their household ornaments were of gold and silver; in their houses they had wine cellars which contained three hundred vats, each holding a hundred hogsheads of wine. In Sybaris this luxury reached its height, for the Sybarites would not allow any trade which caused a disagreeable sound, such as that of the blacksmith, carpenter, or mason, to be carried on in their city limits. They dressed in garments of deep purple, tied their hair in gold threads, and the city was famed for its incessant banqueting and merrymaking. It was such luxury as this that Pindar found at the court of Hiero, at Syracuse, whither Æschylus had retired after his defeat by Sophocles at the Dionysian Festival at Athens.

The worship of Bacchus being at its height at that time, it may be imagined that wine formed the principal element of their feasts. And even as the dithyramb had been pressed into the service of poetry, so was drinking made rhythmic by music. For even the wine was mixed with water according to musical ratios; for instance, the pæonic or 3 to 2, ‿‿‿—= ₵ ₵ ₵ ₣ ; the iambic or 2 to 1, —‿ = ₣ ₵; dactylic or 2 to 2, —‿‿ = ₣ · ₵ ₵. The master of the feast decided the ratio, and a flute girl played a prescribed melody while the toast to good fortune, which commenced every banquet, was being drunk. By the time the last note had sounded, the great cup should have gone round the table and been returned to the master. And then they had the game of the cottabos, which consisted of throwing the contents of a wine cup high in the air in such a manner that the wine would fall in a solid mass into a metal basin. The winner was the one who produced the clearest musical sound from the basin.

We see from all this that music was considered rather a beautiful plaything or a mere colour. By itself it was considered effeminate; therefore the early Greeks always had the flute player accompanied by a singer, and the voice was always used with the lyre to prevent the latter appealing directly to the senses. The dance was corrected in the same manner; for when we speak of Greek dances, we always mean *choric* dances. Perhaps the nearest approach to the effect of what we call music was made by Æschylus, in the last scene of his "Persians," when Xerxes and the chorus end the play with one continued wail of sorrow. In this instance the words take second place, and the actual sound is depended upon for the dramatic effect.

The rise and fall of actual instrumental music in Greece may be placed between 500 and 400 B. C. After the close of the Peloponnesian War (404 B. C.), when Sparta supplanted Athens as the leader of Greece, art declined rapidly, and at the time of Philip of Macedon (328 B. C.) may be said to have been practically extinct. Then, in place of the dead ashes of art, the cold fire of science arose; for we have such men as Euclid (300 B. C.) and his school applying mathematics to musical sounds, and a system of cold calculation to an art that had needed all the warmth of emotional enthusiasm to keep it alive. Thus music became a science. Had it not been for the little weeds of folk song which managed with difficulty to survive at the foot of this arid dust heap, and which were destined to be transformed and finally to bloom into such lovely flowers in our times, we might yet have been using the art to illustrate mathematical calculations.

The teaching of Pythagoras was the first step in this classification of sounds; and he went further than this, for he also classified the *emotions* affected by music. It was therefore a natural consequence that in his teaching he should forbid music of an emotional character as injurious. When he came to Crotona, it was to a city that vied with Agrigentum, Sybaris, and Tarentum in luxury; its chief magistrate wore purple garments, a golden crown upon his head, and white shoes on his feet. It was said of Pythagoras that he had studied twelve years with the Magi in the temples of Babylon; had lived among the Druids of Gaul and the Indian Brahmins; had gone among the priests of Egypt and witnessed their most secret temple rites. So free from care or passion was his face that he was thought by the people to be Apollo; he was of majestic presence, and the most beautiful man they had ever seen. So the people accepted him as a superior being, and his influence became supreme over science and art, as well as manners.

He gave the Greeks their first scientific analysis of sound. The legend runs that, passing a blacksmith's shop and hearing the different sounds of the hammering, he conceived the idea that sounds could be measured by some such means as weight is measured by scales, or distance by the foot rule. By weighing the different hammers, so the story goes, he obtained the knowledge of harmonics or overtones, namely, the fundamental, octave, fifth, third, etc. This legend, which is stated seriously in many histories of music, is absurd, for, as we know, the hammers would not have vibrated. The anvils would have given the sound, but in order to produce the octave, fifth, etc., they would have had to be of enormous proportions. On the other hand, the monochord, with which students in physics are familiar, was his invention; and the first mathematical demonstrations of the effect on musical pitch of length of cord and tension, as well as the length of pipes and force of breath, were his.

These mathematical divisions of the monochord, however, eventually did more to stifle music for a full thousand years than can easily be imagined. This division of the string made what we call harmony impossible; for by it the major third became a larger interval than our modern one, and the minor third smaller. Thus thirds did not sound well together, in fact were dissonances, the only intervals which *did* harmonize being the fourth, fifth, and octave. This system of mathematically dividing tones into equal parts held good up to the middle of the sixteenth century, when Zarlino, who died in 1590, invented the system in use at the present time, called the *tempered scale*, which, however, did not come into general use until one hundred years later.

Aristoxenus, a pupil of Aristotle, who lived more than a century after Pythagoras, rejected the monochord as a means for gauging musical sounds, believing that the ear, not mathematical calculation, should be the judge as to which interval sounds "perfect." But he was unable to formulate a system that would bring the third (and naturally its inversion the sixth) among the harmonizing intervals or consonants. Didymus (about 30 B. C.) first discovered that two different-sized whole tones were necessary in order to make the third consonant; and Ptolemy (120 A. D.) improved on this system somewhat. But the new theory remained without any practical effect until nearly the seventeenth century, when the long respected theory of the perfection of mathematical calculation on the basis of natural phenomena was overthrown in favour of actual effect. If Aristoxenus had had followers able to combat the crushing influence of Euclid and his school, music might have grown up with the other arts. As it is, music is still in its infancy, and has hardly left its experimental stage.

Thus Pythagoras brought order into the music as well as into the lives of people. But whereas it ennobled the people, it killed the music, the one vent in life through which unbounded utterance is possible; its essence is so interwoven with spirituality that to tear it away and fetter it with human mathematics is to lower it to the level of mere utilitarianism. And so it was with Greek music, which was held subordinate to metre, to poetry, to acting, and finally became a term of contempt. Pythagoras wished to banish the flute, as Plato also did later, and the name of flute player was used as a reproach. I fancy this was because the flute, on account of its construction, could ignore the mathematical divisions prescribed for the stringed instruments, and therefore could indulge in purely emotional music. Besides, the flute was the chosen instrument of the orgiastic Bacchic cult, and its associations were those of unbridled license. To be sure, the voice was held by no mathematical restrictions as to pitch; but its music was held in check by the words, and its metre by dancing feet.

Having measured the musical intervals, there still remained the task of classifying the different manners of singing which existed in Greece, and using all their different notes to form a general system. For just as in different parts of Greece there existed different dances, the steps of which were known as Lydian, Ionian, Locrian, and Dorian feet, and so on, so the melodies to which they were danced were known as being in the Lydian,

Ionian, Locrian, or Dorian scale or mode. In speaking of Hindu music, I explained that what we call a mode consists of a scale, and that one mode differs from another *only* in the position of the semitones in this scale. Now in ancient Greece there were in use over fifteen different modes, each one common to the part of the country in which it originated. At the time of Pythagoras there were seven in general use: the Dorian, Lydian, Æolian or Locrian, Hypo- (or low) Lydian, Phrygian, Hypo- (or low) Phrygian, and Mixolydian or mixed Lydian. The invention of the latter is attributed to Sappho by Plutarch, quoting Aristoxenus.

These modes were all invested with individual characters by the Greeks, just as in the present day we say our major mode is happy, the minor sad. The Dorian mode was considered the greatest, and, according to Plato, the only one worthy of men. It was supposed to have a dignified, martial character. The Lydian, on the other hand, was all softness, and love songs were written in it. The Phrygian was of a violent, ecstatic nature, and was considered as being especially appropriate for dithyrambs, the metre for the wild bacchanalian dances. For instance, Aristotle tells how Philoxenus attempted to set dithyrambic verse to the Dorian mode, and, failing, had to return to the Phrygian. The Mixolydian, which was Sappho's mode, was the mode for sentiment and passion. The Dorian, Phrygian, and Lydian were the oldest modes.

Each mode or scale was composed of two sets of four notes, called tetrachords, probably derived from the ancient form of the lyre, which in Homer's time is known to have had four strings.

Leaving the matter of actual pitch out of the question (for these modes might be pitched high or low, just as our major or minor scale may be pitched in different keys), these three modes were constructed as follows:

Greek.... Dorian   E͡F G A B͡C D E, that is, semi-
                    tone, tone, tone.

Asiatic   ⎰ Phrygian D E͡F G A B͡C D,
           ⎨   or F♯G͡♯A B C♯D͡♯E F♯, that
           ⎪   is, tone, semitone, tone.
           ⎩ Lydian   C D E͡F G A B͡C, that is, tone,
                        tone, semitone.

Thus we see that a tetrachord commencing with a half-tone and followed by two whole tones was called a Dorian tetrachord; one commencing with a tone, followed by a half-tone, and again a tone, constituted a Phrygian tetrachord. The other modes were as follows: In the Æolian or Locrian the semitones occur between the second and third notes, and the fifth and sixth:

Theraclides Ponticus identifies the Hypodorian with the Æolian, but says that the name "hypo-" merely denoted a likeness to Doric, not to pitch. Aristoxenus denies the identity, and says that the Hypodorian was a semitone below the Dorian or Hypolydian. In the Hypophrygian, the semitones occur between the third and fourth, and

sixth and seventh degrees:

In the Hypolydian, the semitones occur between the fourth and fifth, and seventh and eighth:

The Dorian (E), Phrygian (commencing on F♯ with the fourth sharped), and the Lydian (A♭ major scale) modes we have already explained. In the Mixolydian, the semitones occur between the first and second, and fourth and

fifth degrees:

According to the best evidence (in the works of Ptolemy, "Harmonics," second book, and Aristides), these were approximately the actual pitch of the modes as compared one to another.

And now the difficulty was to weld all these modes together into one scale, so that all should be represented and yet not be complicated by what we should call accidentals. This was accomplished in the following manner, by simple mathematical means:

We remember that the Dorian, which was the most greatly favoured mode in Greece, was divided into two tetrachords of exactly the same proportions, namely, semitone, tone, tone. By taking the lowest note of the Mixolydian, B, and forming a Dorian tetrachord on it, B C D E were acquired. Adding to this another Dorian tetrachord, E F G A (commencing on the last note of the first), and repeating the same series of tetrachords an octave higher, we have in all four Dorian tetrachords, two of which overlap the others. The two middle tetrachords, constituting the original Dorian mode, were called *disjunct*, the two outer ones which overlap the middle ones were called *conjunct* or *synemmenon* tetrachords.

If we consider this new scale from octave to octave, commencing with the lowest note, that is to say from B to B, we find that it coincides exactly with the Mixolydian mode; therefore this was called the Mixolydian octave. The octave in this scale from the second note, C to C, coincides exactly with the Lydian mode, and was called the Lydian octave; from the third note, D, up to its octave gives the Phrygian; from the fourth note, E, the Dorian; from the fifth, F, the Hypolydian; from the sixth, G, the Hypophrygian; and from the seventh, A, the Æolian or Hypodorian octave. Add one note to the lower end of this universal Greek scale, as it was called, and we see that the whole tonal system was included within two octaves. To each of the notes comprising it was given a name partly derived from its position in the tetrachords, and partly from the fingering employed in lyre playing, as shown in the diagram on page 87.

The fifteen strings of the *kithara* were tuned according to this scale, and the A, recurring three times in it, acquired something of the importance of a tonic or key note. As yet, however, this scale allowed of no transposition of a mode to another pitch; in order to accomplish this the second tetrachord was used as the first of another

similar system. Thus, considering the second tetrachord,
E F G A, as first of the new scale, it would be followed
by A B♭ C D, and the two disjunct tetrachords would
be formed. Followed by the two upper conjunct tetrachords, and the *proslambanómenos* added, our system on
a new pitch would be complete. This procedure has
come down almost unchanged to our times; for we have
but two modes, major and minor, which are used on every
pitch, constituting various keys. These Greek modes
are the basis on which all our modern ideas of tonality
rest; for our major mode is simply the Greek Lydian, and
our minor mode the Æolian.

LIST OF NOTES IN THE GREEK SCALE

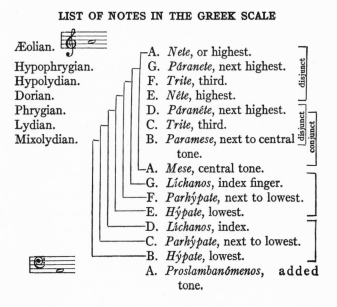

Æolian.

Hypophrygian.
Hypolydian.
Dorian.
Phrygian.
Lydian.
Mixolydian.

A. *Nete*, or highest.
G. *Páranete*, next highest.
F. *Trite*, third.
E. *Nête*, highest.
D. *Páranête*, next highest.
C. *Trite*, third.
B. *Paramese*, next to central tone.
A. *Mese*, central tone.
G. *Lichanos*, index finger.
F. *Parhýpate*, next to lowest.
E. *Hýpate*, lowest.
D. *Lichanos*, index.
C. *Parhýpate*, next to lowest.
B. *Hýpate*, lowest.
A. *Proslambanómenos*, added tone.

To go into detailed explanation of the Greek enharmonic and chromatic pitch will scarcely be worth while, and I will therefore merely add that the instruments were sometimes tuned differently, either to relieve the inevitable monotony of this purely diatonic scale or for purposes of modulation. A Dorian tetrachord is composed of semitone, tone, tone; to make it chromatic, it was changed as follows: , the *lichanos*, or index finger string, being lowered a semitone.

The enharmonic pitch consisted of tuning the *lichanos* down still further, almost a quarter-tone below the second string, or *parhýpate*, thus making the tetrachord run quarter-tone, quarter-tone, two tones. Besides this, even in the diatonic, the Greeks used what they called soft intervals; for example, when the tetrachord, instead of proceeding by semitone, tone, tone (which system was called the hard diatonic), was tuned to semitone, three-quarter-tone, and tone and a quarter. The chromatic pitch also had several forms, necessitating the use of small fractional tones as well as semitones.

Our knowledge of the musical notation of the Greeks rests entirely on the authority of Alypius, and dates from about the fourth century A. D. That we could not be absolutely sure of the readings of ancient Greek melodies, even if we possessed any, is evident from the fact that these note characters, which at first were derived from the signs of the zodiac, and later from the letters of the alphabet, indicate only the relative pitch of the sounds; the rhythm is left entirely to the metrical value of the words in the lines to be sung. Two sets of signs were used for musical notation, the vocal system consisting of writing the letters of the alphabet in different positions, upside down, sideways, etc.

Of the instrumental system but little is known, and that not trustworthy.

VII

THE MUSIC OF THE ROMANS — THE EARLY CHURCH

THE art history of the world makes it clear to us that when the art of a country turns to over-elaboration of detail and mechanical dexterity, when there is a general tendency toward vividness of *impression* rather than poignancy and vitality of *expression*, then we have the invariable sign of that decadence which inevitably drifts into revolution of one kind or another. Lasus (500 B. C.), who, as previously mentioned, was a great flute and lyre player as well as poet, betrays this tendency, which reached its culmination under the Romans. Lasus was more of a virtuoso than a poet; he introduced into Greece a new and florid style of lyre and harp playing; and it was he who, disliking the guttural Dorian pronunciation of the letter S, wrote many of his choric poems without using this letter once in them. Pindar, his pupil, followed in his footsteps. In many of his odes we find intricate metrical devices; for instance, the first line of most of the odes is so arranged metrically that the same order of accents is maintained whether the line be read backward or forward, the short and long syllables falling into exactly the same places in either case. The line "Hercules, the patron deity of Thebes," may be taken as an

example, ⌣⌣⌣⌣⌣⌣⌣. Such devices occur
all through his poems. We find in them also that magnificence of diction which is the forerunner of "virtuosity"; for he speaks of his song as "a temple with
pillars of gold, gold that glitters like blazing fire in the
night time."

In the hands of Aristophanes (450–380 B. C.), the
technique of poetry continued to advance. In "The
Frogs," "The Wasps," and "The Birds" are to be found
marvels of skill in onomatopoetic* verse. His comedies
called for many more actors than the tragedies had required, and the chorus was increased from fifteen to twenty-
four. Purple skins were spread across the stage, and the
parabasis (or topical song) and satire vied with the noble
lines of Æschylus and Sophocles for favour with the
public.

Meanwhile, as might have been expected, instrumental
music became more and more independent, and musicians,
especially the flute players, prospered; for we read in
Suidas that they were much more proficient and sought
after than the lyre and kithara players. When they
played, they stood in a conspicuous place in the centre
of the audience. Dressed in long, feminine, saffron-
coloured robes, with veiled faces, and straps round their
cheeks to support the muscles of the mouth, they exhibited
the most startling feats of technical skill. Even women
became flute players, although this was considered dis-
graceful. The Athenians even went so far that they

---

* Imitating the sound of the thing signified. Poe's "Raven"
has much of this character.

built a temple to the flute player Lamia, and worshipped her as Venus. The prices paid to these flute players surpassed even those given to virtuosi in modern times, sometimes amounting to more than one thousand dollars a day, and the luxury in which they lived became proverbial.

During this period, Aristophanes of Alexandria (350 B. C.), called "the grammarian," devised a means for indicating the inflection of the voice in speaking, by which the cadences which orators found necessary in impassioned speech could be classified, at least to some extent. When the voice was to fall, a downward stroke \ was placed above the syllable; when the voice was to be raised, an upward stroke / indicated it; and when the voice was to rise and fall, the sign was ∧, which has become our accent in music. These three signs are found in the French language, in the accent *aigu*, or high accent, as in *passé*; the accent *grave*, or low accent, as in *sincère*; or *circonflexe*, as in *Phâon*. The use of dots* for punctuation is also ascribed to Aristophanes; and our dots in musical notation, as well as the use of commas to indicate breathings, may be traced to this system.

As I have said, all this tended toward technical skill and analysis; what was lacking in inventive power it was sought to cover by wonderful execution. The mania for flute playing, for instance, seemed to spread all over the world; later we even hear that the king of Egypt, Ptolemy Auletes (80–51 B. C.), Cleopatra's father, was nicknamed " the flute player."

---

* ċ, perfect pause; c·, short; c., shortest; breathings: ' hard; ' soft.

In Rome, this lack of poetic vitality seemed evident from the beginning; for while Greece was represented by the tragedy and comedy, the Romans' preference was for mere pantomime, a species of farce of which they possessed three kinds: (1) The simple pantomime without chorus, in which the actors made the plot clear to the audience by means of gestures and dancing. (2) Another which called for a band of instrumental musicians on the stage to furnish an accompaniment to the acting of the pantomimist. (3) The chorus pantomime, in which the chorus and the orchestra were placed on the stage, supplementing the gestures of the actors by singing a narrative of the plot of the pantomime, and playing on their instruments. The latter also were expressive of the non-ideal character of the pantomime, as is indicated by the fact that the orchestra was composed of cymbals, gongs, castanets, foot castanets, rattles, flutes, bagpipes, gigantic lyres, and a kind of shell or crockery cymbals, which were clashed together.

The Roman theatre itself was not a place connected with the worship of the gods, as it was with the Greeks. The altar to Dionysus had disappeared from the centre of the orchestra, and the chorus, or rather the band, was placed upon the stage with the actors. The bagpipe now appears for the first time in musical history, although there is some question as to whether it was not known to the Assyrians. It represents, perhaps, the only remnant of Roman music that has survived, for the modern Italian peasants probably play in much the same way as did their forefathers. The Roman pipes were bound with brass, and had about the same power of tone as was obtained from the trumpet.

It is easy to see that an orchestra thus constituted would be better adapted for making a great noise than for music, while the pantomime itself was of such a brutal nature that the degradation of art may be said to have been complete. As the decay of art in Egypt culminated under Ptolemy Auletes, so in Rome it culminated in the time of Caligula (12–41 A. D.), and Nero (37–68 A. D.).

The latter, as we learn from Suetonius, competed for prizes in the public musical contests, and was never without a slave at his elbow to warn him against straining his voice. In his love of magnificence he resembled a Greek flute player, with unbounded means to gratify it. His palace, the "Golden House," had triple porticos a mile in length, and enclosed a lake surrounded by buildings which had the appearance of a city. Within its area were corn fields, vineyards, pastures, and woods containing many animals, both wild and tame. In other parts it was entirely overlaid with gold, and adorned with jewels and mother-of-pearl. The porch was so high that a colossal statue of himself, one hundred and twenty feet in height, stood in it. The supper rooms were vaulted, and compartments of the ceiling, inlaid with ivory, were made to revolve and scatter flowers; they also contained pipes which shed perfumes upon the guests.

When the revolt under Vindex broke out (68 A. D.), a new instrument had just been brought to Rome. Tertullian, Suetonius, and Vitruvius agree in calling it an organ. This instrument, which was the invention of

Ctesibus of Alexandria, consisted of a set of pipes through which the air was made to vibrate by means of a kind of water pump operated by iron keys. It was undoubtedly the direct ancestor of our modern organ. Nero intended to introduce these instruments into the Roman theatre. In planning for his expedition against Vindex, his first care was to provide carriages for his musical instruments; for his intention was to sing songs of triumph after having quelled the revolt. He publicly vowed that if his power in the state were reestablished, he would include a performance upon organs as well as upon flutes and bagpipes, in the exhibitions he intended to institute in honour of his success.

From a musical point of view, Suetonius's biography of Nero is interesting chiefly on account of its giving us glimpses of the life of a professional musician of those days. We read, together with many other details, that it was the custom for a singer to lie on his back, with a sheet of lead upon his breast, to correct unsteadiness in breathing, and to abstain from food for two days together to clear his voice, often denying himself fruit and sweet pastry. The degraded state of the theatre may well be imagined from the fact that under Nero the custom of hiring professional applause was instituted. After his death, which is so dramatically told by Suetonius, music never revived in Rome.

In the meanwhile, however, a new kind of music had begun; in the catacombs and underground vaults, the early Christians were chanting their first hymns. Like all that we call "new," this music had its roots in the old. The hymns sung by the Christians were mainly Hebrew temple songs, strangely changed into an uncouth imitation of the ancient Greek drama or worship of Dionysus; for example, Philo of Alexandria, as well as Pliny the Younger, speaks of the Christians as accompanying their songs with gestures, and with steps forward and backward. This Greek influence is still further implied by the order of one of the earliest of the Church fathers, Clement of Alexandria (about 300 A. D.), who forbade the use of the chromatic style in the hymns, as tending too much toward paganism. Some writers even go so far as to identify many of the Christian myths and symbols with those of Greece. For instance, they see, in the story of Daniel in the lions' den, another form of the legend of Orpheus taming the wild beasts; in Jonah, they recognize Arion and the dolphin; and the symbol of the Good Shepherd, carrying home the stray lamb on his shoulders, is considered another form of the familiar Greek figure of Hermes carrying the goat.

Be this as it may, it is certain that this crude beginning of Christian music arose from a vital necessity, and was accompanied by an indomitable faith. If we look back, we note that until now music had either been the servant of ignoble masters, looked upon as a mathematical problem to be solved scientifically, or used according to methods prescribed by the state. It had been dragged down to the lowest depths of sensuality by the dance, and its divine origin forgotten in lilting rhythms and soft, lulling rhymes.

On the other hand, the mathematicians, in their cold calculation, reduced music to the utilitarianism of algebra, and even viewed it as a kind of medicine for the nerves and mind. When we think of the music of Pythagoras and his school, we seem to be in a kind of laboratory in which all the tones are labelled and have their special directions for use. For the legend runs that he composed melodies in the diatonic, chromatic, and enharmonic styles as antidotes for moods such as anger, fear, sorrow, etc., and invented new rhythms which he used to steady and strengthen the mind, and to produce simplicity of character in his disciples. He recommended that every morning, after rising, they should play on the lyre and sing, in order to clear the mind. It was inevitable that this half mathematical, half psychologically medicinal manner of treating music would, in falling into the hands of Euclid (300 B. C.) and his school, degenerate into a mere peg on which to hang mathematical theorems. On the other hand, when we think of Greek dances, we seem to pass into the bright, warm sunshine. We see graceful figures holding one another by the wrist, dancing in a circle around some altar to Dionysus, and singing to the strange lilt of those unequal measures. We can imagine the scheme of colour to be white and gold, framed by the deep-blue arch of the sky, the amethyst sea flecked with glittering silver foam, and the dark, sombre rocks of the Cretan coast bringing a suggestion of fate into this dancing, soulless vision. Turning now to Rome, we see that this same music has fallen to a wretched slave's estate, cowering in some corner until the screams of Nero's living torches need to be drowned; and then, with brazen clangour and unabashed rhythms, this brutal music flaunts forth with swarms of dancing slaves, shrilling out the praises of Nero; and the time for successful revolution is at hand.

The first steps toward actually defining the new music took place in the second century, when the Christians were free to worship more openly, and, having wealthy converts among them, held their meetings in public places and basilicas which were used by magistrates and other officials during the day. These basilicas or public halls had a raised platform at one end, on which the magistrate sat when in office. There were steps up to it, and on these steps the clergy stood. The rest of the hall was called the "nave" (ship), for the simile of "storm-tossed mariners" was always dear to the early Christian church. In the centre of the nave stood the reader of the Scriptures, and on each side of him, ranged along the wall, were the singers. The Psalms were sung antiphonally, that is, first one side would sing and the other side would answer. The congregations were sometimes immense, for according to St. Jerome (340–420 A. D.) and St. Ambrose (340–397 A. D.) "the roofs reechoed with their cries of 'Alleluia,' which in sound were like the great waves of the surging sea."

Nevertheless this was, as yet, only sound, and not music. Not until many centuries later did music become distinct from chanting, which is merely intoned *speech*. The disputes of the Arians and the Athanasians also affected the music of the church, for as early as 306 A. D., Arius introduced many secular melodies, and had them sung by women.

Passing over this, we find that the first actual arrangement of Christian music into a regular system was attempted by Pope Sylvester, in 314 A. D., when he instituted singing schools, and when the heresy of Arius was formally condemned.

Now this chanting or singing of hymns was more or less a declamation, thus following the Greek tradition of using one central note, somewhat in the nature of a keynote.

Rhythm, distinct melody, and even metre were avoided as retaining something of the unclean, brutal heathenism against which the Christians had revolted. It was the effort to keep the music of the church pure and undefiled that caused the Council of Laodicea (367 A. D.) to exclude from the church all singing not authorized from the pulpit.

A few years later (about 370 A. D.) Ambrose, the Archbishop of Milan, strove to define this music more clearly, by fixing upon the modes that were to be allowed for these chants; for we must remember that all music was still based upon the Greek modes, the modern major and minor being as yet unknown. In the course of time the ancient modes had become corrupted, and the modes that Ambrose took for his hymns were therefore different from those known in Greece under the same names. His Dorian is what the ancients called Phrygian, dominant, A; his Phrygian was the ancient Dorian, dominant, C; his Lydian corresponded to the old Hypolydian, dominant, C; and his

Mixolydian to the old Hypophrygian,  dominant, D. These modes were accepted by the church and were called the Authentic modes.

Almost two centuries later, Gregory the Great added four more modes, which were called Plagal or side modes (from *plagios* — oblique). These were as follows:

Hypodorian, dominant, F.

Hypophrygian, dominant, A.

Hypolydian, dominant, A.

Hypo-mixolydian, dominant, C.

It is easy to see that these so-called new modes are simply new versions of the first four; although they are lowered a fourth beneath the authentic modes (hence the *hypo*), the *keynote remains the same* in each instance. Still later two more modes were added to this list, the Ionic, dominant, G, which corresponded to the ancient Greek Lydian; and the Æolian, dominant, E, which, strange to say, was the only one of these newer modes which corresponded to its Greek namesake. Naturally these two newly admitted modes were also accompanied by their lower pitched attendant modes, the Hypoionic, dominant, E, and the Hypoæolian, dominant, C.

SUMMARY

Mode.	Key.	Dominant.
Dorian........................	D	A
Hypodorian	D	F
Phrygian.....................	E	C
Hypophrygian.................	E	A
Lydian.......................	F	C
Hypolydian...................	F	A
Mixolydian...................	G	D
Hypo-mixolydian..............	G	C
Æolian.......................	A	E
Hypoæolian...................	A	C
Ionian.......................	C	G
Hypoionian...................	C	E

Dominants

Now all these lower, or derived modes, Hypodorian, Hypophrygian, Hypolydian, etc., received the name Plagal modes, because there was but one tonic or keynote in the scale; consequently a melody starting on any degree of the scale would invariably return to the same tonic or keynote. They differed from the authentic modes, inasmuch as in the latter a melody might end either on the upper or lower tonic or keynote. Thus the melody itself was said to be either authentic or plagal, according to whether it had one or two tonics. The theme of Schumann's "Etudes symphoniques" is authentic, and the first variation is plagal.

Between the sixth and tenth centuries there was much confusion as to the placing of these modes, but they finally stood as given above. The Greek names were definitely accepted in the eleventh century, or thereabouts; previously, they were known also as the first, second, third, etc., up to the twelfth, church tones or Gregorian modes.

At this point it is necessary to refer again to Ambrose. Apart from having brought the first four authentic modes into church music, he composed many hymns which had this peculiarity, namely, that they were modelled more on the actual declamation of the words to be sung than had hitherto been the case. We are told that his chants — to use the phrase of his contemporary, Francis of Cologne — were "all for sweetness and melodious sound"; and St. Augustine (354–430 A. D.), speaks of them with ecstasy. The words in these hymns were used in connection with small groups of notes; consequently they could be understood as they were sung, thus returning in a measure to the character of the music of the ancients, in which the word and declamation were of greater importance than the actual sounds which accompanied them. But now a strange thing was to happen that was to give us a new art. Now, at last, music was to be separated from language and dance rhythms, and stand alone for the first time in the history of civilization as *pure music*.

To appreciate the change made by Gregory (540–604 A. D.), it is necessary to bear in mind the state of the church just before his time. As the Ambrosian chant had brought something of the old declamation and sweetness back into the church ceremonial, so also in the church itself there was a tendency to sink back into the golden shimmer that had surrounded the ancient pagan rites. Already Paul of Samosata, Bishop of Antioch (260 A. D.), had striven to bring a certain Oriental magnificence into the church ceremonials. He had a canopied throne erected for himself, from which he would address his congregation; he introduced applause into the church, after the fashion of the Roman theatres; he also had a chorus of women singers, who, as Eusebius tells us, sang not the Christian hymns, but pagan tunes. Later, in Constantinople, even this luxury and pomp increased; the churches had domes of burnished gold, and had become gigantic palaces, lit by thousands of lamps. The choir, dressed in glittering robes, was placed in the middle of the church, and these singers began to show the same fatal sign of decadence that we saw before in Rome and Greece. According to St. Chrysostom (347-407 A. D.), they used unguents on their throats in order to make the voice flexible, for by this time the singing had become a mere vehicle for virtuosity; when they sang their *tours de force*, the people applauded and waved their handkerchiefs, as they did also when the preaching pleased them. The pagans pointed the finger of scorn at the Christians, as being mere renegades from the old religion, and said, plausibly enough, that their worship was merely another form of the Dionysus tragedy. There was the same altar, the same chorus, the priest who sang and was answered by the chorus; and the resemblance had grown to such an extent that St. Chrysostom (350 A. D.) complained that the church chorus accompanied its singing with theatrical gestures, which, as we know, is simply the first step towards the dance.

This was the state of things when Gregory became Pope in 590 A. D. His additions to the modes already in use have been explained. His great reform lay in severing the connection between the music of the church and that of the pagan world before it. Casting aside the declamation and rhythm, which up to now had always dominated pure sound, he abolished the style of church singing in vogue, and substituted for it a system of chanting in which every tie between the words and music was severed.

The music was certainly primitive enough, for it consisted merely of a rising and falling of the voice for the space of many notes on one single syllable, as, for instance,

Glo - - - ri - a . . . .

The difference between this and the Ambrosian chant is evident if we look at the following; and we must also bear in mind that the Ambrosian chants were very simple in comparison with the florid *tours de force* of the Byzantine church:

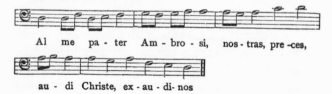

Al me pa - ter Am - bro - si, nos - tras, pre -ces,

au - di Christe, ex - au - di- nos

Now this reform could not be carried out at once; it was only through the medium of Charlemagne (742–814 A. D.), a hundred years later, that the Gregorian chant was firmly established. Authorized by a synod of bishops, called together from all parts of Europe by Pope Adrian I, Charlemagne, in 774, caused all the chant and hymn books of the Ambrosian system throughout Italy to be burned. So completely was this accomplished that only one Ambrosian missal was found (by St. Eugenius at Milan), and from this work alone can we form any idea as to the character of the music used by the followers of Ambrose, who were much retarded by the lack of a musical notation, which was the next factor needed to bring music to an equality with the other arts.

VIII

FORMATION OF THE SCALE — NOTATION

In comparing the Ambrosian chant with that of Gregory, it may be said that we have touched upon the vital principle of modern music. The novelty in the Gregorian chant consisted in its absolute emancipation from the tyranny of actual words and declamation; while the idea, the poetic principle, or religious ecstasy still remained the ideal to be expressed in the music. Before this, as already explained, music was either a mathematical problem, a rhythm to mark the time in dancing, or a vehicle serving for the display of clever *tours de force*, the music of the tragedies being merely a kind of melodious declamation. To quote Goethe, "having recognized the fact, it still remains for us to see how it developed." Let us now consider this point.

Three things were necessary before these Gregorian chants could develop at all: (1) A simple, clean-cut musical scale or systematized table of musical sounds. (2) Some definite manner of symbolizing sounds, so that they could be accurately expressed in writing. (3) A cultivation of the sense of hearing, in order that mankind might learn to distinguish between sounds that are discordant and those that sound well together; in other words, harmony.

We will begin with the scale, and review what we know of the Greek modes in order to show how they were amalgamated into our present octave system of scales.

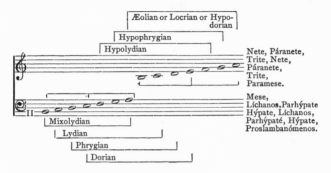

Under Ambrose and Pope Gregory, these modes had taken a different form.   The chromatic and enharmonic styles had been abandoned in theory, the portamento which the singers introduced into their chants being the only principle retained.   The new system was as follows:

In order to complete the story of the evolution of scales and clefs, we must add that the Flemish monk, Hucbald (900 A. D.), divided this scale into regular tetrachords, beginning at G, with the succession, tone, semitone, tone, forming four disjunct tetrachords,

This division remained without influence on the development of the scale.

The first change in the *tetrachord* system of reckoning tones and dividing the scale was made by Guido d'Arezzo (first half of eleventh century), who divided it into hexachords or groups of six notes each. Up to that time, each note of the scale had had a letter of the alphabet for its symbol. It was Guido who conceived the idea of using syllables for these notes. The story of how it occurred to him is well known: On one occasion, hearing his brethren in the monastery choir of Arezzo, in Tuscany, sing a hymn to St. John the Baptist, he noticed that the first syllable of each line came on regularly ascending notes of the scale, the first syllable coming on C, the first of the next line on D, the first of the third on E, etc., up to A on the sixth line. As all these syllables happened to differ one from the other, and, moreover, were very easy to sing, he hit upon the idea of using them to distinguish the notes on which they fell in the hymn.

Ut queant   la - xis *Re*sonare   fibris

Mi - ra ges - torum *Fa* - mu - li tu - o - rum

Sol - ve polluti *La*bi - i re - a - tum Sancte Joannes

Furthermore, as there were six of these syllables, he arranged the musical scale in groups of six notes instead of four, hexachords instead of tetrachords. Commencing with G, which was the lowest note of the system in Hucbald's time, the first hexachord was formed of G A B C D E; the second, following the example of the Greeks, he made to overlap the first, namely, C D E F G A; the third, likewise overlapping the second, commenced on F. In order to make this hexachord identical in structure with the first and second, he flatted the B, thus making the succession of notes, F G A B♭ C D. The next three hexachords were repetitions of the first three, namely, G A B C D E, C D E F G A, F G A B♭ C D; the last was again a repetition of the first, G A B C D E.

THE GAMUT.

Hard Low	Natural Low	Soft Low
Ut re mi fa sol la	Ut re mi fa sol la	Ut re mi fa sol la

Γ A B C D E C D E F G a F G a b c d
Gamma

Hard High	Natural High
Ut re mi fa sol la	Ut re mi fa sol la

G a b c d e c d e f g aa

	Soft High					Hard Super Acute				
Ut	re	mi	fa	sol	la	Ut	re	mi	fa	sol	la

| f | g | aa | bb | cc | dd | g | aa | bb | cc | dd | ee |

To the lowest note of this scale, which was foreign to the Greek system, he gave a special name, *gamma*, after the Greek letter G. From this we get our word for the scale, the gamut. The other notes remained the same as before, only that for the lowest octave capital letters were used; in the next octave, the notes were designated by small letters, and in the last octave by double letters, aa, bb, etc., as in the following example.

Capitals.   Small letters   Double or very small letters

PRESENT SCALE.

Contra   Great   Small   1st c'   2nd c''   3rd c'''   4th c''''   8

Following out his system, he applied the newly acquired syllables to each of the hexachords — for instance, the lowest hexachord, G A B C D E, which was called hard, became *ut re mi fa sol la;* the second, which was called natural, C D E F G A, also became *ut re mi fa sol la;*

and the third, which was called soft, F G A B♭ C D, became likewise *ut re mi fa sol la*. The next three hexachords were treated in the same manner; the last or seventh hexachord was merely a repetition of the first and the fourth.

Now in the hymns, and also in the sequences, as they were called (which were simply a series of notes forming a little melody sung to two or three words), the voice was rarely called upon to progress more than the interval of a sixth, and so this solmization, as the new system was called, was very valuable; for one had only to give the pitch, and *ut* always meant the keynote, *re* the second, *mi* the third, etc., etc. In time *ut* was found to be a difficult syllable to sing, and *do* was substituted. This change, however, was made after the scale was divided into a system of octaves instead of hexachords. The improvement in singing soon made the limits of the hexachords too small to be practical; therefore another syllable was added to the hexachordal system, *si*, and with this seventh note we have our modern scale. From this we see that the scale in present use is composed of octaves, just as the older scales were composed of hexachords, and before that tetrachords. Just as in mediæval times each hexachord commenced with *ut*, so now every octave of our tonal system commences with *do*.

Before leaving the hexachordal system, it may be as well to explain the mode of procedure when the voice had to go beyond the interval of the sixth. We know that the first of every set of six notes was called *ut*, the second, *re*, the third, *mi*, etc. When the voice had to go beyond *la*, the sixth note, to B♮, that sixth note was always called *re*, and was considered the second note of a new hexachord. If, on the other hand, the voice had to go beyond *a*, to B♭, the fifth note was called *re*, since the syllables *mi fa* must always come on the half-tone.

In a study of our system of writing music, it may be as well to begin with the derivation of our sharps and flats. Observing the third hexachord on our list we see that in order to make it identical in structure with the first and second, the B had to be lowered a semitone. Now the third hexachord was called soft. The B♭ in it was accordingly called a soft B or B *molle*, which is still the name in France for a flat, and *moll* in German still means minor, or "soft" or "lowered." For the fourth hexachord, which was called hard, this B was again raised a semitone. But the flatted B was already indicated by the letter *b* or round *b*, as it was called; hence this B natural was given a *square* shape and called B *carré*, ♮. The present French word for natural (when it is specially marked) is *bécarré;* the German word for major also comes indirectly from this, for *dur* means "hard."

An explanation of the modern German names for notes will be easily understood in this connection. In the German nomenclature the letters of the alphabet stand for the notes of the scale as in the English, with the exception of B. This B, or "round" B, in the German system stands for B♭, which is more logical than our English usage, since our flat is merely a slightly modified form of *b*. The German B natural is our letter *h*, which is merely a corruption of the square *b*, ♮, which by the addition of a line in time became our ♮. The Germans have carried the flatting and sharping of tones to a logical conclusion in their present nomenclature, for by "sharping" the sound of a single letter it is raised a semitone from its normal diapason, thus F becomes *Fis*, G *Gis*. On the other hand, in order to lower a tone, the letter representing it is "flatted," and F is called *Fes*, G *Ges*, the only exception to these rules being the B which we have already considered.

In France the Guidonian system was adhered to closely, and to this day the *bécarré* is used only as an accidental, to indicate that the note to which it refers has been flatted before. The *naturel* (which has the same shape) is used to designate a note that is natural to the key; thus the distinction is made between an accidental and a note that is common to the key. In F major, for instance, B♮ is *si bécarré*, A♮ would be *la naturel*. Our modern sharp is merely another form of the natural or square B (♮) which gradually came to be used before *any* note, signifying that it was raised or sharped a halftone; the flat lowered it a semitone, and after a while the natural received its present place between the sharp and flat. The first instance we have of the sharp being used is in the thirteenth century, when (in the Rondels of Adam de la Hale) it takes the form of a cross × (the German word for the sharp still remains *kreuz*). The French word *diese* (sharp) comes from the Greek *diesis*, a term used to indicate the raising of the voice in the chromatic scale.

And now we have to speak of notation and its development. Thus far we have found only two ways in which musical sounds were indicated by the ancients. First, we remember the invention of Aristophanes of Alexandria, his accents, high, low, and circumflex. Then we know from Ptolemy, Bœthius, and Alypius that letters were used to designate the different tones; but as there is no music extant in this notation to prove the theory, we need not trouble ourselves with it.

The system of Aristophanes, however, was destined to become the nucleus from which our modern notation sprang. We know that an elementary idea, clearly expressed, has more chances of living than has a more complicated system, however ingenious the latter may be. Now this system is so plain that we will find it is common to many aboriginal peoples, for instance the American Indians have a system very similar.

In the period now under consideration (from the third to the tenth century), music was noted in this way: an upstroke of the pen meant a raising of the voice, a downstroke lowered it, a flat stroke meant a repetition of the same note, thus / \ — . Gradually it became necessary to indicate the contour of the melodies with more accuracy; therefore the circumflex was added ⌢ and reversed ⌣ . Still later a sign for two steps was invented ⌐ and when the progression was to be diatonically stepwise

the strokes were thicker ⌐ [musical notation]. So this notation developed, and by combining the many signs together,
simple non-rhythmic melodies could be indicated with com-
parative clearness and simplicity.   The flat stroke for a
single note –, indicating [musical notation], eventually became smaller
and thicker, thus ▬.   By combining these different signs,
a skip of a third and back came to be noted ▬⌐▬ , and
if the note came down on a second instead of the original
note it became ▬⌐▬ [musical notation].   The *quilisma* (ᗡ) indicated a repetition of two notes, one above the other, and
we still use much the same sign for our trill.   Also the two
forms of the circumflex, ⌒ ⌣, were joined (ᗕ) and thus
we have the modern turn, so much used by Wagner.

Now while this notation was ingenious, it still left much
to be desired as to pitch.   To remedy this a red line was
drawn before writing these signs or *neumes*, as they were
called.   This line represented a given pitch, generally E;
above and below it were then written the signs for the
notes, their pitch being determined by the relative position
they held in regard to the *line*.   Thus ▬⌐▬ᗡᴬᴬ was the
equivalent of [musical notation], considering the line as being middle C pitch, a fourth higher F.
This was the condition of musical notation in 1000 A. D.

To Guido d'Arezzo is ascribed its development up to
some semblance of our present system, although the

claim has often been denied. It is certain, however, that the innovations were made at this period. In the first place Guido made the red line *always* stand for the pitch of F, and at a little distance above it he added another line, this time yellow, which was to indicate the pitch of C. Thus the signs began to take very definite meaning as regards pitch; for, given a sign extending from one line to the other, the reader could see at a glance that the music progressed a fifth, from F to C, or *vice-versa*. And now the copyists, seeing the value of these lines in determining the pitch of the different signs, of their own account added two more in black ink, one of which they drew between the F and the C line, and the other above the

C line, thus ≣≣≣≣. By doing this they accurately decided the pitch of every note, for the lowest line, being F, the line between that and the C line must stand for A, and the two spaces for G and B; the top line would stand for E, and the space between it and the yellow line for D.

Little by little these copyists grew careless about making the lines in yellow, red, and black, and sometimes drew them all in black or red, thereby losing the distinguishing mark of the F and C lines. In order to remedy this, Guido placed the letters F and C before the lines representing these notes, thus ₣≣. In this way our modern *clefs* (*clavis* or key) originated, for the C clef, as it is called, gradually changed its shape to C ⊏ Ƒ and ⊨ Ҟ, and the F clef changed to ꝯꝍ =ꟸ, which is our bass clef in a rudimentary form.

Later, still another line was added to the set, thus giving us our modern staff, and another clef, $\int$, was added on the next to the lowest line. This, in turn, became our present treble clef, 𝄞. In the course of time the signs themselves underwent many changes, until at last from ┏┓, etc., they became our modern signs.

Before this, however, a grave defect in the notation had to be remedied. There was as yet no way of designating the length of time a note was to be sustained; something definite in the way of noting *rhythm* was necessary. This was accomplished by Franco of Cologne, in the beginning of the thirteenth century. By disconnecting the parts of the sign ┏┛ one from another, the following individual signs were acquired ▮ ◗ ▪. In order to have two distinct values of length, these signs were called longs and shorts, *longa* ◗, and *brevis* ▪, to which was added the *brevis* in another position ◆, called *semibrevis*. The *longa* was twice the value of the *brevis*, and the *semibrevis* was half the length of the *brevis* (◗ = ▪ ▪   ▪ = ◆ ◆). When notes of equal length were slurred, they were written ┏▛. When two or more notes were to be sung to one syllable in quicker time, the *brevi* were joined one to the other ▜▪, as for instance in the songs of the thirteenth century,

DIRGE FOR KING RICHARD'S DEATH
GAUCELM FAIDIT.

Fortz chose est que tot le maur ma - jor dam

Roi Thibaut de Navarre (1250).

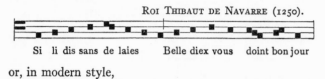

Si li dis sans de laies   Belle diex vous   doint bon jour

or, in modern style,

In this example we find the first indication of the measuring off of phrases into bars. As we see, it consisted of a little stroke, which served to show the beginning of a new line, and was not restricted to regularity of any kind except that necessitated by the verse.

The use of the *semibrevis* is shown in the following chanson of Raoul de Coucy (1192):

Quant li   ros - sig - nol   jo - lis chan - te

Seur la   flor d'este   que n'est la   rose   et le   lis

The French troubadours and the German minnesingers of the thirteenth century used these forms of notes only, and even then restricted themselves to two kinds, either the *longa* and *brevis*, or *brevis* and *semibrevis*.

The necessity for rests very soon manifested itself, and the following signs were invented to correspond to the *longa, brevis,* and *semibrevis* ▬▬▬▬▬. Also the number of note symbols was increased by the *maxima* or double *longa* ▬, and the *minima* ♩, which represented half the value of the *semibrevis.*

Now that music began taking a more definite rhythmic form than before, a more regular dividing off of the phrases became necessary. This was accomplished by the use of a dot, and another form, the perpendicular line, which we have noticed in the song of the King of Navarre (1250). At first a means to indicate triple time was invented, and the measure corresponding to our $\frac{9}{8}$ was indicated by placing the sign ⊙ at the beginning of the line. This was called perfect. Then, for plain triple time the dot was omitted ○; for $\frac{6}{8}$ time the sign ℂ was adopted, and for ordinary common time C was taken. Consequently, when these signs were placed at the beginning of the line they changed the value of the notes to correspond to the time marked. Thus in ⊙ (*tempus perfectum, prolatio major*) or $\frac{9}{8}$, the *brevis* was reckoned worth three *semibrevi* ▪ = ♦ ♦ ♦ (𝅝 = ♩. ♩. ♩.); the *semibrevis* three *minimi* ♦ = ♩ ♩ ♩ (♩ = ♫♫♩). In ○ or $\frac{3}{4}$ time ▪ = ♦ ♦ ♦ (𝅗𝅥 = ♩ ♩ ♩); but the *semibrevis* was only as long as two *minimi* ♦ = ♩ ♩ (♩ = ♫♩). In ℂ or $\frac{6}{8}$ time ▪ = ♦ ♦ (𝅗𝅥. = ♩. ♩.), but ♦ = ♩ ♩ ♩ (♩. = ♫♫♩). In C or $\frac{2}{2}$ time ▪ = ♦ ♦ (𝅝 = 𝅗𝅥 𝅗𝅥), and ♦ = ♩ ♩ (𝅗𝅥 = ♩ ♩).

In the beginning of the fifteenth century the notes began to be written in an open form

    ⬒   *Maxima.*

    ◲   *Longa.*

    □   *Brevis.*

    ◇   *Semibrevis.*

    ♩   *Minima.*

    ♪   *Semiminima*, which was added later.

As still smaller units of value were added, the *semiminima* was replaced by ♩, and the half *semiminima* thus became ♪, and the next smaller values, ♪ and ♪. The rest to correspond to the *semiminima* was ᚱ; for the *semibrevis* ▬, and *minima* ▬.

Thus we have the following values and their corresponding rests:

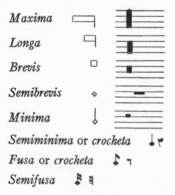

Maxima	⬒	
Longa	◲	
Brevis	□	
Semibrevis	◇	
Minima	♩	

Semiminima or *crocheta*   ♩ ᚱ

Fusa or *crocheta*   ♪ ᚱ

Semifusa   ♪ ᚱ

The rests for the *fusa* and *semifusa* were turned to the left in order to avoid the confusion that would ensue if the rest ♭ stood for ♪. Besides, the sign would have easily become confused with the C clef ⮡.

Signs for the changes of *tempo*, that is to say changes from quick to slow, etc., were introduced in the fifteenth century. The oldest of them consists of drawing a line through the *tempus* sign ⓒ. This meant that the notes were to be played or sung twice as rapidly as would usually be the case, without, however, affecting the relative value of the notes to one another.   Now we remember that the sign **C** stood for our modern $\frac{4}{4}$ time; when a line was drawn through it, ⓒ, it indicated that two *brevi* were counted as one, and the movement was said to be *alla breve*. This is the one instance of time signatures that has come down to us unaltered.

IX

THE SYSTEMS OF HUCBALD AND GUIDO D' AREZZO—THE BEGINNING OF COUNTERPOINT

WE have seen that by order of Charlemagne, Ambrosian chant was superseded by that of Gregory, and from any history of music we may learn how he caused the Gregorian chant to be taught to the exclusion of all other music. Although Notker, in the monastery of St. Gall, in Switzerland, and others developed the Gregorian chant, until the time of Hucbald this music remained mere wandering melody, without harmonic support of any kind.

Hucbald (840–930) was a monk of the monastery of St. Armand in Flanders. As we know from our studies in notation, he was the first to improve the notation by introducing a system of lines and spaces, of which, however, the spaces only were utilized for indicating the notes, viz.:

His attempt to reconstruct the musical scale was afterwards overshadowed by the system invented by Guido
d'Arezzo, and it is therefore unnecessary to describe it
in detail. His great contribution to progress was the
discovery that more than one sound could be played or
sung simultaneously, thus creating a composite sound,
the effect which we call a chord. However, in deciding
which sounds should be allowed to be played or sung
together, he was influenced partly by the mysticism of
his age, and partly by a blind adherence to the remnants
of musical theory which had been handed down from the
Greeks. As Franco of Cologne, later (1200), in systema-
tizing rhythm into measure, was influenced by the idea
of the Trinity in making his $\frac{3}{8}$ or $\frac{9}{8}$ time *tempus perfectum*,
and adopting for its symbol the Pythagorean circle ⊙
or ○, so Hucbald, in choosing his series of concords or
sounds that harmonize well together, took the first
three notes of the overtones of every sonorous fundamental, or, to express it differently, of the series of natural
harmonics, that is to say, he admitted the octave and fifth:

. But from the fifth to the octave gives
the interval of the fourth, therefore he permitted this
combination also.

From the works of Bœthius (*circa* 400) and others, he
had derived and accepted the Pythagorean division of
the scale, making thirds and sixths dissonant intervals;
and so his perfect chord (from which our later triad gets
its name of *perfect*) was composed of a root, fifth or fourth,
and octave.

Hucbald, as I have already explained, changed the Greek tone system somewhat by arranging it in four regular disjunct tetrachords, namely:

This system permitted the addition of a fifth to each note indiscriminately, and the fifths would always be *perfect;* but in regard to the octaves it was faulty, for obvious reasons. As his system of notation consisted of merely writing T for tone and S for semitone between the lines of his staff, it was only necessary to change the order of these letters for the octave at the beginning of each line. With the fourth, however, this device was impossible, and therefore he laid down the rule that when the voices proceeded in fourths, and a discord (or augmented fourth) was unavoidable, the lower voice was to remain on the same note until it could jump to another fourth forming a perfect interval:

This at least brought into the harmony an occasional third, which gradually became a recognized factor in music.

We probably know that the year 1000 was generally accepted as the time when the world was to come to an end. In the *Bibliothèque Nationale* in Paris there is a manuscript containing the prophecy which had been handed down for many centuries; also the signs for the notes to which it was to be sung, viz.:

The text is:

The Judge will speak and the earth shall tremble with awe. The stars shall be destroyed and the glory of the moon shall die, the mountains shall be crushed and the world with all in it shall utterly perish.

With the opening of the eleventh century, such was the relief from this fear which had been oppressing Christendom, that even the church reflected it in such strange rites as the *Feast of Asses* (January 14th), which was a burlesque of the Mass.

In this travesty of the Mass a young girl, dressed to represent the Virgin, riding on an ass and carrying a child in her arms, was conducted to the church door. Upon being admitted and riding up the aisle to the altar, the girl tethered the ass to the railing and sat on the steps until the service was finished. The *Credo, Gloria,* etc., all ended with a "hee-haw," and at the conclusion of the service the officiating priest brayed three times, and was answered by the congregation. The mixing of the vernacular with Latin in this service is the first instance of the use of any language but Latin in church music.

This quasi-symbolical pantomime gave rise in time to the mediæval Passion Plays, or Mysteries, as they were called. That these travesties of the Mass took different forms in various countries is very evident when we remember the description of the "Abbot of Unreason," in Scott's "Abbot." In England, among other absurdities such as the "Pope of Fools," the "Ball Dance," etc., they also had the festival of the "Boy Bishop," in which, between the sixth and twenty-eighth of December, a boy was made to perform all the functions of a bishop.

It would seem that all this has but little bearing upon the development of music. As a matter of fact it was a most potent factor in it, for music was essentially and exclusively a church property. By permitting the people to secularize the church rites at certain seasons, it was inevitable that church music would also become common property for a time, with this difference, however, that the common people could carry the tunes away with them, and the music would be the only thing remaining as a recollection of the carnival. Indeed, the prevalence of popular songs soon became such that writers of church music began to use them instead of their being derived from church music, as was originally the case. This continued to such an extent that almost up to 1550 a mass was known by the name of the popular song it was based upon, as, for instance, the mass of the "Man in Armour," by Josquin dés Pres, and those entitled "*Je prends conge*" and "*Je veult cent mille ecus.*"

Now we know that the *tempus perfectum* was *par excellence* $\frac{9}{8}$ and $\frac{3}{4}$ time. It was natural therefore that these first church tunes should have been changed to dances in the hands of the common people. Even in these dances it is interesting to note that the same symbolic significance appears to be present, for the earliest form of these dances was the "round song," or roundelay, and it was danced in a circle.

Duple time did not come into general use until the beginning of the fourteenth century. About the same time, the organum (as it was called) or system of harmonization of Hucbald was discarded, and Johannes de Muris and Philippe de Vitry championed the consonant quality of the third and sixth, both major and minor. The fifth was retained as a consonant, but the fourth was passed over in silence by the French school of writers, or classed with the dissonants. Successive fifths were prohibited as being too harshly dissonant, but successive fourths were necessarily permitted, as it would be an impossibility to do without them. Nevertheless, the fourth was still considered a dissonance, and was permitted only between the upper parts of the music. Thus the harsh consecutive passages in fifths and fourths of the organum of Hucbald disappeared in favour of the softer progressions of thirds and sixths.

In order to make clear how the new science of counterpoint came into existence, I must again revert to Hucbald.*

Before his time, all "recognized" music was a more or less melodious succession of tones, generally of the same

* There is much question as to Hucbald's organum. That actually these dissonances were used even up to 1500 is proved by Franco Gafurius of Milan, who mentions a Litany for the Dead (*De Profundis*) much used at that time:

De   profundis, etc.

length, one syllable being sometimes used for many notes. He discovered that a melody might be sung by several singers, each commencing at a different pitch instead of all singing the same notes at the same time. He also laid down rules as to how this was to be done to produce the best effect. We remember why he chose the fourth, fifth, and octave in preference to the third and sixth. He called his system an "organum" or "diaphony," and to sing according to his rules was called to "organize" or "organate." We must remember that at that time fourths and fifths were not always indicated in the written music; only the melody, which was called the principal or subject. By studying the rules prescribed for the organum, the singers could add the proper intervals to the melody. We must keep in mind, however, that later fourths were preferred to fifths (being considered less harsh), and that the musical scale of the period compelled the different voices to vary slightly, that is to say, two voices could not sing exactly the same melody at the interval of a fourth without the use of sharps or flats; therefore one voice continued on the same note until the awkward place was passed, and then proceeded in fourths again with the other voice as before:

On account of the augmented fourth that would occur by a strict adherence to the melodic structure of the subject, the

following would have been impossible:

Thus we find the first instance of the use of thirds, and also of oblique motion as opposed to the earlier inevitable parallel motion of the voices. This necessary freedom in singing the organum or diaphony led to the attempt to sing two *different* melodies, one against the other — "note against note," or "point counter point,"* point or *punct* being the name for the written note. There being now two distinct melodies, both had to be *noted* instead of leaving it to the singers to add their parts extemporaneously, according to the rules of the organum, as they had done previously. Already earlier than this (in 1100), owing to the tendency to discard consecutive fourths and fifths, the intermovement of the voices, from being parallel and oblique, became *contrary*, thus avoiding the parallel succession of intervals. The name "organum" was dropped and the new system became known as tenor and descant, the tenor being the principal or foundation melody, and the descant or descants (for there could be as many as there were parts or voices to the music) taking the place of the organum. The difference between *discantus* and *diaphony* was that the latter consisted of several parts or voices, which, however, were more or less exact reproductions, at different pitch, of the principal or given melody, while the former was composed of entirely different melodic and rhythmic material. This gave rise to the science of counterpoint, which, as I have said, consists of the trick of making a number of voices sing different melodies at the same time without violating certain given rules. The given melody or "principal"

* Counterpoint is first mentioned by Muris (1300).

soon acquired the name of *cantus firmus*, and the other parts were each called *contrapunctus*,* as before they had been called tenor and descant. These names were first used by Gerson, Chancellor of Notre Dame, Paris, about 1400.

In the meantime (about 1300–1375), the occasional use of thirds and sixths in the diaphonies previously explained led to an entirely different kind of singing, called *falso bordone* or *faux bourdon* (*bordonizare*, "to drone," comes from a kind of pedal in organum that first brought the third into use). This system, contrary to the old organum, consisted of using only thirds and sixths together, excluding the fourth and fifth entirely, except in the first and last bars. This innovation has been ascribed to the Flemish singers attached to the Papal Choir (about 1377), when Pope Gregory XI returned from Avignon to Rome. In the British Museum, however, there are manuscripts dating from the previous century, showing that the *faux bourdon* had already commenced to make its way against the old systems of Hucbald and Guido. The combination of the *faux bourdon* and the remnant of the organum gives us the foundation for our modern tone system. The old rules, making plagal motion of the different voices preferable to parallel motion, and contrary motion preferable to either, still hold good in our works on theory; so also in regard to the rules forbidding consecutive fifths and octaves, leaving the question of the fourth in doubt.

To sum up, we may say, therefore, that up to the sixteenth century, all music was composed of the slender

* Only principal (tenor or cantus firmus) was sung to words.

material of thirds, sixths, fifths, and octaves, fourths being permitted only *between* the voices; consecutive successions of fourths, however, were permitted, a license not allowed in the use of fifths or octaves. This leads us directly to a consideration of the laws of counterpoint and fugue, laws that have remained practically unchanged up to the present, with the one difference that, instead of being restricted to the meagre material of the so-called consonants, the growing use of what were once called dissonant chords, such as the dominant seventh, ninth, diminished seventh, and latterly the so-called altered chords, has brought new riches to the art.

Instead of going at once into a consideration of the laws of counterpoint, it will be well to take up the development of the instrumental resources of the time. There were three distinct types of music: the ecclesiastical type (which of course predominated) found its expression in melodies sung by church choirs, four or more melodies being sometimes sung simultaneously, in accordance with certain fixed rules, as I have already explained. These melodies or chants were often accompanied by the organ, of which we will speak later. The second type was purely instrumental, and served as an accompaniment for the dance, or consisted of *fanfares* (ceremonial horn signals), or hunting signals. The third type was that of the so-called *trouvères* or *troubadours*, with their *jongleurs*, and the minnesingers, and, later, the mastersingers. All these "minstrels," as we may call them, accompanied their singing by some instrument, generally one of the lute type or the psaltery.

X

MUSICAL INSTRUMENTS — THEIR HISTORY
AND DEVELOPMENT

In church music, the organ is perhaps the first instrument to be considered. In 951, Elfeg, the Bishop of Winchester had built in his cathedral a great organ which had four hundred pipes and twenty-six pairs of bellows, to manage which seventy strong men were necessary. Wolstan, in his life of St. Swithin, the Benedictine monk, gives an account of the exhausting work required to keep the bellows in action.

Two performers were necessary to play this organ, just as nowadays we play four-hand music on the piano. The keys went down with such difficulty that the players had to use their elbows or fists on each key; therefore it is easy to see that, at the most, only four keys could be pressed down at the same time. On the other hand, each key when pressed down or pushed back (for in the early organs the keyboard was perpendicular) gave the wind from the bellows access to ten pipes each, which were probably tuned in octaves or, possibly, according to the organum of Hucbald, in fifths or fourths. This particular organ had two sets of keys (called manuals), one for each player; there were twenty keys to each manual, and every key caused ten pipes to sound. The compass of this organ was restricted to ten notes, repeated at the distance of an octave, and, there being four hundred pipes, forty pipes were available for each note. On each key was inscribed the name of the note. As may be imagined, the tone of this instrument was such that it could be heard at a great distance.

There were many smaller organs, as, for instance, the one in the monastery of Ramsey, which had copper pipes. Pictures of others from the twelfth century show that even where there were only ten pipes, the organ had two manuals, needed two players, and at least four men for the bellows. The great exertion required to play these instruments led to the invention of what is called "mixtures." From the moment fifths and fourths were considered to sound better together than the simple notes, the pipes were so arranged that the player did not need to press two of the ponderous organ keys for this combination of sounds. One key was made to open the valves of the two sets of pipes, so that each key, instead of sounding one note, would, at will, sound the open fifth, fourth, or octave. With the addition of the third, thus constituting a perfect major triad, this barbarous habit has come down to our present day almost unchanged, for by using what is called the "mixture stop" of our modern organs, each key of the manual gives not only the original note, but also its perfect major triad, several octaves higher.

Originally the organ was used only to give the right intonation for the chanting of the priests. From the twelfth century, small portable organs of limited compass were much used; although the tone of these instruments was necessarily slight, and, owing to the shortness of the pipes, high in pitch, the principle of the mechanism was similar to that of the larger instruments. They were hung by means of a strap passed over the shoulders; one hand pressed the keys in front of the pipes (which were arranged perpendicularly), and the other hand operated the small bellows behind the pipes. These small instruments rarely had more than eight pipes, consequently they possessed only the compass of an octave. With slight variations, they were quite universally used up to the seventeenth century. Organ pedals were invented in Germany about 1325. Bernhard, organist of St. Mark's, Venice (1445–1459), has been credited with the invention of organ pedals, but it is probable that he merely introduced them into Italy.

As the Greek modes formed the basis for the musical system of the church, so the Greek monochord is the type from which the monks evolved what they called the clavichord. The monochord has a movable bridge, therefore some time is lost in adjusting it in order to get the different tones. To obviate this inconvenience, a number of strings were placed side by side, and a mechanism inserted which, by pressing a key (*clavis*), would move the bridge to the point at which the string must divide to give the note indicated by the key. This made it possible to use one string for several different notes, and explains why the clavichord or clavicembalo needed comparatively few strings. This instrument became obsolete toward the end of the eighteenth century.

The other species of instrument, the harpsichord,

which was invented about 1400, and which may be considered as having sprung from the clavichord, consisted of a separate string for each sound; the key, instead of setting in action a device for striking and at the same time *dividing* the strings, caused the strings to be plucked by quills. Thus, in these instruments, not only was an entirely different quality of tone produced, but the pitch of a string remained unaltered. These instruments were called *bundfrei*, "unbound," in opposition to the *clavicembalo*, which was called *gebunden*, or "bound." The harpsichord was much more complicated than the clavichord, in that the latter ceased to sound when the key which moved the bridge was released, whereas the harpsichord required what is called a "damper" to stop the sound when the key came up; once the string was touched by the quill, all command of the tone by the key was lost. To regulate this, a device was added to the instrument by means of which a damper fell on the string when the key was released, thereby stopping the sound.

We have now to consider the instrumental development of the Middle Ages.

An instrument of the harpsichord family which has significance in the development of the instruments of the Middle Ages is the spinet (from *spina*, "thorn"; it had leather points up to 1500), first made by Johannes Spinctus, Venice, 1500. It was a harpsichord with a *square* case, the strings running diagonally instead of lengthwise. When the spinet was of very small dimensions it was called a virginal; when it was in the shape of our modern grand piano, it was, of course, a harpsichord; and when the strings and sounding board were arranged perpendicularly, the instrument was called a clavicitherium. As early as 1500, then, four different instruments were in general use, the larger ones having a compass of about four octaves. The connecting link between the harpsichord, the clavichord, and the piano, was the dulcimer or hack-brett, which was a tavern instrument. Pantaleon Heben-streit, a dancing master and inventor of Leipzig, in 1705 added an improved hammer action, which was first applied to keyboard instruments by Cristofori, an instru-ment maker at Florence (1711). His instrument was called *forte-piano* or *pianoforte*, because it would strike loud or soft.

These instruments all descended from the ancient lyre, the only difference being that instead of causing the strings to vibrate by means of a plectrum held in the hand, the plectrum was set in motion by the mechanism of the *claves* or keys. The system of fingering employed in playing the harpsichord, up to 1700, did not make use of the thumb. J. S. Bach, F. Couperin, and J. P. Rameau were the pioneers in this matter. The first published work on piano technique and fingering was that by C. P. E. Bach (1753).

With the advent of bowed instruments the foundation was laid for the modern orchestra, of which they are the natural basis. The question of the antiquity of the bowed instrument has often been discussed, with the result that the latter has been definitely classed as essen-tially modern, for the reason that it did not become known in Europe until about the tenth to the twelfth centuries. As a matter of fact, the instrument is doubtless of Persian or Hindu origin, and was brought to the West by the Arabs, who were in Spain from the eighth to the fifteenth centuries; in fact, most of our stringed instruments, both the bowed and those of the lyre type, we owe to the Arabs — the very name of the lute, *el oud* ("shell" in Arabic) became *liuto* in Italian, in German *laute*, and in English lute. There were many varieties of these bowed instruments, and it is thought that the principle arose from rubbing one instrument with another. The only other known examples of bowed instruments of primitive type are (1) the *ravanastron*, an instrument of the monochord type, native to India, made to vibrate by a kind of bow with a string stretched from end to end; (2) the Welsh *chrotta* (609 A. D.), a primitive lyre-shaped instrument, with which, however, the use of the bow seems to have been a much later invention. Mention should also be made of the marine trumpet, much in vogue from the fourteenth to the sixteenth centuries; it consisted of a long, narrow, resonant box, composed of three boards, over which was stretched a single string; other unchangeable strings, struck with the bow, served as drones. Only the harmonics were played on the marine trumpet.

The principle of procuring the vibrations in stringed instruments by means of a bow was, of course, applied to the monochord class of keyed instruments, and was thus the origin of the hurdy-gurdy, which consisted of a wheel covered with resined leather and turned by a crank.

The bowed instruments were originally of two types, the first in the form of the lute or mandolin; the second probably derived from the Welsh *crwth*, consisting of a flat, long box strung with strings (called fidel from *fides*, " string "). The combination of these types, which were subjected to the most fantastic changes of shape, led eventually to the modern violin family.

We know that the highest plane of perfection in the violin was reached in Italy about 1600. The Cremona makers, Amati, Guarnerius, and Stradivarius, made their most celebrated instruments between 1600 and 1750.

The violin bow, in its earliest form, was nothing more than an ordinary bow with a stretched string; Corelli and Tartini used a bow of the kind. The present shape of the bow is due to Tourte, a Paris maker, who experimented in conjunction with Viotti, the celebrated violinist.

By looking at the original lute and the Arabian *rebeck* or Welsh *crwth* (originally Latin *chorus*), we can see how the modern violin received its generally rounded shape from the lute, its flatness from the *rebeck*, the sides of the instrument being cut out in order to give the bow free access to the side strings. The name too, *fidula* or *vidula*, from mediæval Latin *fides*, " string," became fiddle and viola, the smaller viola being called violino, the larger, violoncello and viola da gamba.

In the Middle Ages, the different species of bowed instrument numbered from fifteen to twenty, and it was not until between 1600 and 1700 that the modern forms of these instruments obtained the ascendancy.

Of the wind instruments it was naturally the flute that retained its antique form; the only difference between the modern instrument and the ancient one being that the former is blown crosswise, instead of perpendicularly. Quantz, the celebrated court flute player to Frederick the Great of Prussia, was the first to publish, in 1750, a so-called "method" of playing the traversal (crosswise) flute.

With the reed instruments the change in modern times is more striking. The original form of the reed instruments was of the double-reed variety. The oldest known mention of them dates from 650 A. D., when the name applied is *calamus* (reed); later the names *shalmei* (*chalumeau*, "straw," from German *halm*) and *shawm* were used. These instruments were played by means of a bell-shaped mouthpiece, the double reed being fixed inside the tube. It was not until toward the end of the sixteenth century that the bell-shaped mouthpiece was dispensed with and the reed brought directly to the lips, thus giving the player greater power of expression. The oboe is a representative type of the higher pitched double-reed instruments. In its present shape it is about two hundred years old. As the deeper toned instruments were necessarily very long, six to eight and even ten feet, an assistant had to walk before the performer, holding the tube on his shoulder. This inconvenience led to bending the tube back on itself, making it look somewhat like a bundle of sticks, hence the word *faggot*; although it is commonly known in this country by the French name, *bassoon*. This manner of arranging the instrument dates from about the year 1550. The clarinet is an essentially modern instrument, the single beating reed and cylindrical tube coming into use about 1700, the invention of a German named Denner, who lived at Nuremberg.

All the brass instruments of the Middle Ages seem to have been very short, therefore high in pitch. We remember that the Romans had trumpets (chiefly used in signalling) called *buccina*, and we may assume that the whole modern family of brass instruments has descended from this primitive type. As late as 1500, the hunting horn consisted of but one loop which passed over the shoulder and around the body of the player. A horn of from six to seven feet in length was first used about 1650; and we know that, owing to the small-ness of the instruments and their consequent high pitch in those days, many of Bach's scores contain parts abso-lutely impracticable for our modern brass instruments. The division of these instruments into classes, such as trumpets, horns, trombones, etc., is due to the differences in shape, which in turn produce tones of different quality. The large bore of the trombone gives great volume to the tone, the small bore of the trumpet great brilliancy, the medium bore of the horn veils the brilliancy on one hand and lightens the thickness of tone on the other.

The horn, called *cor de chasse*, was first used in the orches-tra in 1664, in one of Lully's operas, but its technique (stopped tones and crooks) was only properly understood about 1750; the present-day valve horn did not come into general use until within the last half century. Fifty years before the principle had been applied to the horn the trumpet had crooks and slides, a mechanism which, in the trumpet, is still retained in England, pointing to the fact that the trombone is, after all, nothing but a very large kind of trumpet.

XI

FOLK SONG AND ITS RELATION TO NATIONALISM IN MUSIC

In order to understand as well as to feel music, we must reduce it to its primary elements, and these are to be found in folk song, or, to go further back, in its predecessor, the chant of the savages.

Folk music may be likened to a twig which has fallen into a salt mine, to borrow an expression from Taine; every year adds fresh jewels to the crystals that form on it until at last the only resemblance to the original is in the general contour. We know that the nucleus of melody lies in one note, just as the origin of language is to be sought for in the word. Therefore folk music proper must be separated from what may be called barbaric music, the most primitive type of the latter being the "one-note" strain from which spring the melodies of the people. This one-note form passes through many rhythmical changes before song becomes developed to the extent of adding several notes to its means of expression. The next development of savage chanting (which is the precursor of folk song) may be traced back to its two elements, one of which was a mere savage howl, and the other, that raising of the voice under stress of strong emotion which still constitutes one of our principal means of expression.

Thus, in this barbaric music we invariably find three principles: 1, rhythm; 2, the howl or descending scale of undefined intervals; and 3, the emotional raising of the voice. The rhythm, which characterizes the most primitive form of song or chant, consists of the incessant repetition of a very small group of rhythmic sounds. This incessant recurrence of one idea is characteristic of primitive, weak, or insane natures. The second principle, which invariably includes the first (pointing to a slightly more advanced state of development), is met with in many folk songs of even modern times. The third principle is one which indicates the transition stage from primitive or barbaric music to folk music.

To the primitive savage mind, the smallest rhythmic phrase is a wonderful invention, therefore it is repeated incessantly. Add to that a certain joy in mere sound, and we have the howl, which certainly follows the sequence of nature, for a thunder clap, or the phenomenon of echo, is its prototype, being a loud explosion followed by a more or less regular sequence of minor reverberations. When the accent of passion is added to these two principles — will and nature — we have laid the æsthetic foundation for all that we call music.* The example of a loud tone with gradually ascending inflections has only been found in the most perverted types of humanity; for instance, an English writer quaintly alludes to the songs of the Polynesian cannibals as consisting of "gruesomely suggestive passages of rising quarter-tones sung

* The antiquity of any melody (or its primitiveness) may be established according to its rhythmic and melodic or human attributes.

gloatingly before their living captives who are soon to be devoured."

Now traces of these three elements are to be found in every folk song known, and we may even trace their influence in modern music, the lowest or most primitive being, as I have said, the "one-note" type, the next what I have called the "howl" type, the third the highest or "emotional" type.

Specimens of the first type, chants such as these [musical notation], are to be heard in every part of the globe, the rhythmic figure being necessarily short and repeated incessantly.

The next step was a tremendous advance, and we find its influence permeating all music. The most primitive specimens of this type we find among the Jute Indians [musical notation], a mixture of one and two.

The same is to be found in Australia, slightly modified:

The Caribs have the same song [musical notation, marked "Chromatic"]. We find it again in Hungary, although in a still more modified form, thus:

[musical notation]

And last of all we meet with it in its primitive state in the
folk song used by Bizet in "Carmen." We can even see
traces of it in the quasi-folk song of the present century:

The third element of folk song shows again a great
advance, for instead of the mere howl of pleasure or pain,
we have a more or less exactly graded expression of
feeling. In speaking of impassioned speech I explained
the relative values of the inflections of the voice, how the
upward skip of the fourth, fifth, and octave indicates the
intensity of the emotion causing the cry. When this element is brought into music, it gives a vitality not before
possessed, for by this it becomes speech. When in such
music this inflection rhymes with the words, that is to
say, when the speech finds its emotional reflection in the
music, we have reached the highest development of folk
song. In its best state, this is immeasurably superior
to much of our "made" music, only too often false in
rhythm, feeling, and declamation.

Among the different nations, these three characteristics
often become obscured by national idiosyncracies. Much
of the Chinese music, the "Hymn to the Ancestors," for
instance, seemingly covers a number of notes, whereas,
in fact, it belongs to the one-note type. We find that
their melodies almost invariably return to the same note,
the intervening sounds being more or less merely variations
above and below the pitch of the principal sound. For
example:

Hungarian folk music has been much distorted by the oriental element, as represented by the *zingari* or gypsies. The Hungarian type of folk music is one of the highest, and is extremely severe in its contours, as shown in the following:

The gypsy element as copied by Liszt has obscured the folk melodies by innumerable arabesques and ornaments of all sorts, often covering even a "one-note" type of melody until it seems like a complicated design.

This elaboration of detail and the addition of passing and ornamental notes to every melody is distinctly an oriental trait, which finds vent not only in music but also in architecture, designing, carving, etc. It is considered by many an element of weakness, seeking to cover a poverty of thought by rich vestments. And yet, to my mind, nothing can be more misleading. In spite of Sir Hubert Parry and other writers, I cannot think that the Moors in Spain, for instance, covered poverty of thought beneath superficial ingenuity of design. The Alhambra outdoes in "passage work," in virtuoso arabesques, all that an army of Liszts could do in piano literature; and yet the Arabs were the saviours of science, and promoted the greatest learning and depth of thought known in Europe in their time. As for Liszt, there is such an astounding wealth of poetry and deep feeling beneath the somewhat "flashy," bombastic trick of speech he inherited, that the true lover of music can no more allow his feelings to be led astray by such externals than one would judge a man's mind by the cut of his coat or the hat he wears.

Thus we see the essence of folk song is comprised in the three elements mentioned, and its æsthetic value may be determined by the manner in which these elements are combined and their relative preponderance.

One point must be very distinctly understood, namely, that what we call harmonization of a melody cannot be admitted as forming any part of folk song. Folk melodies are, without exception, homophonous. This being the case, perhaps my statement that the vital principle of folk music in its best state has nothing in common with nationalism (considered in the usual sense of the word), will be better understood. And this will be the proof that nationalism, so-called, is merely an extraneous thing that has no part in pure art. For if we take any melody, even of the most pronounced national type, and merely eliminate the characteristic turns, affectations, or mannerisms, the theme becomes simply music, and retains no touch of nationality. We may even go further; for if we retain the characteristic mannerisms of dress, we may harmonize a folk song in such a manner that it will belie its origin; and by means of this powerful factor (an essentially modern invention) we may even transform a Scotch song, with all its "snap" and character, into a Chinese song, or give it an Arabian flavour. This, to be sure, is possible only to a limited degree; enough, however, to prove to us the power of harmony; and harmony, as I have said, has no part in folk song.

To define the *rôle* of harmony in music is no easy matter. Just as speech has its shadow languages, gesture and expression; just as man is a duality of idealism and materialism; just as music itself is a union of the emotional and the intellectual, so harmony is the shadow language of melody; and just as in speech this shadow language overwhelms the spoken word, so in music harmony controls the melody. For example: Imagine the words "I will kill you" being said in a jesting tone of voice and with a pleasant expression of the face; the import of the words would be lost in their expression; the mere words would mean nothing to us in comparison with the expression that accompanied them.

Take away the harmonic structure upon which Wagner built his operas and it would be difficult to form a conception of the marvellous potency of his music. Melody, therefore, may be classed as the gift of folk song to music; and harmony is its shadow language. When these two powers, melody and harmony, supplement each other, when one completes the thought of the other, then, provided the thought be a noble one, the effect will be overwhelmingly convincing, and we have great music. The contrary results when one contradicts the other, and that is only too often the case; for we hear the mildest waltzes dressed up in tragic and dramatic chords, which, like Bottom, "roar as gently as any sucking dove."

In discussing the origin of speech, mention was made of those shadow languages which accompany all our spoken words, namely, the languages of expression and gesture. These were surely the very first auxiliaries of uttered speech, and in the same way we find that they constitute the first sign of advance in primitive melody. Savages utter the same thought over and over again, evidently groping after that semblance of Nirvana (or perhaps it may be better described as "hypnotic exaltation") which the incessant repetition of that one thought, accompanied by its vibrating shadow, sound, would naturally occasion.

It was also stated that the relative antiquity or primitivity of a melody is invariably to be discovered by its degree of relationship to the original type, one note, one rhythm, the emotional, the savage howl, or, in other words, the high note followed by a gradual descent. To confirm this theory of the origin of folk song, we need only look at the aboriginal chants of widely separated peoples to find that the oldest songs all resemble one another, despite the fact that they originated in widely separated localities.

Now the difference between this primitive music and that which we call folk song is that the latter is characterized by a feeling for design, in the broadest sense of the word, entirely lacking in the former. For we find that although folk song is composed of the same material as savage music, the material is arranged coherently into sentences instead of remaining the mere exclamation of passion or a nerve exciting reiteration of unchanging rhythms and vibrations, as is the case in the music of the savage.

Before proceeding further, I wish to draw the line which separates savage from folk music very plainly.

We know that the first stage in savage music is that of one note. Gradually a tone above the original is added on account of the savage being unable to intone correctly; through stress of emotion the fifth and octave come into the chant; the sixth, being the note above the fifth, is added later, as is the third, the note above the second. Thus is formed the pentatonic scale as it is found all over the world, and it is clear, therefore, that the development of the scale is due to emotional influences.

The development of rhythm may be traced to the words sung or declaimed, and the development of design or form to the dance. In the following, from Brazil, we find a savage chant in almost its primitive state:

The next example, also from Brazil, is somewhat better, but still formless and unemotional.

Let this be danced to, however, and the change is very marked, for immediately form, regularity, and design are

noticeable:

On the other hand, the emotional element marks another very decided change, namely, by placing more sounds at the command of the singer, and also by introducing words, which necessarily invest the song with the rhythm of language.

Thus the emotional and declamatory elements heighten the powers of expression by the greater range given to the voice, and add the poignancy and rhythm of speech to song.   On the other hand, the dance gives regularity to the rhythmic and emotional sequences.

In the following examples we can see more clearly the elements of folk song as they exist in savage music:

Three or four note (simple)
South America

Nubia

Emotional (simple)
Samoa

Emotional and Composite
Hudson's Bay

Soudan

Howl and Emotion
Chromatic

The fact that so many nations have the pentatonic or
five-note scale (the Chinese, Basque, Scotch, Hindu, etc.),
would seem to point to a necessary similarity of their
music. This, however, is not the case. In tracing the
differences we shall find that true folk song has but few
marked national traits, it is something which comes from
the heart; whereas nationalism in music is an outward
garment which is a result of certain habits of thought,
a *mannerism* of language so to speak. If we look at the
music of different nations we find certain characteristics; divest the music of these same characteristics
and we find that the figure upon which this garment of
nationalism has been placed is much the same the world
over, and that its relationship to the universal language
of savage music is very marked. Carmen's song, divested
of the mixture of triplets and dual rhythms (Spanish or
Moorish) is akin to the "howl."

Nationalism may be divided into six different classes:

First we have what may be broadly termed "oriental-
ism," which includes the Hindu, Moorish, Siamese, and
Gypsy, the latter embracing most of southeastern European
(Roumania, etc.) types. Liszt's "Second Rhapsody,"

opening section, divested of orientalism or gypsy characteristics, is merely of the savage three-note type.

Our second division may be termed the style of reiteration, and is to be found in Russia and northern Europe.

The third consists of the mannerism known as the "Scotch snap," and is a rhythmic device which probably originated in that trick of jumping from one register of the voice to another, which has always had a fascination for people of simple natures. The Swiss *jodel* is the best illustration of this in a very exaggerated form.

The fourth consists of a seemingly capricious intermixture of dual and triple rhythm, and is especially noticeable in Spanish and Portuguese music as well as in that of their South American descendants. This distinction, however, may be traced directly back to the Moors. For in their wonderful designs we continually see the curved line woven in with the straight, the circle with the square, the *tempus perfectum* with the spondee. This would bring this characteristic directly under the head of orientalism or ornamental development. Yet the peculiarity is so marked that it seems to call for separate consideration.

The fifth type, like the fourth, is open to the objection that it is merely a phase of the oriental type. It consists of the incessant use of the augmented second and diminished third, a distinctively Arabian characteristic, and is to be found in Egypt, also, strange to say, occasionally among our own North American Indians. This, however, is not to be wondered at, considering that we know nothing of their ancestry. Only now and then on that broad sea of mystery do we see a half submerged rock, which gives rise to all sorts of conjectures; for example, the custom of the Jutes to wear green robes and use fans in certain dances, the finding in the heart of America of such an Arab tune as this:

or such a Russian tune as this:

The last type of nationalism in folk song is almost a negative quality, its distinguishing mark being mere simplicity, a simplicity which is affected, or possibly assimilated, by the writer of such a song; for German folk song proper is a made thing, springing not from the people, but from the many composers, both ancient and modern, who have tried their hands in that direction.

While this of course takes nationalism out of the composition of German folk song so-called, the latter has undoubtedly gained immensely by it; for by thus divesting music of all its national mannerisms, it has left the thought itself untroubled by quirks and turns and a restricted musical scale; it has allowed this thought to shine out in all its own essential beauty, and thus, in this so-called German folk song, the greatest effects of poignancy are often reached through absolute simplicity and directness.

Now let us take six folk songs and trace first their national characteristics, and after that their scheme of design, for it is by the latter that the vital principle, so to speak, of a melody is to be recognized, all else being merely external, costumes of the different countries in which they were born. And we shall see that a melody or thought born among one people will change its costume when it migrates to another country.

Arab Song

Scheme

Russia—Reiteration

Red Sarafan

Scotch

Irish—Emotional in character, with greater perfection in design

Spanish

Egyptian

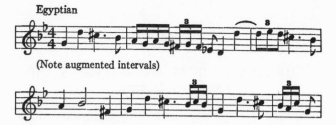

(Note augmented intervals)

The characteristics of German and English folk songs may be observed in the familiar airs of these nations.

The epitome of folk song, divested of nationalism, is shown in the following:

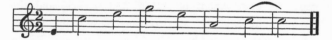

XII

THE TROUBADOURS, MINNESINGERS AND MASTERSINGERS

ALTHOUGH wandering minstrels or bards have existed since the world began, and although the poetry they have left is often suggestive, the music to which the words were sung is but little known.

About 700–800 A. D., when all Europe was in a state of dense ignorance and mental degradation, the Arabs were the embodiment of culture and science, and the Arab empire extended at that time over India, Persia, Arabia, Egypt (including Algeria and Barbary), Portugal, and the Spanish caliphates, Andalusia, Granada, etc. The descriptions of the splendour at the courts of the Eastern caliphs at Bagdad seem almost incredible.

For instance, the Caliph Mahdi is said to have expended six millions of dinars of gold in a single pilgrimage to Mecca. His grandson, Almamon, gave in alms, on one single occasion, two and a half millions of gold pieces, and the rooms in his palace at Bagdad were hung with thirty-eight thousand pieces of tapestry, over twelve thousand of which were of silk embroidered with gold. The floor carpets were more than twenty thousand in number, and the Greek ambassador was shown a hundred lions, each with his keeper, as a sign of the king's royalty, as well as a wonderful tree of gold and silver, spreading into eighteen large, leafy branches, on which were many birds made of the same precious metals. By some mechanical means, the birds sang and the leaves trembled. Naturally such a court, particularly under the reign of Haroun-al Raschid (the Just), who succeeded Almamon, would attract the most celebrated of those Arabian minstrels, such as Zobeir, Ibrahim of Mossoul, and many others who figure in the "Arabian Nights," real persons and celebrated singers of their times. We read of one of them, Serjab, who, by court jealousy and intrigues, was forced to leave Bagdad, and found his way to the Western caliphates, finally reaching Cordova in Spain, where the Caliph Abdalrahman's court vied with that of Bagdad in luxury. Concerning this we read in Gibbon that in his palace of Zehra the audience hall was incrusted with gold and pearls, and that the caliph was attended by twelve thousand horsemen whose belts and scimiters were studded with gold.

We know that the Arabian influence on the European arts came to us by the way of Spain, and although we can see traces of it very plainly in the Spanish music of to-day, the interim of a thousand years has softened its characteristics very much. On the other hand, the much more pronounced Arabian characteristics of Hungarian music are better understood when we recall that the Saracens were at the gates of Budapesth as late as 1400. That the European troubadours should have adopted the Moorish *el oud* and called it "lute" is therefore but natural. And in all the earlier songs of the troubadours we shall find many traces of the same influence; for their *albas* or *aubades* (morning songs) came from the Arabic, as did their *serenas* or serenades (evening songs), *planhs* (complaints), and *coblas* (couplets). The troubadours themselves were so called from *trobar*, meaning to invent.

In the works of Fauriel and St. Polaye, and many others, may be found accounts of the origin of the Provençal literature, including, of course, a description of the troubadours. It is generally admitted that Provençal poetry has no connection with Latin, the origin of this new poetry being very plausibly ascribed to a gypsy-like class of people mentioned by the Latin chroniclers of the Middle Ages as *joculares* or *joculatores*. They were called *joglars* in Provençal, *jouglers* or *jougleors* in French, and our word "juggler" comes from the same source. What that source originally was may be inferred from the fact that they brought many of the Arab forms of dance and poetry into Christian Europe. For instance, two forms of Provençal poetry are the counterpart of the Arabian *cosidas* or long poem, all on one rhyme; and the *maouchahs* or short poem, also rhymed. The *saraband*, or Saracen dance, and later the morris dance (*Moresco* or *Fandango*) or Moorish dance, seem to point to the same origin. In order to make it clearer I will quote an Arabian song from a manuscript in the British Museum, and place beside it one by the troubadour Capdeuil.

Arabian Melody

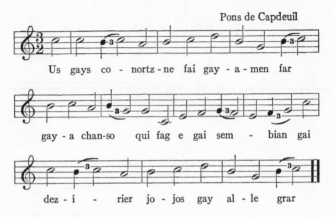

Pons de Capdeuil

Us gays co - nortz - ne fai gay - a - men far

gay - a chan-so   qui fag e gai sem - bian gai

dez - i - rier jo - jos gay al - le grar

The troubadours must not be confounded with the *jougleurs* (more commonly written *jongleurs*). The latter, wandering, mendicant musicians, ready to play the lute, sing, dance, or "juggle," were welcomed as merry-makers at all rich houses, and it soon became a custom for rich nobles to have a number of them at their courts. The troubadour was a very different person, generally a noble who wrote poems, set them to music, and employed *jongleurs* to sing and play them. In the South these songs were generally of an amorous nature, while in the North they took the form of *chansons de geste*, long poems recounting the feats in the life and battles of some hero, such as Roland (whose song was chanted by the troops of William the Conqueror), or Charles Martel.

And so the foundations for many forms of modern music were laid by the troubadours, for the *chanson* or song was always a narrative. If it were an evening song it was a *sera* or serenade, or if it were a night song, *nocturne;* a dance, a *ballada;* a round dance, a *rounde* or *rondo;* a country love song, a *pastorella.* Even the words descant and treble go back to their time; for the *jongleurs,* singing their masters' songs, would not all follow the same melody; one of them would seek to embellish it and sing something quite different that still would fit well with the original melody, just as nowadays, in small amateur bands we often hear a flute player adding embellishing notes to his part. Soon, more than one singer added to his part, and the new voice was called the triple, third, or treble voice. This extemporizing on the part of the *jongleurs* soon had to be regulated, and the actual notes written down to avoid confusion. Thus this habit of singing merged into *faux bourdon,* which has been discussed in a former chapter. Apart from these forms of song, there were some called *sirventes* — that is "songs of service," which were very partisan, and were accompanied by drums, bells, and pipes, and sometimes by trumpets. The more warlike of these songs were sung at tournaments by the *jongleurs* outside the lists, while their masters, the troubadours, were doing battle, of which custom a good description is to be found in Hagen's book on the minnesingers.

In France the Provençal poetry lasted only until the middle of the fourteenth century, after the troubadours had received a crushing blow at the time the Albigenses were extirpated in the thirteenth century.

In one city alone (that of Beziers), between 30,000 and 40,000 people were killed for heresy against the Pope. The motto of the Pope's representatives was "God will know His Own," and Catholics as well as Albigenses (as the sect was called) were massacred indiscriminately. That this heresy against the Pope was vastly aided by the troubadours, is hardly open to doubt. Such was their power that the rebellious, antipapal *sirventes* of the troubadours (which were sung by their troops of *jongleurs* in every market place) could be suppressed only after the cities of Provence were almost entirely annihilated and the population destroyed by the massacre, burning alive, and the Inquisition.

A review of the poems of Bertran de Born, Bernart de Ventadour, Thibaut, or others is hardly in place here. Therefore we will pass to Germany, where the spirit of the troubadours was assimilated in a peculiarly Germanic fashion by the minnesingers and the mastersingers.

In Germany, the troubadours became minnesingers, or singers of love songs, and as early as the middle of the twelfth century the minnesingers were already a powerful factor in the life of the epoch, counting among their number many great nobles and kings. The German minnesingers differed from the French troubadours in that they themselves accompanied their songs on the viol, instead of employing *jongleurs*. Their poems, written in the Swabian dialect, then the court language of Germany, were characterized by greater pathos and purity than those of the troubadours, and their longer poems, corresponding to the *chansons de geste* of the north of France, were also superior to the latter in point of dignity and strength. From the French we have the "Song of Roland" (which William the Conqueror's troops sang in their invasion of England); from the Germans the "Nibel-ungen Song," besides Wolfram von Eschenbach's "Par-zival" and Gottfried von Strasburg's "Tristan." In contradistinction to the poetry of the troubadours, that of the minnesingers was characterized by an undercurrent of sadness which seems to be peculiar to the Germanic race. The songs are full of nature and the eternal strife between Winter and Summer and their prototypes Death and Life (recalling the ancient myths of Maneros, Bacchus, Astoreth, Bel, etc.).

After the death of Konrad IV, the last Swabian emperor of the House of Hohenstaufen, minnesinging in Germany declined, and was succeeded by the movement represented by the *meister* or mastersingers. During the fourteenth and fifteenth centuries, when Germany was broken up into countless small duchies and kingdoms, many of the German nobles became mere robbers and took part in the innumerable little wars which kept the nation in a state of ferment. Thus they had neither time nor inclination to occupy themselves with such pursuits as poetry or music. In the meanwhile, however, the incessant warfare and brigandage that prevailed in the country tended to drive the population to the cities for protection. The latter grew in size, and little by little the tradespeople began to take up the arts of poetry and music which had been discarded by the nobles.

Following their custom in respect to their trades, they formed the art companies into guilds, the rules for ad-mittance to which were very strict. The rank of each member was determined by his skill in applying the rules of the "Tabulatur," as it was called. There were five grades of membership: the lowest was that of mere admittance to the guild; the next carried with it the title of scholar; the third the friend of the school; after that came the singer, the poet; and last of all the mastersinger, to attain which distinction the aspirant must have invented a new style of melody or rhyme. The details of the contest we all know from Wagner's comedy; in a number of cases Wagner even made use of the sentences and words found in the rules of the mastersingers. Although the mastersingers retained their guild privileges in different parts of Germany almost up to the middle of the present century, the movement was strongest in Bavaria, with Nuremberg as its centre.

Thus we see that the mastersingers and the minnesingers were two very different classes of men. The mastersingers are mainly valuable for having given Wagner a pretext for his wonderful music. Hans Sachs was perhaps the only one of the mastersingers whose melodies show anything but the flattest mediocrity. The minnesingers and their immediate predecessors and successors, on the other hand, furnished thought for a great part of our modern art. To put it in a broad manner, it may be said that much of our modern poetry owes more than is generally conceded to the German mediæval romance as represented in the works of Wolfram von Eschenbach, Gottfried of Strasburg, and the unknown compilers of the "Nibelungenlied" and "Gutrune." Music owes more to the troubadours, for, from what we know of the melodies of the minnesingers, they cannot compare in expressiveness with those of their French *confrères*.

In closing this consideration of the minnesingers, I will quote some of their verses and melodies, giving short accounts of the authors.

The best known of the minnesingers were Walther von der Vogelweide, Heinrich Frauenlob, Tannhäuser, Nithart, Toggenburg, etc. We first hear of Walther von der Vogelweide in 1200, as a poet attached to the court of Philip of Hohenstaufen, the German Kaiser, and shortly after to that of his successors Otto and Friedrich. He accompanied Kaiser Friedrich to the Crusade of 1228, and saw him crowned in Jerusalem. He died in Würzburg, Bavaria. In accordance with his dying request, food and drink for the birds were placed on his tomb every day; the four holes carved for that purpose being still visible. The pictures in Hagen's work on the mastersingers were collected in the fifteenth century by Manasses of Zorich, and have served as the basis for all subsequent works on the subject. The picture of Von der Vogelweide (page 21) shows him sitting in an attitude of meditation, on a green hillock, beside him his sword and his coat of arms (a caged bird on one side and his helmet on the other), and in his hand a roll of manuscript. One of his shorter poems begins:

> Neath the lindens
> In the meadow
> Seek I flowers sweet;
> Clover fragrant,
> Tender grasses,
> Bend beneath my feet.

See, the gloaming,
Softly sinking,
Covers hill and dale.
Hush! my lover —
Tandaradei!
Sweet sings the nightingale.

We all are familiar with Tannhäuser (plate 35), through Wagner's opera; therefore it is unnecessary to say more than that he was a real person, a minnesinger, and that the singing tournament at the Wartburg (the castle of the Thüringen family) really took place in 1206–07. This tournament, which Wagner introduces into his "Tann-häuser," was a trial of knightly strength, poetry, and music, between the courts of Babenhausen and Thüringen, and was held in Erfurt. Among the knights who competed were Klingsor of Hungary, a descendant of the Klingsor who figures in the "Parzival" legend, Tannhäuser, Walther von Eschenbach, Walther von der Vogelweide, and many others. Tannhäuser was a follower, or perhaps better, the successor of Walther von der Vogelweide, like him, a crusader, and lived in the first half of the thirteenth century. Toggenburg and Frauenlob were both celebrated minnesingers, the former (plate 7) being the subject of many strange legends. The simplicity and melodious charm of his verses seem to contradict the savage brutality ascribed to him in the stories of his life.

Frauenlob (plate 44), as Heinrich von Meissen was called, represents the minnesingers at the height of their development. He died about 1320, and his works, as his nickname suggests, were imbued with *das ewig weibliche* in its best sense. He was called the Magister of the seven free arts, and was given the position of Canon of the Cathedral of Mayence, with the title of Doctor of Divinity. He also wrote a paraphrase on the "Song of Solomon," turning it into a rhapsodical eulogy of the Virgin Mary, carrying versification to what seemed then its utmost limits. The picture shows him playing and singing to some prince, the carpet on which he stands being lifted by the attendants. It makes plain the difference between the minnesingers and the troubadours. In this picture the singer is seen to be accompanying himself before the king, whereas in plate 28 we see two troubadours in the lists, their *jongleurs* playing or singing the songs of their masters, while the latter engage each other in battle. In order to give one more example we will take the pictures of Conrad, the son of Conrad IV, and the last of the Hohenstaufens (plate 11). He was born about 1250, and was beheaded in the market place at Naples in 1268. The story of Konradin, as he was called, is familiar; how he lived with his mother at the castle of her brother, Ludwig of Bavaria, how he was induced to join in a rebellion of the two Sicilies (to the crown of which he was heir) against France, his defeat and execution by the Duke of Anjou, himself a well-known troubadour. The text accompanying his picture in Hagen's work describes him as having black eyes and blonde hair, and wearing a long green dress with a golden collar. His gray hunting horse is covered with a crimson mantle, has a golden saddle and bit, and scarlet reins. Konradin wears white hunting gloves and a three-cornered king's

crown.   Above the picture are the arms of the kingdom
of Jerusalem (a golden crown in silver ground), to which
he was heir through his grandmother, Iolanthe.   One of
his songs runs as follows, and it may be accepted as
a fair specimen of the style of lyric written by the
minnesingers:

> The lovely flowers and verdure sweet
> That gentle May doth slip
> Have been imprisoned cruelly
> In Winter's iron grip;
> But May smiles o'er the green clad fields
> That seemed anon so sad,
> And all the world is glad.
>
> No joy to me the Summer brings
> With all its bright long days.
> My thoughts are of a maiden fair
> Who mocks my pleading gaze;
> She passes me in haughty mood,
> Denies me aught but scorn,
> And makes my life forlorn.
>
> Yet should I turn my love from her,
> For aye my love were gone.
> I'd gladly die could I forget
> The love that haunts my song.
> So, lonely, joyless, live I on,
> For love my prayer denies,
> And, childlike, mocks my sighs.

The music of these minnesingers existing in manuscript
has been but little heeded, and only lately has an attempt
been made to classify and translate it into modern notation.   The result so far attained has been unsatisfactory,

for the rhythms are all given as spondaic. This seems
a very improbable solution of the mystery that must
inevitably enshroud the musical notation of the eleventh,
twelfth, and thirteenth centuries.

Nithart (plate 36), by whom a number of melodies or
"tones" are given in Hagen's book (page 845), has been
dubbed the second "Till Eulenspiegel." He was a Bavarian, and lived about 1230, at the court of Frederick of
Austria. He was eminently the poet and singer of the
peasants, with whom, after the manner of Eulenspiegel, he
had many quarrels, one of which is evidently the subject
of the picture. His music, or melodies, and the verses
which went with them, form the most complete authentic
collection of mediæval music known. In considering the
minnelieder of the Germans it is very interesting to compare them with the songs of the troubadours, and to
note how in the latter the Arab influence has increased
the number of curved lines, or arabesques, whereas the
German songs may be likened to straight lines, a characteristic which we know is a peculiarity of their folk
song.

PASTORELLA BY THIBAUT II, KING OF NAVARRE, 1254.

L'Au - tri-er par la ma - ti-née En - tre sen bos et un

Vergier   Une   past - ore   ai trou-neé chan-tant pour

soi   en   voi - sier.

Example from NITHART

In speaking of the straight lines of the melodies of the minnesingers and in comparing them with the tinge of orientalism to be found in those of the troubadours, it was said that music owes more to the latter than to the former, and this is true. If we admit that the straight line of Grecian architecture is perfect, so must we also admit that mankind is imperfect. We are living beings, and as such are swayed to a great extent by our emotions. To the straight line of purity in art the tinge of orientalism, the curved line of emotion, brings the flush of life, and the result is something which we can *feel* as well as worship from afar. Music is a language, and to mankind it serves as a medium for saying something which cannot be put into mere words. Therefore, it must contain the human element of mere sensuousness in order to be intelligible.

This is why the music of the troubadours, although not so pure in style as that of the minnesingers, has been of the greatest value in the development of our art. This orientalism, however, must not mask the straight line; it must be the means of lending more force, tenderness, or what not, to the figure. It must be what the poem is to the picture, the perfume to the flower; it must help to illustrate the thing itself. The moment we find this orientalism (and I am using the word in its broadest sense) covering, and thus distorting the straight line of pure music, then we have national music so-called, a music which derives its name and fame from the clothes it wears and not from that strange language of the soul, the "why" of which no man has ever discovered.

XIII

EARLY INSTRUMENTAL FORMS

REFERRING to some newspaper reports which he knew to be without foundation, Bismarck once said, " Newspapers are simply a union of printer's ink and paper." Omitting the implied slur we might say the same of printed music and printed criticism; therefore, in considering printed music we must, first of all, remember that it is the letter of the law which kills. We must look deeper, and be able to translate sounds back into the emotions which caused them. There is no right or wrong way to give utterance to music. There is but *one* way, namely, through the living, vital expression of the content of the music; all else is not music but mere pleasure for the ear, a thing of the senses. For the time being we must see through the composer's eyes and hear through his ears. In other words, we must think in his language. The process of creating music is often, to a great extent, beyond the control of the composer, just as is the case with the novelist and his characters. The language through which musical thought is expressed, however, is a different thing, and it is this process of developing musical speech until it has become capable of saying for us that which, in our spoken language, must ever remain unsaid, that I shall try to make clear in our consideration of form in music.

Until the very end of the fifteenth century, music, so far as we know, had no language of its own, that is to say, it was not recognized as a medium for expressing thought or emotion. Josquin des Prés (born at Conde in the north of France in 1450, died 1521) was the first to attempt the expression of thought in sound. Luther, in rebelling against Rome, also overturned the music of the church in Germany. He incorporated many folk songs into the music of the Protestant church and discarded the old Gregorian chant (which was vague in rhythm, or, rather, wholly without rhythm), calling it asinine braying.

While Luther was paving the way for Bach by encouraging church music to be something more than merely the singing of certain melodies according to prescribed rules, in Italy (at the time of his death in 1546) the Council of Trent was already trying to decide upon a style of music proper for the church. The matter was definitely settled in 1562 or 1563 by the adoption of Palestrina's style.* Thus, while in Germany ecclesiastical music was being broadened and an opening offered for the development of the dramatic and emotional side of music, in Italy, on the contrary, the emotional style of music was being neglected and an absolutely serene style of what may be called " impersonal " music encouraged. Italy, however, soon had opera on which to fall back, and thus music in both countries developed rapidly, although on different lines.

In England, the budding school of English art, as exemplified by Purcell, was soon overwhelmed by the

* Pier Luigi, born in Palestrina, near Rome.

influence of Händel and the all-pervading school of Italian opera, which he brought with him.

In France, up to 1655, when Cardinal Mazarin sent to Italy for an opera troupe with the purpose of entertaining Anne of Austria (the widow of Louis XIII), there was practically no recognized music except that imported from other countries. Under Louis XI (d. 1483) Ockeghem, the Netherland contrapuntist, was the chief musician of the land.

The French pantomimes or masques, as they were sometimes called, can hardly be said to have represented a valuable gain to art, although their prevalence in France points directly to their having been the direct descendants of the old pantomime on one hand, and on the other, the direct ancestor of the French opera. For we read that already in 1581 (twenty years before Caccini's " Euridice " at Florence), a ballet entitled " Circe " was given on the occasion of the marriage of Margaret of Lorraine, the stepsister of Henry III. The music to it was written by Beaulieu and Salmon, two court musicians. There were ten bands of music in the cupola of the ballroom where the ballet was given. These bands included hautbois, cornets, trombones, violas de gamba, flutes, harps, lutes, flageolets. Besides all this, ten violin players in costume entered the scene in the first act, five from each side. Then a troupe of Tritons came swimming in, playing lutes, harps, flutes, one even having a kind of 'cello. When Jupiter makes his appearance, he is accompanied by forty musicians. The festivities on this occasion are said to have cost over five million francs. Musically, the ballet was no advance towards expressiveness in art. An air which accompanied " Circe's " entrance, may be cited as being the original of the well-known "Amaryllis," which is generally called *Air Louis XV*. Baltazarini calls it *un son fort gai, nomme la clochette.*

Music remained inert in France until 1650, when the Italians gained an ascendancy, which they retained until 1732, when Rameau's first opera " Hyppolyte et Aricie " was given in Paris. Rameau had already commenced his career by gaining great success as a harpsichord player and instrumental composer, mostly for the harpsichord. By his time, however, music, that is to say, secular music, was already becoming a new art, and the French merely improved upon what already existed.

Now this new art was first particularly evident in the dances of these different peoples. These dances gave the music *form*, and held it down to certain prescribed rhythms and duration. Little by little the emotions, the natural expression of which is music, could no longer be restricted to these dance forms and rhythms; and gradually the latter were modified by each daring innovator in turn. This " daring " of human beings, in breaking through the trammels of the dance in order to express what lay within their souls in the language that properly belonged to it, would seem almost ludicrous to us, were we not even to-day trying to get up courage to do the same thing. The modifications of dance forms led up to our sonata, symphony, and symphonic poem, as I hope to show. Opera was a thing apart, and, being untrammelled either by dance rhythms or church laws, developed gradually and normally. It cannot, however, be said to have developed side by side with purely instrumental music, for the latter is only just beginning to emancipate itself from its dance clothes and to come forth as a language for the expression of all that is divine in man. First we will consider the forms and rhythms of these dances, then the awakening of the idea of design in music, and its effect in modifying these forms and laying the foundation for the sonata of the nineteenth century.

The following shows the structure of the different dance forms up to about 1750.

OLD DANCE FORMS (1650–1750).

A phrase may be three or four measures, and the sections may be unequal

This period might be repeated or extended to sixteen measures and still remain a period.

In all these forms each period may be repeated.

Often the first, third, and fourth periods are repeated, leaving the second period as it is. This happens especially when the second period is longer than the first. In Nos. 2, 4, 6, 7, a few bars are often added at *Fine* as a coda.

ANALYSIS OF OLD DANCES

1. SARABANDE. — $\frac{3}{2}$ $\frac{3}{4}$ lento. Rhythm ‖ ... ‖. Form 1, sometimes Form 2. This is of Spanish origin (*Saracen* dance), and is generally accompanied by variations called *partita* or doubles.

2. MUSETTE (*cornemusa* or bagpipe). — $\frac{3}{4}$ $\frac{2}{4}$ allegretto. Form 1. Always written over or under a pedal note, which is generally sustained to the end. It generally forms the second part (not period) to the gavotte.

3. GAVOTTE. — $\frac{4}{4}$ allegro moderato. Rhythm ‖ ... | or | ... |. Always commences on the third beat. Form 3 or 5. When accompanied by a musette, the gavotte is always repeated.

4. BOURREE. — ₵ allegro. Rhythm ₵ ... |. Form 3 or 5. Generally faster than the gavotte, and commences on the fourth beat.

5. RIGAUDON. — Similar to the bourrée, but slower.

6. LOURE. — Similar to the bourrée, but slower. (In French the verb *lourer* means " to hold," which may have been a characteristic of the *loure* bass).

7. TAMBOURIN. — ₵ allegro. In form and rhythm like the gavotte, but faster. Usually founded on a rhythmic pedal note imitating a tambourine.

8. CORRENTE, COURANTE. — $\frac{3}{4}$ allegretto.

Rhythm $\frac{3}{4}$ ♪ ♪♪♪ | ♪♪♪♪♪♪ | or $\frac{3}{4}$ ♩ | ♪♪♪♪♪♪ |
(does not usually commence on the beat). Form 1,
sometimes Form 2. The rhythm is usually uniform, a
kind of perpetual motion, though not in one voice.

9. MINUET. — $\frac{3}{4}$ generally a little slower than moderato,
although in later minuets the tempo became allegretto.

Rhythm, generally, ‖$\frac{3}{4}$ ♩ | ♩ ♩ ♩ | ♩ ♪♪♪♪ | etc. Old
minuets often began on the first beat. Form 4; the
third and fourth periods being generally in a different
mode from the first and second periods, and called Trio or
Minuet 2. Minuets exist also without the Trio, and are
in Form 1 or 2.

10. CHACONNE. — $\frac{3}{4}$ moderato. Form undecided; has
sometimes even only one period, sometimes three or two.
It is generally accompanied by doubles or variations, and
is invariably written on a ground bass or *basso ostinato.*
The rhythm is often syncopated.

PASSACAILLE, $\frac{3}{4}$, resembles a chaconne but is more
stately.

11. WALTZ (old German). — $\frac{3}{4}$ andante moderato.
Generally Form 6. Rhythm ‖$\frac{3}{4}$ ♩· ♩ ♪♪ | ♪♪ ♩ ♪♪ |
approximately.

12. MARCH. — $\frac{4}{4}$ allegro moderato.

Rhythm ‖$\frac{4}{4}$ ♪♪ | ♩ ♪♪ ♩ ♩ | ♩· ♪♪♪ | etc., or ‖♩ |
♩ ♪♪ ♩ ♩ | etc. Form 6. Generally all the periods are
repeated and consist of eight measures each; third and
fourth periods change the key and rhythm.

13. ALLEMANDE. — $\frac{4}{4}$ moderato.   Rhythm generally uniform sixteenth notes.   Form 1.

14. PASSEPIED. — Quick minuet.

15. PAVANE, PADVANA, or PAVO (peacock). — $\frac{4}{4}$ andante moderato.   Rhythm ‖ $\frac{4}{4}$ 𝅘𝅥 𝅘𝅥𝅮𝅘𝅥𝅮 𝅘𝅥· 𝅘𝅥 | 𝅘𝅥𝅮𝅘𝅥𝅮𝅘𝅥𝅮𝅘𝅥𝅮 𝅘𝅥 |.
Form 2 or 6.   Sometimes $\frac{2}{4}$; third and fourth periods in different keys.

16. GIGUE. — $\frac{2}{4}$ $\frac{6}{8}$ $\frac{3}{4}$ $\frac{3}{8}$ $\frac{9}{8}$ $\frac{12}{8}$ presto.   Rhythm generally uniform eighth notes.   Forms 1 and 2.

17. POLONAISE. — $\frac{3}{4}$.   Rhythm ‖ $\frac{3}{4}$ 𝅘𝅥𝅮𝅘𝅥𝅮 𝅘𝅥𝅮𝅘𝅥𝅮 𝅘𝅥 | or
‖ 𝅘𝅥𝅮𝅘𝅥𝅮 𝅘𝅥𝅮𝅘𝅥𝅮 𝅘𝅥 | allegro.   Form 1, generally with short coda.

MODERN FORMS (1800).

1. MAZURKA. — $\frac{3}{4}$ allegretto.   Form 6.
Rhythm ‖ $\frac{3}{4}$ 𝅘𝅥 | 𝅘𝅥𝅮𝅘𝅥𝅮 𝅘𝅥 𝅘𝅥 |.

2. POLONAISE (also POLACCA). — $\frac{3}{4}$ allegro maestoso.
Rhythm ‖ $\frac{3}{4}$ 𝅘𝅥𝅮𝅘𝅥𝅮 𝅘𝅥𝅮𝅘𝅥𝅮 𝅘𝅥𝅮𝅘𝅥𝅮𝅘𝅥𝅮 ‖ or 𝅘𝅥 𝅘𝅥 𝅘𝅥𝅮𝅘𝅥𝅮 𝅘𝅥𝅮𝅘𝅥𝅮 |.   The bass is generally | 𝅘𝅥𝅮𝅘𝅥𝅮 𝅘𝅥𝅮𝅘𝅥𝅮𝅘𝅥𝅮 |.   Form 7.

3. BOLERO (CACHUCHA) (Spanish).—Like the polonaise but livelier, and generally containing counter-rhythms in triplets.

4. HABANERA. — $\frac{2}{4}$.   Rhythm ‖ $\frac{2}{4}$ 𝅘𝅥𝅮𝅘𝅥𝅮 𝅘𝅥𝅮𝅘𝅥𝅮 | 𝅘𝅥𝅮𝅘𝅥𝅮 𝅘𝅥𝅮𝅘𝅥𝅮 |
𝅘𝅥𝅮𝅘𝅥𝅮 𝅘𝅥𝅮𝅘𝅥𝅮 | 𝅘𝅥𝅮𝅘𝅥𝅮 𝅘𝅥 |.   The characteristic element is the mixture of triplets and eighth notes.   Time, andante. Form undecided, generally No. 1.   Very often repeated with slight changes.

5. CZARDAS (Hungarian). — First part 𝄵 (*lassan, lento*); second part ²⁄₄ (*friska, presto* and *prestissimo*). For form and rhythm see Liszt's rhapsodies, Nos. 2, 4, and 6.

6. TARANTELLA. — Rhythm ‖ ⁶⁄₈ ♫♫♫ ♫♫♫ | ♫♫♫ ♫♫♫ or ‖ ♫♫♫ ♫♫♫ | ♪ ♪ ♪ ‖. Time, molto allegro to prestissimo. Forms 4 and 6, sometimes 7. In the Trio the movement is often quieter although not necessarily slower. It almost invariably has a Coda. The Finale is usually prestissimo.

7. SALTARELLO. — Similar to the tarantella, with the exception of having more jumps (*salti*).

8. POLKA (about 1840). — ²⁄₄ allegretto. Rhythm ‖ ²⁄₄ ♫ ♪ | ♫ ♪ |. Form 6. Accent is on the second beat. Cuban dances (sometimes called habaneros) are often in polka form and rhythm, with the one exception of the triplets peculiar to almost all Spanish music

‖ ²⁄₄ ♫ ♪̄ | ♫ ♪̄ | ♫♫ ♫ | ♫♫ ♫♫♫ ‖

9. WALTZ. — ³⁄₄. Rhythm (bass) ‖ ³⁄₄ ♩̄ ♩ ♩ | ♩̄ ♩ ♩ |. Faster than the old waltz. Form 2 with a coda. Modern waltzes are often written in sets, or many different waltzes joined together by short modulations or codas, preceded by an introduction, generally in one period, *lento*, and ending with a brilliant coda containing reminiscences of the principal themes.

10. GALOP. — ²⁄₄. Rhythm ‖ ²⁄₄ ♫♫ ♫ | ♫ ♫ | or | ♫ ♫ | ♫ ♫ |. Form 6. Time, presto.

11. MARCH. — Same as the old march, but modified in character and movement according to its title — funeral

march, military march, cortége, festival march, etc. In funeral marches, the third and fourth periods are generally in major.

The modernizing of dance forms has been undertaken by almost every writer from Scarlatti (d. 1757) down to our day. Scarlatti joined sections together with isolated measures, repeated sections and phrases before completing the period, and added short codas to periods indiscriminately. Since his time, everyone has added to or curtailed the accepted forms by putting two forms together; hence the fantaisie-mazurka, etc. Wagner represents the culminating point of the modern tendency to disregard forms which were interpreted differently by every composer, and which had their origin in dances.

The attempt to emancipate music from the dance commenced very early; in fact, most of the earliest secular music we know already shows the tendency towards programme music, for, from an emotional standpoint, secular music began at the very bottom of the ladder. It was made to express *things* at first, just as in learning any new language we naturally first acquire a vocabulary of nouns to express things we see, such as table, chair, etc., in the same way that in *written* language the symbols first take the shape of animals or other things they are meant to represent. This same characteristic naturally showed itself in music before the words for *emotion* came, the common, everyday nouns were sought for in this new language. The madrigals of Weelkes and their word painting show this, and the same occur in instrumental music, as in Byrd's " Carman's Whistle,"

one of the earliest English instrumental works contemporaneous to the madrigals of Morley and others.
In France, many of the earliest clavichord pieces were of
the programme type, and even in Germany, where instrumental music ran practically in the same groove with
church music, the same tendency showed itself.

I have given the forms of most of the old dances, and
also the elements of melodic structure (motive, phrase,
etc.). I must, however, add the caution that this material is to be accepted in a general way, and as representing
the rhythms and forms most frequently used. A French
courante differed from the Italian, and certain dances were
taken at different *tempi* in different countries. Poor, or
at least careless construction, is often the cause of much
confusion. Scarlatti, for instance, is especially loose in
melodic structure.

It was only with Beethoven that the art of musical
design showed anything like complete comprehension by
the composer. Until then, with occasional almost haphazard successes, the art of pushing a thought to its logical
conclusion was seemingly unknown. An emotional passage now and then would often betray deep feeling, but
the thought would almost invariably be lost in the telling,
for the simple reason that the musical sentences were put
together almost at random, mere stress of momentary
emotion being seemingly the only guiding influence. Bach
stands alone; his sense of design was inherent, but, owing
to the contrapuntal tendency of his time, his feeling for
melodic design is often overshadowed, and even rendered
impossible by the complex web of his music. With a

number of melodies sounding together, their individual emotional development becomes necessarily difficult to emphasize.

Bach's art has something akin to that of Palestrina. They both stand alone in the history of the world, but the latter belongs to the Middle Ages. He is the direct descendant of Ambrose, Gregory, Notker, Tutilo, etc., the crowning monument of the Roman Church in music, and represents what may be termed unemotional music. His art was untouched by the strange, suggestive colours of modern harmony; it was pure, unemotional, and serene. One instinctively thinks of Bach, on the other hand, as a kind of musical reflection of Protestantism. His was not a secluded art which lifted its head high above the multitude; it was rather the palpable outpouring of a great heart. Bach also represents all the pent-up feeling which until then had longed in vain for utterance, and had there been any canvas for him to paint on (to use a poor simile), the result would have been still more marvellous. As it was, the material at his disposal was a poor set of dance forms, with the one exception of the fugue, the involved utterance of which precluded spontaneity and confined emotional design to very restricted limits. It is exactly as if Wagner had been obliged to put his thoughts in quadrille form with the possible alternative of some mathematical device of musical double bookkeeping. As it is, Bach's innovations were very considerable. In the first place, owing to the lack of the system of equal temperament, composers had been limited to the use of only two or three sharps and flats; in all the harpsichord music of the pre-Bach period we rarely find compositions in sharp keys beyond G, or flat keys beyond A♭. To be sure, Rameau, in France, began at the same time to see the necessity for equal temperament, but it was Bach who, by his forty-eight "Preludes and Fugues," written in all the keys, first settled the matter definitely.

In the fugue form itself, he made many innovations consisting mainly of the casting aside of formalism.   With Bach a fugue consists of what is called the "exposition," that is to say, the enunciation of the theme (subject), its answer by another voice or part, recurrence of the subject in another part which, in turn, is again answered, and so on according to the number of voices or parts. After the exposition the fugue consists of a kind of free contrapuntal fantasy on the subject and its answer.   By throwing aside the restraint of form Bach often gave his fugues an emotional significance in spite of the complexity of the material he worked with.

XIV

THE MERGING OF THE SUITE INTO THE SONATA

In the previous chapter it was stated that the various dances, such as the minuet, sarabande, allemande, etc., led up to our modern sonata form, or, perhaps, to put it more clearly, they led up to what we call sonata form. As a matter of fact, already in the seventeenth century, we find the word *sonata* applied to musical compositions; generally to pieces for the violin, but rarely for the harpsichord. The word sonata was derived originally from the Italian word *suonare*, "to sound," and the term was used to distinguish instrumental from vocal music. The latter was sung (*cantata*), the former was sounded (*suonata*) by instruments. Thus many pieces were called *suonatas;* the distinguishing point being that they were *played* and not sung. Organ sonatas existed as far back as 1600 and even earlier, but the earliest application of the word seems to have been made in connection with pieces for the violin.

Dances were often grouped together, especially when they had some slight intrinsic musical value. Probably the term *sonata* first designated a composition in one of these dance forms not intended for dancing. Gradually groups of dances were called *suites;* then, little by little, the dance titles of the separate numbers were dropped, and the *suite* was called *sonata*. These different numbers, however, retained their dance characteristics, as we shall see later. The arrangement of the pieces composing the *suites* differed in various countries. There were French, Italian, German, and English suites, generally, however, retaining the same grouping of the different movements. The first movement consisted of an *allemande;* then came a *courante;* then a *minuet;* then a *sarabande;* and last of all a *gigue;* all in the same key. Sometimes the *minuet* and *sarabande* changed places, just as in modern times do the *andante* and *scherzo.*

Already in 1685, when Corelli's sonatas for strings appeared, the custom of decreasing the number of movements to three began to obtain, and a century later this custom was universal. The *allemande, overture,* or *preludio* formed the first movement; the second consisted of the *sarabande,* the ancestor of our *adagio;* and the last part was generally a *gigue.* Even when the dance titles were no more used (the music having long outgrown its original purpose), the distinctive characteristics of these different movements were retained; the *sarabande* rhythm was still adhered to for the *adagio* (even by Haydn) and the triple time and rhythm of the *gigue* were given to the last part. In addition to this, these three movements were often kept in one key. In his first sonatas Beethoven added a movement, generally a *minuet,* to this scheme; but returned to the three-movement structure later. His Op. 111 has only two movements, in a way returning to a still earlier general form of the sonata. Now, as has already been said, some of the earliest examples of instrumental music were mainly descriptive in character, that is to say, consisting of imitations of *things*, thus marking the most elementary stage of programme music. Little by little composers became more ambitious and began to attempt to give expression to the emotions by means of music; and at last, with Beethoven, " programme music " may be said, in one sense, to have reached its climax. For although it is not generally realized, he wrote every one of his sonatas with definite subjects, and, at one time, was on the point of publishing mottoes to them, in order to give the public a hint of what was in his mind when he wrote them.

Analysis may be considered as the reducing of a musical composition to its various elements — harmony, rhythm, melody — and power of expression. Just as melody may be analyzed down to the motives and phrases of which it consists, so may the expressiveness of music be analyzed; and this latter study is most valuable, for it brings us to a closer understanding of the power of music as a language.

For the sake of clearness we will group music as follows:

1. Dance forms.
2. Programme music. (Things. Feelings.)
3. The gathering together of dances in suites.
4. The beginnings of design.
5. The merging of the suite into the sonata.

The dance tunes I need hardly quote; they consist of a mere play of sound to keep the dancers in step, for which purpose any more or less agreeable rhythmical succession of sounds will serve.

If we take the next step in advance of instrumental music we come to the giving of meanings to these dances, and, as I have explained, these meanings will at first.have reference to things; for instance, Couperin imitates an alarm clock; Rameau tries to make the music sound as if three hands were playing instead of two (*Les trois mains*); he imitates sighing (*Les soupirs*); the scolding voice; he even tries to express a mood musically (*L'indifferente*). In Germany, these attempts to make instrumental music expressive of something beyond rhythmic time-keeping continued, and we find Carl Philip Emanuel Bach attempting to express light-hearted amiability (*La complaisance*) and even languor (*Les tendres langueurs*). The suite, while it combined several dances in one general form, shows only a trace of *design*. There was more design in one of the small programme pieces already quoted than in most of the suites of this period (see, for example, Loeilly's " Suite ").

Bach possessed instinctively the feeling for musical speech which seemed denied to his contemporaries whenever they had no actual story to guide their expression; and even in his dance music we find coherent musical sentences as, for instance, in the *Courante* in A.

In art our opinions must, in all cases, rest directly on the thing under consideration and not on what is written about it. In my beliefs I am no respecter of the written word, that is to say, the mere fact that a statement is made by a well-known man, is printed in a well-known work, or is endorsed by many prominent names, means nothing to me if the thing itself is available for examination. Without a thorough knowledge of music, including its history and development, and, above all, musical "sympathy," individual criticism is, of course, valueless; at the same time the acquirement of this knowledge and sympathy is not difficult, and I hope that we may yet have a public in America that shall be capable of forming its own ideas, and not be influenced by tradition, criticism, or fashion.

We need to open our eyes and see for ourselves instead of trusting the direction of our steps to the guidance of others. Even an opinion based on ignorance, frankly given, is of more value to art than a platitude gathered from some outside source. If it is not a platitude but the echo of some fine thought, it only makes it worse, for it is not sincere, unless of course it is quoted understandingly. We need freshness and sincerity in forming our judgments in art, for it is upon these that art lives. All over the world we find audiences listening suavely to long concerts, and yet we do not see one person with the frankness of the little boy in Andersen's story of the "New Clothes of the Emperor." It is the same with the other arts. I have never heard anyone say that part of the foreground of Millet's "Angelus" is "muddy" or that the Fornarina's mysterious smile is anything but "hauntingly beautiful." People do not dare admire the London Law Courts; all things must be measured by the straight lines of Grecian architecture. Frankness! Let us have frankness, and if we have no feelings on a subject, let us remain silent rather than echo that drone in the hive of modern thought, the "*authority* in art."

Every person with even the very smallest love and

sympathy for art possesses ideas which are valuable to that art.   From the tiniest seeds sometimes the greatest trees are grown.   Why, therefore, allow these tender germs of individualism to be smothered by that flourishing, arrogant bay tree of tradition — fashion, authority, convention, etc.

My reason for insisting on the importance of all lovers of art being able to form their own opinions is obvious, when we consider that our musical public is obliged to take everything on trust.   For instance, if we read on one page of some history (every history of music has such a page) that Mozart's sonatas are sublime, that they do not contain one note of mere filigree work, and that they far transcend anything written for the harpsichord or clavichord by Haydn or his contemporaries, we echo the saying, and, if necessary, quote the " authorities."   Now if one had occasion to read over some of the clavichord music of the period, possibly it might seem strange that Mozart's sonatas did not impress with their magnificence. One might even harbour a lurking doubt as to the value of the many seemingly bare runs and unmeaning passages. Then one would probably turn back to the authorities for an explanation and find perhaps the following: " The inexpressible charm of Mozart's music leads us to forget the marvellous learning bestowed upon its construction. Later composers have sought to conceal the constructional points of the sonata which Mozart never cared to disguise, so that incautious students have sometimes failed to discern in them the veritable ' pillars of the house,' and have accused Mozart of poverty of style because he left them boldly exposed to view, as a great architect delights to expose the piers upon which the tower of his cathedral depends for its support." (Rockstro, " History of Music," p. 269.) Now this is all very fine, but it is nonsense, for Mozart's sonatas are anything but cathedrals. It is time to cast aside this shibboleth of printer's ink and paper and look the thing itself straight in the face. It is a fact that Mozart's sonatas are compositions entirely unworthy of the author of the " Magic Flute," or of any composer with pretensions to anything beyond mediocrity. They are written in a style of flashy harpsichord virtuosity such as Liszt never descended to, even in those of his works at which so many persons are accustomed to sneer.

Such a statement as I have just made may be cried down as rank heresy, first by the book readers and then by the general public; but I doubt if anyone among that public would or could actually turn to the music itself and analyze it intelligently, from both an æsthetic and technical standpoint, in order to verify or disprove the assertion.

Once a statement is made it seems to be exceedingly difficult to keep it from obtaining the universal acceptance which it gains by unthinking reiteration in other works. One of the strangest cases of this repetition of a careless statement may be found in the majority of histories of music, where we are told that musical expression (that is to say, the increasing and diminishing of a tone, crescendo and diminuendo) was first *discovered* at Mannheim, in Germany, about 1760. This statement may be found in the works of Burney, Schubart, Reichardt, Sittard, Wasielewski, and even in Jahn's celebrated " Life of Mozart."

The story is that Jommelli, an Italian, first "invented" the crescendo and diminuendo, and that when they were first used, the people in the audience gradually rose from their seats at the crescendo, and as the music "diminuendoed" they sat down again. The story is absurd, for the simple reason that even in 1705, Sperling, in his "Principæ Musicæ," describes crescendos from *ppp* to *fff*, and we read in Plutarch of the same thing.

Shedlock, in his work "The Pianoforte Sonata," quotes as the first sonatas for the clavier those of Kuhnau, and cites especially the six *Bible* sonatas. Now Kuhnau, although he was Bach's predecessor at St. Thomas' Church in Leipzig, was certainly a composer of the very lowest rank. The *Bible* sonatas, which Shedlock paints to us in such glowing colours, are the merest trash, and not to be compared with the works of his contemporaries. I do not think that they have any place whatsoever in the history or development either of music or of that form called the sonata.

The development of the suite from dance forms has already been shown, and we will now trace the development of the sonata from the suite in Italy, Germany, and France. As an example of this development in Italy, a so-called sonata by G. B. Pescetti will serve (the sonatas by Domenico Scarlatti were not originally so named, and the sonatas before that were simply short pieces, so designated to distinguish them from dance music). This sonata was published about 1730, and was one of nine. The first movement is practically of the *allemande* type, and its first period ends in the dominant key. There is but the

slightest trace of a second theme in the first part; yet
the improvement in contrapuntal design over the suites
is evident.   The second movement is in the same key, and
retains the characteristic rhythm of the *sarabande;* at the
end, the improvement, so far as design is concerned, is
very noticeable.   The last movement, still in the same
key, is a *gigue,* thus keeping well in the shadow of the
suite.

A sonata by the German Rolle (1718–1785) is valuable
in that it shows a very decided second theme in the first
period, thus tending toward the development of the
original simple dance form into the more complex sonata
form.   The *adagio,* however, still has the *sarabande* characteristics, and foreshadows many things.   It contains
many *words* that later were shaped into great poems by
others.   " The Erlking " of Schubert is especially hinted
at, just as the first movement was prophetic of Beethoven.
In the last movement we have the *gigue* rhythm again.

In France, music had become merely a court appendage,
as was the case with the other arts, and had long served
as a means for showing the divine grace with which
Louis XIV or XV could turn out his toes in the minuet.
In addition to this, the arranging of a scientific system of
harmonization by Rameau (1683–1764) (which, by the
way, is the basis of most of the treatises of harmony of the
present century), caused the few French composers who
could make headway against the prevailing Italian opera
after Lully to turn their attention away from polyphonic
writing; and having, after all, but little to express in other
than the long-accustomed dance rhythms and tunes, their

music cannot be said to have made any mark in the world. In order to show the poverty of this style, let us take a sonata by Méhul (1763–1817).   The first movement has already a well-defined second theme, but otherwise is a mere collection of more or less commonplace progressions. The second part is a dance tune, pure and simple; indeed the first part had all the characteristics of the *farandole* (see Bizet's "l'Arlesienne").   The last part is entitled rondo, "a round dance," and is evidently one in the literal sense of the word.   In all these sonatas the increasing use of what is called the Alberti bass is noticeable.

To show the last link between the suite and the sonata, reference may be made to the well-known sonata in D major by Haydn.   In this, as in those analyzed above, all the movements are in the same key.   The adagio is a *sarabande*, and the last movement has the characteristics of the *gigue*.   This, however, is only the starting point with Haydn; later we will consider the development of this form into what is practically our modern sonata, which, of course, includes the symphony, quartet, quintet, concerto, etc.

Our path of study in tracing the development of the sonata from the suite leads us through a sterile tract of seemingly bare desert.   The compositions referred to are full of fragments, sometimes fine in themselves, but lying wherever they happened to fall, their sculptors having no perception of their value one with another.   Disconnected phrases, ideas never completed; to quote Hamlet, "Words, words!"   Later we find Beethoven and Schubert constructing wonderful temples out of these same fragments, and shaping these same words into marvellous tone poems.

The music of the period we have been considering is well described by Browning in " A Toccata of Galuppi's ":

> Yes you, like a ghostly cricket,
>   Creaking where a house was burned:
> Dust and ashes, dead and done with,
>   Venice spent what Venice earned.

XV

THE DEVELOPMENT OF PIANOFORTE MUSIC

Up to the time of Beethoven, music for the pianoforte consisted mainly of programme music of the purely descriptive order, that is to say, it was generally imitative of natural or artificial externals. To be sure, if we go back to the old clavecinists, and examine the sonatas of Kuhnau, sundry pieces by Couperin, Rameau, and the Germans, Froberger, C. P. E. Bach and others, we find the beginnings of that higher order of programme music which deals directly with the emotions; and not only that, but which aims at causing the hearer to go beyond the actual sounds heard, in pursuance of a train of thought primarily suggested by this music.

To find this art of programme music, as we may call it, brought to a full flower, we must seek in the mystic utterances of Robert Schumann. It is wise to keep in mind, however, that although Schumann's piano music certainly answers to our definition of the higher programme music, it also marks the dividing line between emotional programme music without a well-defined object and that dramatically emotional art which we have every reason to believe was aimed at by Beethoven in many of his sonatas, and which, in its logical development and broadened out by orchestral colours and other resources, is championed by Richard Strauss at the present day.

We have already learned that C. P. E. Bach had entirely broken with the contrapuntal style of his father and his age in order to gain freer utterance, and that the word " colour " began to be used in his time in connection with music for even one instrument. It is, perhaps, needless to say that the vastly enlarged possibilities, both technical and tonal, of the newly invented *forte-piano* were largely the outcome of this seeking for colour in music. In addition to this, the new art of harmonic dissonances was already beginning to stretch out in the direction of new and strange tonal combinations, thus giving to the music written for the instrument many new possibilities in the way of causing and depicting emotions. That the first experiments were puerile, we know, as, for example, Haydn's attempts, in one of his pianoforte sonatas, to suggest the conversion of an obdurate sinner.

When we consider Mozart, it is impossible to forget the fact that in his piano works he was first and foremost a piano virtuoso, a child prodigy, of whom filigree work was expected by the public for which he wrote his sonatas. (We cannot call this orientalism, for it was more or less of German pattern, traced from the fioriture of the Italian opera singer.) Therefore, emotional utterance or even new or poetic colouring was not to be expected of him.

As has been said before, it remained for Beethoven to weld these new words and strange colours into poems, which, notwithstanding the many barnacles hanging to them (remnants of a past of timid adhesion to forms and fashions), are, in truth, the first lofty and dignified musical utterances with an object which we possess. I mean by this statement that his art was the first to cast aside the iron fetters of what then formed the canons of art. The latter may be described (even in reference to modern days) as constituting the shadow of a great man. And, although this is a digression, I may add that all students of piano music no doubt realize the weighty shadow that Beethoven cast over the first half of the nineteenth century, just as Wagner is doing at the present time.

Our purists are unable to realize that the shadows are the least vital part of the great men who cast them. We remember that the only wish expressed by Diogenes when Alexander came to see him was that the king should stand aside so that he could enjoy the light of the sun.

To return: We find that Beethoven was the first exponent of our modern art. Every revolution is bound to bring with it a reaction which seeks to consolidate and put in safe keeping, as it were, results attained by it. Certainly Beethoven alone can hardly be said to have furthered this end; for his revolt led him into still more remote and involved trains of thought, as in his later sonatas and quartets. Even the Ninth Symphony, hampered as it is by actual words for which declamation and a more or less well-defined form of musical speech are necessary, suffers from the same involved utterance that characterizes his last period.

Schubert, in his instrumental work, was too ardent a seeker and lover of the purely beautiful to build upon the forms of past generations, and thus his piano music, neither restrained nor supported by poetic declamation, was never held within the bounds of formalism.

It was Mendelssohn who first invested old and seemingly worn-out forms of instrumental music (especially for the pianoforte) with the new poetic license of speech, which was essentially the spirit of the age of revolution in which he lived.

In holding up Mendelssohn as a formalist against Beethoven, and at the same time presenting him as the composer directly responsible for our modern symphonic poem, there is a seeming contradiction, which, however, is more apparent than real. While Beethoven never hesitated to overturn form (harmonic or otherwise) to suit the exigencies of his inspiration, Mendelssohn cast all his pictures into well-defined and orthodox forms. Thus his symphonic poems, for example, the overtures to "The Lovely Melusina," "Fingal's Cave," "Ruy Blas," etc., are really overtures in form; whereas, the so-called "Moonlight" sonata of Beethoven, as well as many others, are sonatas only in name. The emotional and problematic significance given by Mendelssohn to many of his shorter piano pieces, including even such works as preludes and fugues, is familiar to us all. These works, however, but rarely departed from the orthodox forms represented by their names. His "Songs without Words" have been so often quoted as constituting a new art form that it is well to remember that they are practically all cast in the same mould, that of the most simple song form, with one, and sometimes two more or less similar verses, preceded by a short introduction and ending with a coda.

We may say then, broadly, that Beethoven invested instrumental music with a wonderful poignancy and power of expression, elevating it to the point of being the medium of expressing some of the greatest thoughts we possess. In so doing, however, he shattered many of the great idols of formalism by the sheer violence of his expression.

Schubert, let me say again, seemed indifferent to symmetry, or never thought of it in his piano music. Mendelssohn, possibly influenced by his early severe training with Zelter, accepted symmetry of form as the cornerstone of his musical edifice; although he was one of the first in the realms of avowed programme music, he never carried it beyond the boundary of good form. And, as in speaking a moment ago of the so-called canons of musical art, we compared them with the shadows that great men have cast upon their times, it may be as well to remember that just this formalism of Mendelssohn overshadowed and still overshadows England to the present day. On the other hand, Beethoven's last style still shows itself in Brahms, and even in Richard Strauss. Schumann was different from these three. His music is not avowed programme music; neither is it, as is much of Schubert's, pure delight in beautiful melodies and sounds. It did not break through formalism by sheer violence of emotion, as did Beethoven's; least of all has it Mendelssohn's orthodox dress. It represents, as well as I can put it, the rhapsodical reverie of a great poet to whom nothing seems strange, and who has the faculty of relating his visions, never attempting to give them coherence, until, perhaps, when awakened from his dream, he naïvely wonders what they may have meant. It will be remembered that Schumann added titles to his music after it was composed.

To all of this new, strange music, Liszt and Chopin added the wonderful tracery of orientalism. As I have said before, the difference between these two is that with Chopin this tracery enveloped poetic thought as with a thin gauze; whereas with Liszt, the embellishment itself made the starting point for almost a new art in tonal combination, the effects of which are seen on every hand to-day. To realize its influence, one need only compare the graceful arabesques of the most simple piano piece of to-day with the awkward and gargoyle-like figuration of Beethoven and his predecessors. We may justly attribute this to Liszt rather than to Chopin, whose nocturne embellishments are but first cousins to those of the Englishman, John Field, though naturally Chopin's Polish temperament gave his work that grace and profusion of design which we have called orientalism.

XVI

THE MYSTERY AND MIRACLE PLAY

It is interesting to recall the origin of our words " treble " and " discant." The latter was derived from the first attempts to break away from the monotony of several persons singing the same melody in unison, octaves, fifths, or fourths. In such cases the original melody was called *cantus firmus* (a term still generally used in counterpoint to designate the given melody of an exercise to which the student is to write other parts), the new melody that was sung with it was called the *discant*, and when a third part was added, it received the name *triplum* or *treble*. As Ambros remarks, this forcible welding together of different melodies, often well-known old tunes, secular or derived from the church chants, was on a direct line with the contemporary condition of the other arts. For instance, on the portal to the left of the Cathedral of Saint Mark, at Venice, is a relief, representing some Biblical scene, which is entirely made up of fragments of some older sculptured figures, placed together without regard to anatomy in much the same brutal fashion that the melodies of the time were sung together. The traces of this clumsy music-making extended down to Palestrina's time, and became the germ of counterpoint, canon, and fugue, constituting (apart from the folk song) the only music known at that time.

This music, however, very soon developed into two styles, one adopted by the church, the other, a secular style, furnishing the musical texture both of opera and other secular music. The opera, or rather the art form we know under that name (for the name itself conveys nothing, for which reason Wagner coined the term "music drama ") broke away from the church in the guise of Mysteries, as they were called in mediæval times. A Mystery (of which our modern oratorio is the direct descendant) was a kind of drama illustrating some sacred subject, and the earliest specimens laid the foundation for the Greek tragedy and comedy. We still see a relic of this primitive art form in the Oberammergau Passion Play.

We read of the efforts made, as early as the fifth century, to hold the people to the church; among other devices employed was that of illustrating the subjects of the services by the priests performing the offices being dressed in an appropriate costume. Little by little the popular songs of the people crept into the church service among the regular ecclesiastical chants, thus foreshadowing the beginnings of modern opera; for after a while, special Latin texts were substituted for the regular service, the mimetic part of which degenerated into the most extraordinary license as, for instance, in the " Feast of Asses " (January 14) which may be called a burlesque of the mass, and which has been described in a former chapter.

With this mixture of the vernacular and the official

Latin,* these Miracle and Passion Plays, as well as the Mysteries and Moralities (as different forms of this ecclesiastical mumming were called) began to be given in other places besides the churches.

In addition to this combination of singing and acting, the *tenson* or poetic debate (which was one form of the troubadour songs, and one very often *acted* by the jongleurs) probably also did its part towards giving stability to this new art form.   The earliest specimen of it, in its purely secular aspect, is a small work entitled " Robin et Marian," by Adam de la Hale, a well-known troubadour (called " the humpback," born at Arras in the south of France in 1240), who followed in the train of that ferocious Duke Charles of Anjou, who beheaded Konradin, the last of the Hohenstaufens, in 1268, and Manfred, both of them minnesingers.

As the Mystery was the direct ancestor of our oratorio, so was the little pastoral of Adam de la Hale the germ of the modern French vaudeville.   One of its melodies is said to be sung to this day in some parts of southern France.

The entire object in this little play being that both words and action should be perfectly understood, it is obvious that as little as possible should be going on dur-

* It is interesting to note as to the prevalence of Latin, that Dante's " Divina Commedia " was the first important poem in Italian.   Latin was used on the stage in Italy up to the sixteenth century; the stationary chorus stationed on the stage remained until the seventeenth century and was not entirely discontinued until the first half of the eighteenth century.

ing the singing. Thus, such melodies as we find in these old pastoral plays would be accompanied by short notes, serving merely to give the pitch and tonality, which would gradually develop into chords, thus laying the foundation for harmony.

If, on the other hand, we look at the " church play " of the same period, the Mystery, and remember that it was sung by men accustomed to singing the *organum* of Hucbald, we have a clue as to what it was and what it led up to. For while one part or voice of the music would give a melody (copied from or at any rate resembling the Gregorian chant or the sequences of Notker of Tubilo), the other voices would sing songs in the vernacular, and, strangest of all, one voice would repeat some Latin word, or even a " nonsense word" (to use Edward Lear's term) but much more slowly than the other voices. Thus the needs of the Mystery were as well met by incipient counterpoint on the one hand, as, on the other, the secular song-play engendered the sense of harmony.

That the early secular forerunner of opera, as represented by "Robin et Marian," was still, to a certain degree, controlled by the church is clear if we remember that at that time the only methods of noting music were entirely in the hands of the clergy. The notation for the lute, for instance, was invented about 1460 to 1500. Thus, we can say that the recording of secular music was not free from church influence until some time after the sixteenth century.

This primitive " opera " music was thus fettered by difficulty of notation and the influence of the ecclesiastical rules until perhaps about 1600, when the first real opera began to find a place in Italy. Jacopo Peri and Caccini were among the first workers in the comparatively new form, and they both took the same subject, *Eurydice*. Of the former the following two short excerpts will suffice; the first is where Orpheus bewails his fate; in the second he expresses his joy at bringing Eurydice back to earth. Caccini's opera was perhaps the first to introduce the many useless ornaments that, up to the middle of this century, were characteristic of Italian opera.

EURYDICE — PERI.

Orpheus bewailing his fate.

I weep not, I am not sigh - ing, tho' thou art . .

. . . from me tak - en. What use to sigh

Orpheus' joy in bringing back Eurydice.

Gio - i-te al can - to mio ser - ve fron - do

di che in su l'au ro - ra

XVII

OPERA

No art form is so fleeting and so subject to the dictates of fashion as opera. It has always been the plaything of fashion, and suffers from its changes. To-day the stilted figures of Hasse, Pergolesi, Rameau, and even Gluck, seem as grotesque to us as the wigs and buckles of their contemporaries. To Palestrina's masses and madrigals, Rameau's and Couperin's claveçin pieces, and all of Bach, we can still listen without this sense of incongruity. On the other hand, operas of Alessandro Scarlatti, Matheson, and Porpora would bore us unmitigatedly. They have gone out of fashion. Even the modern successors of these men, Bellini, Donizetti, and Verdi, in his earlier years, have become dead letters musically, although only as late as 1845, Donizetti was at the very zenith of his fame.

Of all the operas of the past century, our present public has not seen or even heard of one, with the exception of " The Magic Flute," and less probably " Don Juan." This is bad enough; but if we look at works belonging to the first part of the nineteenth century, we find the same state of affairs. The operas of Spontini, Rossini, most of Meyerbeer's, even Weber's " Freischütz," have passed away, seemingly never to return. Even " Cavalleria Rusticana," of recent creation, is falling rapidly into oblivion. Thus the opéra comique early disappeared in favour of the romantic opera and the operetta. The former has already nearly ended its career, and the latter has descended to the level of mere farce. In the course of time, these opera forms become more and more evanescent; for the one-act opera of miniature tragedy, which is practically only a few years old, is already almost extinct.

And yet this art form has vastly more hold on the public than other music destined to outlive it. The fact is, that music which is tied down to the conventionalities and moods of its time and place can never appeal but to the particular time and mood which gave it birth. (Incidentally, I may say the same of music having its roots in the other peculiarities of folk song.)

Now the writers of these operas were great men who put their best into their work; the cause of the failure of these operas was not on account of the music, but the ideas and thoughts with which this music was saddled. What were the books which people read and loved in those days (1750–1800), that is, books upon which operas might be built? In England we find " The Castle of Otranto," " The Mysterious Mother," etc., by Horace Walpole. Now Macaulay says that Horace Walpole's works rank as high among the delicacies of intellectual epicures as the Strasburg pie among the dishes described in the *Almanach des Gourmands*. None but an unhealthy and disorganized mind could have produced such literary luxuries as the works of Walpole.

France had not yet recovered from the empty formalism of the preceding century, Bernardin de St. Pierre was

a kind of colonial Mlle. Scudery, and Jean Jacques
Rousseau, one of the sparks which were to ignite the French
Revolution, writes his popular opera to the silly story of
" The Village Soothsayer." Had not Gluck written to the
classics he would have had to write " à la Watteau."

In Germany, conditions were better; for the so-called
Romantic school had just begun to make headway. In
opera, however, this school of Romanticism only commenced to make itself felt later, when we have a crop of
operas on Fouque's " Undine " as well as " Hofmann's
Tales."

It is as though opera had to dress according to the
prevailing fashion of the day. The very large sleeves
of one year look strange to us a little later. Just so is it
with opera; for those old operas by Méhul, Spontini,
Salieri, and others all wear enormous crinolines, while the
contemporary instrumental works of the same period,
unfettered by fashion, still possess all the freedom which
their limited speech permitted them to have. Thus we
see that opera is necessarily a child of the times in which
it is written, in contrast to other music which echoes but
the thought of the composer, thought that is not necessarily bound down to any time, place, or peculiarity of
diction.

In Germany, Italian opera was never accepted by the
people as it was in France. In the latter country, opera
had to be in the vernacular and practically to become
French. Lully's operas were written to libretti by Quin-
ault and Corneille; and while, as early as 1645, Paris
imported its opera from Italy, this art form was rapidly

modified to suit the public for which it was secured.
Even with Piccini and Gluck, and down to Rossini and
Meyerbeer, this nationalism was infused into the foreign
product. In Germany the case was entirely different,
for up to the very last, Italian opera was a thing apart.
Although German composers, such as Mozart and Paër,
wrote Italian opera, the " Singspiel " (a kind of opéra
comique), found its culminating point in Weber's " Freischütz," which fought against Rossini's operas for supremacy in Germany.

Gluck's victory over the Piccinists gave to the French
form of Italian opera an impetus that caused Cherubini
to proceed on almost the same lines in his operas, the
" Water Carrier," etc. Cherubini was a pupil of Andreas
Sarti, a celebrated contrapuntist and a disciple of the last
of the Italian church composers who looked back to
Palestrina for inspiration. Thus the infusion of a certain
soberness of diction, which we call German, fitted in with
the man's training and predilections.

The first names we meet with in French opera after
Cherubini are those of Grétry, Méhul, and Spontini.
The former was a Frenchman whose works are now
obsolete, although Macfarren, in the " Encyclopedia
Brittanica," says that he is the only French composer
of symphonies that are known and enjoy popularity in
France.

Grétry was born in Liége, about 1740. He walked to
Italy, studied in Rome, and returned to France about 1770.
None of his works have come down to us, but his name is
interesting by reason of a certain contradiction in his

operas.   This contradiction consists in his being one of the
first to revive the idea of the hidden orchestra; it is interesting also to note that in his " Richard Cœur de Lion,"
he anticipated Wagner's use of the *leitmotiv*.   His words
on the hidden orchestra sound strangely modern:

PLAN FOR A NEW THEATRE. — I should like the auditorium of
my theatre to be small, holding at the most one thousand persons
and consisting of a sort of open space, without boxes, small or great;
for these nooks only encourage talking and scandal.   I would like
the orchestra to be concealed, so that neither the musicians nor the
lights on their music stands could be visible to the spectators.

Méhul was born about 1763 in the south of France,
and is celebrated, among other things, as being a pupil
of Gluck, in Paris.   He was also noted for having, at
the request of Napoleon, brought out an opera based on
Macpherson's " Ossian," in which no violins were used
in the orchestra.   " Joseph," another opera of his, is
occasionally given in small German towns.   Méhul died
in 1817.

Spontini, the next representative of opera in France,
was an Italian, born in 1774.   He went to Paris in 1803,
where, through the influence of the Empress Josephine,
he was enabled to have several small operas performed;
finally in 1807 his " Vestal," written to a French text,
was given with great success.   In this, his greatest work,
he followed Gluck's footsteps, not only in the music, but
also in the choice of a classic subject.   In 1809, he branched
out into a more romantic vein with the opera of " Fer-
nando Cortez."   His other works never attained popularity.   After the Restoration in France, he was named

director of the court music in Berlin by the King of Prussia, at an annual salary of ten thousand thalers (about $7,500), a position he held from 1820 to 1840. He died in Italy in 1851. Spontini may be said to have been the last representative of the Gluck opera; but he also brought into it all the magnificence in scenery, etc., that would naturally be expected by the fashion of the First Empire. He made no innovations, and merely served to keep alive the traditions of Grand Opera in France.

The next powerful influence in France, and indeed in all Europe, was that of Rossini. He may be said to have built on Gluck's ideas in many ways. Born in 1792, at Pesaro, in Italy, he wrote many operas of the flimsy Italian style while still a boy. At twenty-one he had already written his " Tancredi " and the opera buffa, " The Italians in Algiers." His best work (besides " William Tell ") was " The Barber of Seville." Other works are " Cinderella " (*La Cenerentola*), " The Thieving Black-bird " (*La Gazza Ladra*), " Moses," and " The Lady of the Lake." These operas were mostly made up of parts of others that were failures, à la Hasse. An engagement being offered him in London, he went there with his wife, and in one season they earned about two hundred thousand francs, which laid the foundation for his future prosperity.

The next year he went to Paris, where, after a few un-important works, he produced " William Tell " with tremendous success (1829). Although he lived until 1868, he never wrote for the operatic stage again, his other works being mainly the well-known " Stabat Mater " and some choruses. He was essentially a writer of light opera, although " William Tell " has many elevated moments. His style was so entirely warped by his love for show and the virtuoso side of singing that the many real beauties of his music are hardly recognizable. His music is so overladen with *fioriture* that often its very considerable value is obscured. He had absolutely no influence upon German music, for the Germans, from Beethoven down, despised the flimsy style and aims of this man, who, by appealing to the most unmusical side of the fashionable audiences of Europe, did so much to discourage the production of operas with a lofty aim. In France, however, his influence was unchallenged, and we may almost say that, with few exceptions, the overture to " William Tell " served as a model for all other operatic overtures which have been written there up to the present day. We have only to look at the many overtures by Hérold, Boieldieu, Auber, and others, to see the influence exerted by this style of overture, which consisted of a slow introduction, followed by a more or less sentimental melody, followed in turn by a galop as a coda.

So fashionable had this kind of thing become that even Weber was slightly touched by it. In the meanwhile, the French composers were producing operas of a smaller kind, but, in many ways, of a better character than the larger works of Rossini, Spontini, and their followers. Had this flimsy Italian influence been lacking, doubtless French opera to-day would be a different thing from what it actually is. For these smaller operas by Hérold, Auber, and Boieldieu had many points in common with the

German *Singspiel*, which may be said to have saved German musical art for Wagner.

What might have developed under better conditions is shown in a work by Halévy entitled, "La juive," in which is to be found promise of a great school of opera, a promise unhappily stifled by the advent of an eclectic, the German Meyerbeer, who blinded the public with unheard of magnificence of staging, just as Rossini before him had blinded it by novel technical feats. Meyerbeer thus drew the art into a new channel, and, unluckily, this new tendency was not so much in the direction of elevation of style as in sensationalism.

To return to the French composers. Hérold was born in 1791, in Paris, and his principal works were "Zampa" and the "Pré aux clercs." The first was produced in 1831, the latter in 1832. He died in 1833. Boieldieu was born in 1775, in Rouen; died 1834. His principal works were "La dame blanche" and "Jean de Paris."

Halévy (Levy) was born in 1799, in Paris, and died in 1862; his father was a Bavarian and his mother from Lorraine. He wrote innumerable operas. His most famous work, "La juive," written in 1835, was killed by Meyerbeer's "Huguenots," and produced a year later. He was professor of counterpoint at the Conservatoire from 1831, among his pupils being Gounod, Massé, Bazin, and Bizet.

Auber was born in 1782, and died in May, 1871. He was practically the last of the essentially French composers. His operas may be summed up as being the perfect translation into music of the witty plays of Scribe, with whom

he was associated all his life. To read a comedy by
Scribe is to imagine Auber's music to it. No one has
excelled Auber in the expression of all the finesse of wit
and lightness of touch. What the union between the two
men was may be inferred from the fact that Scribe wrote
many of his librettos to Auber's music, the latter being
written first, Scribe then adding the words. His principal
works are " Masaniello " or " The Mute," and " Fra
Diavolo." He was appointed director of the Paris Conservatoire, in 1842, in succession to Cherubini.

In speaking of Grétry, I quoted his opinion (given in
one of his essays on music) as to what opera should be
and cited his use of the *leitmotiv* in his " Richard Cœur
de Lion " (which contains the air, *une fièvre brûlante*).
If with this we quote his reasons for writing opéra comique rather than grand opera, we have one of the reasons
why French opera has, as yet, never developed beyond
Massenet's " Roi de Lahore " on one side, and Delibes'
" Lakme " on the other.

Grétry writes that he introduced lyric comedy on the
stage because the public was tired of tragedy, and because
he had heard so many lovers of dancing complain that
their favourite art played only a subordinate rôle in grand
opera. Also the public loved to hear short songs; therefore he introduced many such into his operas.

Even nowadays, this seeming contradiction between
theory and practice is to be found, I think, in the French
successors of Meyerbeer. The public needed dancing,
and all theories must bend to that wish. Even Wagner
succumbed to this influence in Paris; and when Weber's

" Freischütz " was first given at the grand opera, Berlioz was commissioned to arrange ballet music from
Weber's piano works to supply the deficiency.

In France, even to-day, everything gives way to the public, a public whose intelligence from a poetic standpoint
is, in my opinion, lower than that of any other country.
The French composer is dependent on his country (Paris)
as is no musician of other nationality. Berlioz' life was
embittered by the want of recognition in Paris. Although he had been acclaimed as a great musician all over
Europe, yet he returned again and again to Paris, pre-
ferring (as he admits) the approbation of its musically
worthless public to his otherwise world-wide fame.

We remember that Auber never stirred out of Paris
throughout his long life. It was an article in the *Gaz-
ette Musicale* of Paris which was instrumental in calling
Gounod back into the world from his intended priestly
vocation. And this influence of the admittedly ignorant
and superficial French public is the more remarkable when
one considers the fact that it was always the last to admit
the value of the best work of its composers. Thus Berlioz' fame was gained in Russia and Germany while he
was still derided and comparatively unknown in Paris.

The failure of Bizet's " Carmen " is said to have has-
tened the composer's death, which took place within three
months after the first performance of the opera. As Saint-
Saëns wrote at the time, in his disgust at the French public:
" The fat, ugly bourgeois ruminates in his padded stall,
regretting separation from his kind. He half opens a
glassy eye, munches a bonbon, then sleeps again, thinking

that the orchestra is a-tuning." And yet, even Saint-Saëns, whose name became known chiefly through Liszt's help, and whose operas and symphonies were given in Germany before they were known in France, even he is one of the most ardent adherents to the " anti-foreigner " cry in France. In my opinion, this respect for and attempt to please this grossly ignorant French public is and has been one of the great devitalizing influences which hamper the French composer.

Charles Gounod was born in 1818, in Paris. His father was an engraver and died when Gounod was very young. The boy received his first music lessons from his mother. He was admitted to the Conservatoire at sixteen, and studied with Halévy and Lesueur. In 1839 he gained the *Prix de Rome*, and spent three years in Rome, studying ecclesiastical music. In 1846 he contemplated becoming a priest, and wrote a number of religious vocal works, published under the name Abbé C. Gounod. In 1851 the article I referred to appeared, and such was its effect on Gounod, that within four months his first opera " Sapho " was given (April, 1851). A year later this was followed by some music for a tragedy (Poussard's " Ulysse " at the Comédie Française), and in 1854 by the five-act opera "La nonne sanglante." These were only very moderately successful; and so Gounod turned to the opéra comique, and wrote music to an adaptation of Molière's " Medecin malgré lui." This became very popular, and paved the way for his " Faust," which was produced at the Opéra Comique in 1859. In the opéra comique, as we know, the singing was always interspersed with spoken dialogue.

Thus, this opera, as we know it, dates from its preparation for the Grand Opéra ten years later, 1869. Ten months after " Faust " was given he used a fable of Lafontaine for a short light opera, " Philemon and Baucis."

In the meantime, "Faust" began to bring him encouragement, and his next opera was on the subject of the " Queen of Sheba " (1862). This being unsuccessful, he wrote two more light operas, " Mireille " and " La colombe " (1866). The next was " Romeo et Juliette " (1867). This was very successful, and marks the culmination of Gounod's success as an opera composer. In 1870 he went to London, where he made his home for a number of years. His later operas, " Cinq-Mars " (1877), " Polyeucte " (1878), and " Le tribut de Zamora " (1881), met with small success, and have rarely been given.

In his later years, as we know, he showed his early predilection for religious music; and his oratorios " The Redemption," " Mors et Vita," and several masses have been given with varying success. Perhaps one of the greatest points ever made in Gounod's favour by a critic was that by Pougin, who asks what other composer could have written two such operas as " Faust " and " Romeo et Juliette " and still have them essentially different musically. The " Garden Scene " in the one and the " Balcony Scene " in the other are identical, so far as the feeling of the play is concerned; also the duel of Faust and Valentine and Romeo and Tybalt.

Ambroise Thomas's better works, " Mignon " and " Hamlet," may be said to be more or less echoes of

Gounod; and while his " Francesca da Rimini," which was brought out in 1882, was by far his most ambitious work, it never became known outside of Paris. Ambroise Thomas was born in 1811, and died within a year of Gounod. His chief merit was in his successful direction of the Conservatoire, to which he succeeded Auber in 1871.

Georges Bizet (his name was Alexander César Leopold) was born in 1838, in Paris. His father was a poor singing teacher, and his mother a sister-in-law of Delsarte; she was a first-prize piano pupil of the Conservatoire. As a boy, Bizet was very precocious, and entered the Conservatoire as a pupil of Marmontel when he was ten. He took successively the first prizes for solfége, piano, organ, and fugue, and finally the *Prix de Rome* in 1857, when he was nineteen years old. The latter kept him in Rome until 1861, when he returned to Paris and gave piano and harmony lessons and arranged dance music for brass bands, a *métier* not unknown to either Wagner or Raff.

Until 1872, Bizet wrote but small and unimportant works, such as " The Pearl Fisher," " The Fair Maid of Perth," and several vaudeville operettas, some of which he wrote to order and anonymously. He married a daughter of Halévy, the composer, and in 1871–72 served in the National Guard. His first important work was the incidental music to Alphonse Daudet's " L'Arlesienne " and finally his " Carmen " was given (but without success), at the Opéra Comique, in March, 1875. He died June 3, 1875.

Camille Saint-Saëns was born in Paris, in 1835; he commenced studying piano when only three years old. I believe it is mostly through his piano concertos and his symphonic poems that his name will live; for his operas have never attained popularity, with perhaps the one exception of " Samson and Delilah." His other operas are: " The Yellow Princess," " Proserpina," " Etienne Marcel," " Henry VIII," " Ascanio."

Jules Massenet was born in 1852, and at the age of twelve became a pupil of Bezit at the Conservatoire, was rejected by Bezit for want of talent, and afterward studied with Reber and Thomas, and won the *Prix de Rome* in 1863. Upon his return, in 1866, he wrote a number of small orchestral works, including two suites and several sacred dramas, " Marie Magdalen " and " Eve and the Virgin," in which the general Meyerbeerian style militated against any suggestion of religious feeling. His first grand opera, " Le roi de Lahore," was given in 1881. The second was " Herodiade," which was followed by " Manon," " The Cid," " Esclarmonde," " Le mage."

XVIII

OPERA (Continued)

One of the most disputed questions in modern music is that of opera. Although we have many controversies as to what purely instrumental or vocal music may do, the operatic art, if we may call it so, always remains the same. In creating the music drama, Wagner put forth a composite art, something which many declare impossible, and as many others advocate as being the most complete art form yet conceived. We are still in the midst of the discussion, and a final verdict is therefore as yet impossible. On one hand we have Wagner, and against him we have the absolutists such as Brahms, the orthodox thinkers represented by Anton Rubinstein and many others, the new Russian school represented by Cui, Rimsky-Korsakov, Tchaikovsky, and the successors of the French school of Meyerbeer, namely, Saint-Saëns, Massenet, etc.

In order to get a clear idea of the present state of the matter we must review the question from the beginning of the eighteenth century. For many reasons this is not an easy task, first of all because very little of the music of the operas of this period actually exists. We know the names of Hasse, Pergolesi, Matheson, Graun, Alessandro Scarlatti (who was a much greater man than his son the harpsichord player and composer, Domenico), to name only a few. To be sure, a number of the French operas of the period are preserved, owing to the custom in France of engraving music. In Germany and Italy, however, such operas were never printed, and one may safely say that it was almost the rule for only one manuscript copy to be available. Naturally this copy belonged to the composer, who generally led the opera himself, improvising much of it on the harpsichord, as we shall see later. As an instance of the danger which operas, under such conditions, ran of being destroyed and thus lost to the world, we may cite the total destruction of over sixty of Hasse s operas in his extreme old age.

The second point which makes it difficult for us to get an absolutely clear insight into the conditions of opera at the beginning of the eighteenth century lies in the fact that contemporary historians never brought their histories up to their own times. Thus Marpurg, in his history, divides music into four periods; first, that of Adam and Eve to the flood; second, from the flood to the Argonauts; third, to the beginning of the Olympiads; fourth, from thence to Pythagoras. The same may be said of the celebrated histories of Gerbert and Padre Martini.

On the other hand, we are certain that much of the modern speculation was anticipated by these men. For instance, Matheson calls pantomime " dumb music," freed from melodic and harmonic forms. The idea was advanced that music owes its rhythmic regularity and form to dancing, and architecture was called frozen music, a metaphor which, in later days, was considered such an original conception of Goethe and Schlegel. This same inability of historians to bring their accounts up to the contemporary times may be noticed in the later works of Forkel (d. 1818) and Ambros (d. 1876).

Yet a third reason remains which tends to confuse the student as to what really constituted opera. This is owing to the fact that there existed the very important element of improvisation, of which I shall speak later.

In order to see what Gluck, Weber, and Wagner had to break away from, let us look at the condition of opera at the beginning of the eighteenth century. We remember that opera, having become emancipated from the Church long before any other music, developed apace, while instrumental (secular) music was still in its infancy. In Germany, even the drama was neglected for its kindred form of opera; therefore, in studying its development, we may well understand why the dramatic stage considered the opera its deadly enemy.

The life of the German dramatist and actor of the first half of the eighteenth century was one of the direst hardship and poverty. Eckhof, one of the greatest actors of his time, made his entry into Brunswick in a kind of miserable hay cart, in which, accompanied by his sick wife and several dogs, he had travelled over the rough roads. To keep warm they had filled part of the wagon with straw. The German actor and dramatist of that time often died in the hospital, despised by the richer classes; even the village priests and ministers refused to allow them to eat at their tables. Their scenery rarely consisted of more than three rough pieces: a landscape, a large room, and a peasant's hut interior. Many even had only two large cloths which were hung about the stage, one green, which was to be used when the scene was in the open air, and the other yellow, which was used to represent an interior. Shakespeare's "Poor Players" were certainly a stern reality in Germany. In order to attract the public the plays had to consist for the most part of the grossest subjects imaginable, it being barely possible to smuggle some small portion of serious drama into the entertainment.

With opera, however, it was vastly different; opera troupes were met at the city gates by the royal or ducal carriages, and the singers were fêted everywhere. The prices paid them can only be compared with the salaries paid nowadays. They were often ennobled, and the different courts quarrelled for the honour of their presence. The accounts of the cost of the scenery used are incredible, amounting to many thousands of dollars for a single performance.

One of the earliest German kapellmeisters and opera composers was Johann Adolf Hasse, who was born in Dresden about 1700. To show the foundation upon which Gluck built, we will look at opera as it existed in Hasse's time. In 1727 Hasse married at Venice, Faustina Bordoni, the foremost singer of the time. He wrote over one hundred operas for her, and had a salary of thirty-six thousand marks, or nine thousand dollars, yearly. Now these operas were very different from those we know. The arias in them (and, of course, the whole opera was practically but a succession of arias) were only sketched in an extremely vague manner. Much was left to the singer, and the accompaniment was sparsely indicated by figures written above a bass. The recitative which separated one aria from another was improvised by the singer, and was accompanied on the harpsichord by the kapellmeister, who was naturally obliged to improvise his part on the spur of the moment, following the caprice of the singer. There was no creating an atmosphere for a tragic or dramatic situation by means of the accompaniment; as soon as the situation arrived, an aria was sung explaining it. Now, as the singer was given much latitude in regard to the melody, and *absolute* liberty in regard to the recitative, it is easy to see that, with the astounding technical perfection possessed by the singers of the time, this latitude would be used to astonish the hearers by wonderful vocal feats intermingled with more or less passionate declamation.

The composer was merely the excuse for the opera; but he needed to be a consummate musician to conduct and accompany this improvised music, of which his written score was but the nucleus. The wretched acting of opera singers in general has been rather humourously traced back to this epoch. Nowadays, in an opera, when, by way of example, a murder is to be committed, the orchestra paints the situation, and the act is accomplished without delay. In those olden days a singer would have indignantly refused to submit to such a usurpation of his rights; he would have raised his dagger, and then, before striking, would have sung an aria in the regular three parts, after which he would have stabbed his man. The necessity for doing something during this interim is said to be responsible for

those idiotic gestures which used to be such a seemingly
necessary part of the equipment of the opera singer.

In the ordinary opera of the time there was the custom
of usually having about from twenty to thirty such arias
(Hasse's one hundred operas contain about three thousand
arias). Now these arias, although they were intended to
paint a situation, rapidly became simply a means to display the singer's skill. The second part was a melody
with plenty of vocal effects, and the third part a bravura
piece, pure and simple. So there only remained the
recitative in which true dramatic art could find place. As
this, however, was invariably improvised by the singer,
one can see that the composer of music had his cross as
well as his brother the dramatist. The music having no
vital connection with the text, it is easy to see how one
opera could be set to several texts or *vice-versa*, as was
often done.

Another factor also contributed to retard the artistic
development of opera. All these arias had to be constructed and sung according to certain customs. Thus,
the fiery, minor aria was always sung by the villain, the
so-called colorature arias by the tall, majestic heroine, etc.

All this seems childish to us, but it was certainly a
powerful factor in making fame for a composer. For, as
has been said, while a modern composer writes two or
three different operas, Hasse wrote one hundred versions
of one. This also had its effect on instrumental music,
and, in a way, is also the direct cause of that monstrosity
known as " variations " (Händel wrote sixty-six on one
theme.) In our days we often hear the bitter complaint

that opera singers are no longer what they used to be, and that the great art of singing has been lost. If we look back to the period under consideration, we cannot but admit that there is much truth in the contention. In the first place, an opera singer of those days was necessarily an actor of great resource, a thorough musician, a composer, and a marvellous technician. In addition to this, operas were always written for individuals. Thus, all of Hasse's were designed for Faustina's voice; and by examining the music, we can tell exactly what the good and bad points of her voice were, such was the care with which it was written.

Before we leave the subject of Hasse and his operas, I wish to refer briefly to a statement found in all histories and books on music. We find it stated that all this music was sung and played either loud or soft; with no gradual transitions from one to the other. The existence of that gradual swelling or diminishing of the tone in music which we call crescendo and diminuendo, is invariably denied, and its first use is attributed to Jommelli, director of the opera at Mannheim, in 1760. Thus we are asked to believe that Faustina sang either *piano* or *forte*, and still was an intensely dramatic singer.

This seems to me to require no comment; especially as, already in 1676, Matthew Locke, an English writer, uses the ══ sign for the gradual transition from soft to loud. For obvious reasons there could be no such transition in harpsichord music, and this is why, when the same instrument was provided with hammers instead of quills, the name was changed to *pianoforte*, to indicate its power to modify the tone from soft to loud.

Naturally Händel, who was a man of despotic tendencies, could not long submit to the caprices of opera singers. After innumerable conflicts with them, we find him turning back to one of the older forms of opera, the oratorio.

Bach never troubled himself about an art from which he was so widely separated both by training and inclination. Thus the reformation of opera (I mean the old opera of which I have been speaking) devolved upon Gluck. His early operas were entirely on the lines of those of Hasse and Porpora. He wrote operas for archduchesses ("Il Parnasso" was played by four archduchesses and accompanied on harpsichord by the Archduke Leopold), and was music master to Marie Antoinette at Vienna. It was owing to these powerful influences that his art principles had an opportunity to be so widely exploited. For these principles were not new; they formed the basis of Peri's first attempt at opera in 1600, and had been recalled in vain by Marcello in 1720. They were so simple that it seems almost childish to quote them. They demanded merely that the music should always assist, but never interfere with either the declamation or dramatic action of the story. Thus by Gluck's powerful influence with what may be termed the fashion of his day, he did much to relegate to a place of minor importance the singer, who until then had held undisputed sway. This being the case, the great art of singing, which had allowed the artist the full control and responsibility of opera, thus centering all upon the one individuality, degenerated into the more subordinate rôle of following the composer's directions.

It now became the duty of the composer to foresee every

contingency of his work, and it lay with him to give directions for every detail of it. As a result, the singers, having no longer absolute control but still anxious to display their technical acquirements, gradually changed into that now almost obsolete abomination, the " Italian opera singer," an artist, who, shirking all responsibility for the music and dramatic action, neglected the composer so far as possible, and introduced vocal pyrotechnics wherever he or she dared — and their daring was great.

In the meantime, as Gluck was bringing in his reforms, songs were gradually introduced into the *Schauspiel* or drama, the ill-fated brother of opera in Germany; and just as the grand opera reached its highest point with Gluck, so this species of melodrama grew apace, until we see its culmination in Weber's " Freischütz."

The good results of Gluck's innovations and also, to a certain degree, its discrepancies, may be plainly seen in Mozart's operas; for only too often in his operas Mozart was obliged to introduce *fioriture* of the poorest possible description in situations where they were utterly out of place. This, however, may not be entirely laid at the door of the exacting singer, for we find these same *fioriture* throughout his harpsichord music.

We may almost say that the union of drama and music was first definitely given status by Mozart; for a number of his operas, such as the " Schauspieldirektor," etc., were merely a form of the German *Singspiel*, which, as I have said, culminated in " Freischütz."

Thus, at the beginning of our century we find two art forms: First, grand opera of a strange nationality, and second, the small but rapidly developing form of comedy or drama with music.

In order to show how Wagner evolved his art theories from this material, we must consider to some degree the general conditions of this period.

As late as 1853, Riehl wrote that Mendelssohn was the only composer who had the German public, whereas others had only a small section of it. For example, Schumann, whose music he did not like, was accepted as a new Messiah in the Elbe River district; " but who," he asks, " knows anything about him in the south or west of Germany? " And as for Richard Wagner, who, he says, is a man of extravagant ideas and a kind of phenomenon of no consequence artistically, he asks, " who really knows anything about him outside of the little party of fanatics who profess to like his music (so-called)?" Its only chance of becoming known, he says, is in the public's curiosity to hear works which are rarely given. This curiosity, he continues, will be a much more potent factor in his chance of becoming known than all his newspaper articles and the propaganda of his friend, Franz Liszt.

For the German opera there were half a dozen *Boersenplätze* — Berlin for the northwest, Hamburg for the northeast, Frankfort for the southwest, Munich for the southeast. As Riehl says, a success in Frankfort meant a success in all the Frankfort clay deposit and sandstone systems, but in the chalk formation of Munich it stood no chance. Thus Germany had no musical centre. But after Meyerbeer found such a centre in Paris, all other Germans, including Wagner, looked to Paris for fame.

At the end of the eighteenth century, Vienna was the art centre; nevertheless Gluck had to go to Paris for recognition.

Mendelssohn only succeeded by his *Salonfähigkeit*. Always respectable in his forms, no one else could have made music popular among the cultured classes as could Mendelssohn. This also had its danger; for if Mendelssohn had written an opera (the lack of which was so bewailed by the Philistines), it would have taken root all over Germany, and put Wagner back many years. At the death of Mendelssohn, the Philistines heralded the coming of a new German national school, founded on his principles (formalism), one that would clarify the artistic atmosphere of the turgid and anarchistic excesses of Wagner and Berlioz and their followers. These critics found already that Beethoven's melodies were too long and his instrumentation too involved. They declared that the further music departed from its natural simplicity the more involved its utterance became, the less clear, and consequently the poorer it was. Music was compared to architecture, and thus the more Greek it was, the better; forgetting that architecture was tied to utilitarianism and poetry to word-symbols, and that painting is primarily an art of externals.

Riehl says that art is always in danger of ruin when its simple foundation forms are too much elaborated, overlooking the fact that music is not an art, but psychological utterance.

It needed all Wagner's gigantic personality to rise above this wave of formalism that looked to the past for its salvation, a past which was one of childish experimenting rather than of æsthetic accomplishment. The tendency was to return to the dark cave where tangible walls were to be touched by the hands, rather than to emerge into a sunlight that seemed blinding.

XIX

ON THE LIVES AND ART PRINCIPLES OF SOME SEVENTEENTH AND EIGHTEENTH CENTURY COMPOSERS

There is much of value to the student to be derived from a study of the lives and art principles of the composers of the seventeenth and eighteenth centuries. To go back to an earlier period would hardly be worth while, as the music composed in those days is too much obscured by the uncertainty of tradition and the inevitable awkwardness of expression that goes with all primitiveness in art.

The first whom I would mention are Don Carlo Gesualdo, Prince of Venosa, and Ludovico Viadana.

The former was a nephew of the Archbishop of Naples, was born in 1550, and died in 1613. His name is important from the fact that he went boldly beyond Monteverde, his contemporary, in the use of the new dissonant chords (sevenths and ninths) which were just beginning to be employed, and adopted a chromatic style of writing which strangely foreshadowed the chromatic polyphonic style of the present century. He wrote innumerable madrigals for a number of voices, but his innovations remained sterile so far as the development of music is concerned, for the reason that while his music often acquired a wonderful poignancy for his time by the use of chromatics, just as often it led him into the merest bramble bush of sound, real music being entirely absent.

Viadana (1566–1645) has been placed by many historians of music in the same category as Guido d'Arezzo (who is credited with having invented solmization, musical notation, etc.), Palestrina, Monteverde and Peri, who are famed, the one for having discovered the dominant ninth chord, and the other for the invention of opera. Viadana is said to have been the first to use what is called a *basso continuo*, and even the figured bass. The former was the uninterrupted repetition of a short melody or phrase in the bass through the entire course of a piece of music. This was done very often to give a sense of unity that nowadays would be obtained by a repetition of the first thought at certain intervals through the piece. The figured (or better, ciphered) bass was an entirely different thing. This device, which is still employed, consisted of the use of figures to indicate the different chords in music. These figures or ciphers were written over or under the bass note on which the chord represented by the figures was to be played or sung. A 5 over or under a bass note meant that with that note a perfect major triad was to be sounded, considering the note written as the root of the chord; a 3 was taken to stand for a perfect minor triad; a 6 for the chord of the sixth (first inversion of a triad), and $\frac{6}{4}$ for the second inversion; a line through a 5 or 7 meant that the triad was a diminished fifth or a diminished seventh chord; a cross indicated a leading tone; a 4 stood for the third inversion of the dominant seventh chord. This system of shorthand, as it may be called, was and is still of tremendous value to composers. In the olden days, particularly, when many of the composers engraved their own music for publication, it saved a great deal of labour.   It is probably not generally known that the engraving of music by the composer was so common; but such was the case with Bach, Rameau, and Couperin.

And this reminds me that the embellishments, as they were called, which are so common in all harpsichord and clavichord music, were also noted in a kind of shorthand, and for precisely the same reason.   The embellishments themselves originated from the necessity for sustaining in some way the tone of the instrument, which gave out little, dry, clicklike sounds; if the melody were played in simple notes, these sounds would mingle with the accompaniment and be lost in it.   Therefore, the embellishments served to sustain the tones of the melody, and thus cause them to stand out from the accompaniment.   Their notation by means of symbols copied from the primitive *neumes* vastly facilitated the work of engraving.   Much confusion arose in the notation of embellishments, owing to the fact that each composer had his own system of symbols.

Alessandro Scarlatti and his son Domenico, both celebrated in their day, are the next to demand attention. The former was born about 1650 and died about 1725.   He wrote many operas of which we know practically nothing. His son was born about 1685 and died in 1757.   He was the most celebrated harpsichord player of his time; and although his style, which was essentially one of virtuosity, was not productive of direct results, it did nevertheless foreshadow the wonderful technical achievements of Liszt in our own times. It is indeed a great pity that Domenico Scarlatti's work did not bear more direct fruit in his day, for it would have turned Mozart, as well as many others, from the loose, clumsy mannerisms of the later virtuoso style, which ran to the Alberti bass and other degrading platitudes, paralleled in our comparatively modern days by the Thalberg arpeggios, repeating notes, Döhler trill, etc.

Two masters in music, Händel and J. S. Bach, were born the same year, 1685; their great French contemporary, Rameau, was born two years earlier and died in 1764; while Händel died in 1759, and Bach in 1750. Bach was destined to give to the world its first glimpse of the tremendous power of music, while Rameau organized the elements of music into a scientific harmonic structure, laying the foundation for our modern harmony. Händel's great achievement (besides being a fine composer) was to crush all life out of the then promising school of English music, the foundation for which had been so well laid by Purcell, Byrd, Morley, etc.

Jean Philippe Rameau was born in Dijon, and after travels in Italy and a short period of service as organist at Clermont, in Auvergne, went to Paris. There he wrote a number of small vaudevilles or musical comedies, which were successful; and his music for the harpsichord, consisting almost exclusively of small pieces with descriptive titles, soon began to be widely played in France. Much later in life he succeeded in obtaining a hearing for his operas, the first of which, " Hippolyte et Aricie," was given in 1732, when he was fifty years old. For thirty-two years his operas continued to hold the French stage against those of all foreigners.

His style marked a great advance over that of Lully, the Italian, of the century before. Rameau aimed at clearness of diction and was one of the first to attempt to give individuality to the different orchestral instruments. By some strange coincidence, his first opera had much the same dramatic situation that all the early operas seemed to have, namely, a scene in the infernal regions. Rameau's operas never became the foundation for a distinctly French opera, for at the time of his death (1764), Italian opera troupes had already introduced a kind of comedy with music, which rapidly developed into opéra comique; it was reserved for Gluck, the German, to revive grand opera in France.

As a theoretician, Rameau exerted tremendous influence upon music. He discovered that the chord which we call the perfect major triad was not merely the result of an artificial training of the ear to like certain combinations of sounds, but that this chord was inherent in every musical sound, constituting, as it does, the first four harmonics or overtones. All chords, therefore, that were not composed of thirds placed one above the other, were inversions of fundamental chords. This theory holds good in the general harmonic system of to-day. But although the major triad and even the dominant seventh chord could be traced back to the harmonics, the minor triad proved a different matter; after many experiments Rameau gave it up, leaving it unaccounted for.

Rameau was also largely instrumental in gaining recognition for the desirability of dividing the octave into twelve equal parts, making all the so-called half-tones recur at mathematically equal distances from each other in the chromatic scale. In 1737 his work on the generation of chords through overtones caused the equal temperament system of tuning to be generally accepted, and the old modes, with the exception of the Ionian and Æolian, to be dropped out of use. The former became known as major and the latter as minor, from the third, which was large in the Ionian and small in the Æolian.

Händel, as before stated, was born in 1685 (February 23), in Halle, in the same year as J. S. Bach, who was a month younger (born March 21). His father was a barber, who, as was common in those days, combined the trade of surgery, cupping, etc., with that of hairdressing. He naturally opposed his son's bent toward music, but with no effect. At fifteen years of age, Händel was beginning to be well known as a clavichord and organ player, in the latter capacity becoming specially celebrated for his wonderful improvisations. In spite of an attempt to make a lawyer of him, he persisted in taking music as his vocation, after the death of his father.

In Hamburg, whither he went in 1703, he obtained a place among the second violins in the opera orchestra.* Realizing that in Germany opera was but a reflection of Italian art, he left Hamburg in 1707 and went to Italy,

* At that time the harpsichord player was a very important member of an orchestra, as he accompanied the recitative from figured bass and was practically the conductor. On one occasion when the harpsichordist was absent Händel took his place with so much success that it paved the way for a hearing of his operas.

where he soon began to make a name for himself, both as performer and composer. One of his operas, " Agrippa," was performed at Venice during the Carnival season of 1710.

The Hanoverian kapellmeister, Staffani, was present and invited him to Hanover, whither he went, becoming Staffani's successor in the service of the Elector of Hanover. Several trips to England, where he was warmly welcomed, resulted in his accepting from Queen Anne, in 1713, a salary of two hundred pounds yearly, thus entering her service, notwithstanding his contract with the Elector. In 1714 the Queen died, and the Elector of Hanover was called to the English throne under the title of George I. Händel, in order to escape the impending disgrace occasioned by having broken faith with his former employer, wrote some music intended to be particularly persuasive, and had it played on a barge that followed a royal procession up the Thames. This " Water Music," as it was called, procured for him the King's pardon.

From this time he lived in England, practically monopolizing all that was done in music. In 1720 a company for the giving of Italian opera was formed, and Händel placed at its head. In 1727, on the occasion of the accession of George II, Händel wrote four anthems, one of which " Zadok the Priest," ends with the words " God save the King," from which it has been erroneously stated that he wrote the English national hymn.

In 1737 Händel gave up the writing of operas, after sinking most of his own savings in the undertaking, and began to write oratorios, the germs of which are found in the old Mysteries and Passion plays performed on a platform erected in the chapel or oratory of a church. Much has been written about Händel's habit of taking themes from other composers, and he was even dubbed the " grand old robber." It must not be overlooked, however, that although he made use of ideas from other composers, he turned them to the best account. By 1742 Händel was again in prosperous circumstances, his " Messiah " having been a tremendous success. From that time until his death he held undisputed sway, although his last years were clouded by a trouble with his eyes, which were operated upon unsuccessfully by an English oculist, named Taylor, who had also operated on Bach's eyes with the same disastrous result. Händel became completely blind in 1752. Up to the last year of his life he continued to give oratorio concerts and played organ concertos, of which only the *tutti* were noted, he improvising his part.

Händel's strength lay in his great ability to produce overwhelming effects by comparatively simple means. This is especially the case in his great choruses which are massive in effect and yet simple to the verge of barrenness. This, of course, has no reference to the absurd *fioriture* and long passage work given to the voices, — an Italian fashion of the times, — but to the contrapuntal texture of the work. Of his oratorios, " The Messiah " is the best known. Two of his " Concerti Grossi," the third and sixth, are sometimes played by string orchestras. Of his harpsichord music we have the eight " Suites " of 1720 (among which the one in E is known as having the variations called " The Harmonious Blacksmith "), and a number of " Harpsichord Lessons," among which are six fugues. All these may be said to have little value.

J. S. Bach differed in almost every respect from Händel, except that he was born in the same year and was killed by the same doctor. While Händel left no pupils, with perhaps the exception of his assistant organist, Bach aided and taught his own celebrated sons, Krebs, Agricola, Kittel, Kirnberger, Marpurg, and many other distinguished musicians. Bach twice made an effort to see Händel at Halle, but without success. On the other hand, there are reasons for believing that Händel never took the trouble to examine any of Bach's clavichord music. He lived like a conqueror in a foreign land, writing operas, oratorios, and concertos to order, and stealing ideas right and left without compunction; whereas Bach wrote from conviction, and no charge of plagiarism was ever laid at his door. Händel left a great fortune of twenty thousand pounds. Bach's small salary at the St. Thomas Church in Leipzig made it necessary for him to do much of his own engraving; and at his death, though he had helped many young struggling artists, his widow was left so poor that she had to be supported by public benevolence. Bach's works were neglected by his contemporaries, and it was only in the nineteenth century that he began to be appreciated in a way commensurate with his worth.

Bach was born in Eisenach, in Thuringia, and it is of interest to know that as far back as his great grandfather, Veit Bach (born about 1550), music had been the profession of the family. Bach's parents died when he was a boy of ten, and his education was continued by his elder brother, Johann Christoph, at a town near Gotha, where he held a position as organist. The boy soon outstripped his brother in learning, and continued his studies wholly by himself.

After filling a position as organist at Weimar, in 1703 he accepted one at a small town, Arnstadt, at a salary of about fifty-seven dollars yearly. He had already begun to compose, and possibly in imitation of Kuhnau, whose so-called " Bible " sonatas were at the time being talked about, he wrote an elaborate clavichord piece to illustrate the departure of his brother, Johann Jakob, who had entered the service of Charles XII of Sweden as oboist. This composition is divided into five parts, each bearing an appropriate superscription and ending with an elaborate fugue to illustrate the postillion's horn. I believe this is the only instance of his having written actual programme music. After leaving Arnstadt he filled positions as organist at Mühlhausen, Weimar, Coethen, etc. It was before 1720 that he paid his two visits to Halle in the hope of seeing Händel. At this time he had already written the first part of the " Wohltemperierte Clavier," the violin sonatas, and many other great works. Ten years later, when Händel again came to Germany, Bach was too ill to go to see him personally, but sent his eldest son to invite Händel to come and see him, although without success.

In 1723 he obtained the position of Cantor at the St. Thomas School, in Leipzig, left vacant by the death of Kuhnau; here he remained until his death. In 1749 the

English oculist, Taylor, happened to be in Leipzig.   On
the advice of friends, Bach submitted to an operation on
his eyes, which had always troubled him.   The failure of
this operation rendered him totally blind and the accompanying medical treatment completely broke him down.
On the eighteenth of July, 1750, he suddenly regained his
sight, but it was accompanied by a stroke of paralysis
from which he died ten days later.

So far as his church music is concerned, Bach may
be considered as the Protestant compeer of the Roman
Catholic, Palestrina, with the difference that his music
was based on the tonalities of major and minor and that
his harmonic structure was founded on a scientific basis.
What is mere wandering in Palestrina, with Bach is
moving steadily forward with a well-defined object in
view.   With Bach, music is cast in the definite mould
of tonality, while with Palestrina the vagueness of the
modes lends to his music something of mystery and a
certain supernatural freedom from *human will*, so prominent a characteristic of Bach's compositions.   In considering Bach's music we must forget the technique,
which was merely the outside dress of his compositions.
His style was the one of the period, just as he wore a wig,
and buckles on his shoes.   His music must not be confounded with the contrapuntal style of his utterance, and
although he has never been surpassed as a scientific writer
of counterpoint, it would be unjust to look there for his
chief glory.   As a matter of fact, when his scientific
speech threatened to clash with the musical idea in his
composition, he never hesitated to sacrifice the former to

the latter. Thus Bach may be considered the greatest musical scientist of his time as well as the greatest breaker of mere rules.

Of his sons, Carl Philipp Emanuel is the most celebrated, and did much to prepare the way for Haydn in the development of the sonata. J. S. Bach wrote many sonatas, but none for the clavichord; his sonatas were for the violin and the 'cello alone, a great innovation. The violin sonatas bring into play all the resources of the instrument; indeed it is barely possible to do them justice from the technical standpoint. His "Wohltemperierte Clavier" naturally was a tremendous help to clavichord technique, and even now the " Chromatic Fantaisie " and other works require fine pianists to perform them properly.

In considering the development of music, it must always be remembered that Haydn, Mozart, and their contemporaries knew little or nothing of Bach's works, thus accounting for what otherwise would seem a retrograde movement in art. C. P. E. Bach (born 1714) was much better known than his father; even Mozart said of him, " He is the father, and we are mere children." He was renowned as a harpsichord player, and wrote many sonatas which form the connecting link between the suite and the sonata. He threw aside the polyphonic style of his father and strove to give his music new colour and warmth by means of harmony and modulation. He died in 1788 in Hamburg, where he was conductor of the opera. It should be mentioned that he wrote a method of clavichord playing on which, in later days, Czerny said that Beethoven based his piano teaching.

Up to the period now under consideration, music for the orchestra occupied a very small part in the composer's work. To be sure, J. S. Bach wrote some suites, and separate movements were written in the different dance forms for violins, with sometimes the addition of a few reed instruments, and possibly flutes and small horns or trumpets. It is in the works of C. P. E. Bach, however, that we find the germ of symphonic orchestral writing that was to be developed by Haydn, Mozart, and Beethoven. The so-called "symphonies" by Emanuel Bach are merely rudimentary sonatas written for strings, with flutes, oboes, bassoons, trumpets, etc., and have practically no artistic significance except as showing the inevitable trend of musical thought toward greater power of expression. In Germany (and indeed everywhere else) the Italian element had full sway over opera, and non-Italian musicians were forced into writing for the concert room instead of the stage. Even Beethoven had many disappointments in connection with his one opera "Fidelio," and so strong was the Italian influence, that here in America we are only just now (1897) recovering from the effects of it.

Franz Joseph Haydn was born near Vienna, in 1732, of humble parents, his mother a cook in a count's family, and his father a wheelwright and sexton of the parish church. When a young boy Haydn had a fine voice, on account of which he was admitted as a member of the choir at St. Stephen's Cathedral in Vienna. This entitled him to admission to St. Stephen's School, connected with the cathedral, in which the city paid for the board and lodging as well as the instruction of the singers. When the boys' voices changed or " broke," however, they were turned adrift. On leaving the cathedral, Haydn suffered the direst poverty, engaging himself at one time as valet to the Italian singing teacher, Porpora, in order to secure some lessons.

He gradually managed to make himself known, and was engaged by Count Morzin, a rich nobleman, to organize an orchestra of about eighteen, which the count retained in his service with Haydn as leader. Here he wrote his first symphony (for strings, two oboes and two horns, in three movements) and a number of smaller works. When he was twenty-nine, Count Morzin gave up his establishment and Haydn entered the service of Prince Paul Esterhazy, in Eisenstadt, Hungary, in the same capacity. Here he had an orchestra of sixteen, composed of good musicians, whom he could call up at any hour of the night to play if he wished, and over whom he had complete control. Although the contract by which he was engaged names the most degrading conditions, and places Haydn on a par with all the other servants, the pay, though small (two hundred dollars yearly), was certain and regular. From this time Haydn was free from the hardships of poverty. His salary was soon increased to five hundred dollars, and he made as much more from his compositions. He wrote over one hundred and twenty-five symphonies, sixty-eight trios, seventy-seven quartets, fifty-seven concertos, fifty-seven sonatas, eight oratorios and cantatas, and nineteen operas, besides innumerable smaller things, for instance, between five hundred and six hundred vocal pieces. His operas, of course, are mere trifles compared with our more modern ones.

His friendship for Mozart is well known. As for his relations with Beethoven, it is probable that their disagreement was merely the effect of pride, and perhaps a certain amount of laziness on one side and youthful bumptiousness on the other. Haydn was returning to Vienna *via* Bonn, from England, where he had been welcomed by the wildest enthusiasm, when Beethoven called on him to ask for his opinion as to his talent as a composer. It resulted in Beethoven's going to Vienna. After taking a few lessons of Haydn he went to another teacher and made all manner of contemptuous remarks about Haydn, declaring he had not learned anything from him.

After two highly successful visits to England, in 1792 and 1794, Haydn returned to Vienna and wrote his two celebrated cantatas, " The Creation " and " The Seasons." His last appearance in public was when he attended a performance of " The Creation " in 1808, at the age of seventy-six. He was received with a fanfare of trumpets and cheers from the audience. After the first part he was obliged to leave, and as he was being carried out by his friends, he turned at the door and lifted his hands towards the orchestra, as if in benediction; Beethoven kissed his hand, and everyone paid him homage. He died during the bombardment of Vienna by the French, May 31, 1809.

Haydn's later symphonies have been very cleverly compared with those of Beethoven by the statement that the latter wrote tragedies and great dramas, whereas Haydn wrote comedies and charming farces.   As a matter of fact, Haydn is the bridge between the idealized dance and independent music.   Although Beethoven still retained the form of the dance, he wrote great poems, whereas the music of Haydn always preserves a tinge of the actual dance.   With Haydn, music was still an art consisting of the weaving together of pretty sounds, and although *design*, that is to say, the development of the emotional character of a musical thought, was by no means unknown to him, that development was never permitted to transcend the limits of a certain graceful euphony which was a marked characteristic of his style.   His use of orchestral instruments represents a marked advance on that of C. P. E. Bach, and certainly very materially helped Mozart.

Of Mozart we probably all know something.   Born at Salzburg, in 1756, his was a short life, for he died in 1791. We know of his great precocity; his first compositions were published when he was six years old, at which age he was already playing in concerts with his eleven-year old sister, and was made much of by the titled people before whom he played.   The rest of his life is one continual chronicle of concerts given all over Europe, interrupted at intervals by scarlet fever, smallpox, and other illnesses, until the last one, typhoid fever, caused his death.   During his stay in Italy he wrote many operas in the flowery Italian style which, luckily, have never been revived to tarnish his name.

His first works worthy of mention are the clavier

concertos and several symphonies and quartets, which date
from about 1777. His first important opera is " Idomeneo,
King of Crete," written for the Munich opera. In this he
adopts the principles of Gluck, thus breaking away from
the wretched style of the Italian opera of the period,
although the work itself was written in Italian. His next
opera was in German, " Die Entführung aus dem Serail,"
and was given with great success at Vienna, in 1782. It
was followed by " The Marriage of Figaro," " Don Juan,"
and the " Magic Flute."

The story of his death is well known. A stranger, who
turned out to be the steward of Count Walsegg, came to
him and ordered a requiem, which was played in 1793 as
Walsegg's own composition. Mozart thought the man a
messenger from the other world. He died before he
completed the work. So great was his poverty that it
was difficult to get a priest to attend him, and a physician
who was summoned would come only after the play
he was attending was ended. He had a " third class "
funeral, and as a fierce storm was raging, no one accompanied the body to the grave. His widow gave a concert,
and with the help of the Emperor money enough was raised
to pay the outstanding debts.

It is difficult to give an adequate idea of Mozart's
works. He possessed a certain simple charm of expression
which, in its directness, has an element of pathos lacking
in the comparatively jolly light-heartedness of Haydn.
German opera profited much from his practically adopting
the art principles of Gluck, although it must be confessed
that this change in style may have been simply a phase

of his own individual art development. His later symphonies and operas show us the man at his best. His piano works and early operas show the effect of the "virtuoso "style, with all its empty concessions to technical display and commonplace, ear-catching melody.

XX

DECLAMATION IN MUSIC

THERE is one side of music which I am convinced has never been fully studied, namely, the relation between it and declamation. As we know, music is a language which may delineate actual occurrences by means of onomato-poetic sounds. By the use of more or less suggestive sounds, it may bring before our minds a quasi-visual image of things which we more or less definitely feel.

Now to do all this, there must be rules; or, to put it more broadly, there must be some innate quality that enables this art of sounds to move in sympathy with our feelings. I have no wish to go into detailed analysis of the subject; but a superficial survey of it may clear up certain points with regard to the potency of music that we are too often willing to refer back to the mere pleasing physical sensations of sound.

Some consideration of this subject may enable us to understand the much discussed question of programme music. It may also help us to recognize the astonishing advance we have made in the art; an advance, which, strange to say, consists in successively throwing off all the trammels and conventionalities of what is generally considered artificial, and the striking development of an art which, with all its astounding wealth of exterior means, aims at the expression of elemental sensations.

Music may be divided into four classes, each class marking an advance in receptive power on the part of the listener and poetic subtlety on that of the composer. We may liken the first stage to that of the savage Indians who depict their exploits in war and peace on the rocks, fragments of bone, etc. If the painter has in mind, say, an elephant, he carves it so that its principal characteristics are vastly exaggerated. A god in such delineation is twice the size of the ordinary man, and so it is in descriptive music. For instance, in Beethoven's "Pastoral" symphony, the cuckoo is not a bird which mysteriously hides itself far away in a thicket, the sound of whose voice comes to one like a strange, abrupt call from the darkness of the forest; no, it is unmistakably a cuckoo, reminding one strangely of those equally advanced and extremely cheap art products of Nuremberg, made of pine wood, and furnished with a movable tail.

The next stage is still a question of delineation; but of delineation that leads us into strange countries, and the sounds we hear are but the small door through which we pass. This music *suggests;* by way of example, the opening of the last movement of the " Pastoral " symphony, the march from Tchaïkovsky's "Symphonie Pathétique," the opening of Raff's "Im Walde," and Goldmark's " Sakuntala." Such music hints, and there is a certain potency in its suggestion which makes us see things. These two divisions of music have been termed " programme " or " objective " music.

The other two classes of music have been termed subjective. The first is declamation, pure and simple; the singer may be telling a lie, or his sentiment may be insincere or false; what these sounds stand for, we know from the words, their grade of passion, etc. The last phase of our art is much more subtle, and is not amenable to such accurate analysis. If we may liken music to painting, we may, I think, compare the latter to the first three stages of this new language of music; but it can go no further. For that art must touch its audience through a palpable delineation of something more or less material; whereas music is of the stuff dreams are made of. It is hardly necessary to say, however, that our dreams are often much more poignant than the actual sensations caused by real occurrences would be. And it is because of this strange quality, I think, that dreams and music affect us in much the same manner.

The vital principle of Wagner's art was that he not only made startlingly vivid pictures in his music, but that he made the people in these pictures actually walk out of the frame and directly address the audience. In other words, his orchestra forms a kind of pictorial and psychological background from which his characters detach themselves and actually speak. If they speak falsely, the ever present orchestra, forming as it were a halo, unmercifully tears away the mask, like the mirror in old fairy tales.

In Wagner's operas, however, the intrusion of gross palpable machinery of the stage, as well as that of the actor's art, too often clouds the perfect working of this wonderful art conception. It is just this intrusion of materialism in Wagner's music dramas which constitutes their only weakness.

At this point I wish to insist upon the fact that in music it is always through declamation that the public is addressed most directly; not only that, but declamation is not necessarily tied by any of the fetters of the spoken word; nor is it subservient to any of the laws of articulate speech as we meet with them in language. This being admitted, I have no hesitation in giving my opinion that opera, or rather the music drama, is not the highest or the most perfect form of our art. The music drama as represented by Wagner (and he alone represents it) is the most perfect union of painting, poetry, and music imaginable to our nineteenth-century minds. But as regards representing the highest development of music, I find it too much hampered by the externals of art, necessary materialism in the production of palpable acts, and its enforced subjection to the laws that govern the spoken word.

Music is universal; Wagner's operas, by the inherent necessities of speech, are necessarily and irrevocably Germanic. " Les Maitres Chanteurs," " The Dwarfs of Niebelheim," " Elizabeta," are impossibilities, whereas, for instance, Beethoven's " Eroica " labours under no such disadvantage. " Goodbye, My Dearest Swan," invests part of " Lohengrin " with a certain grotesque colour that no one would ever dream of if there were no necessity for the singer to be tied down to the exigencies of palpable and certainly most materialistic language. The thought in itself is beautiful, but the necessity for the words drags it into the mud.

This certainly shows the difference between the language of music and what is called articulate speech, the purely symbolic and artificial character of the latter, and the direct, unhampered utterance of the former. Music can invariably heighten the poignancy of mere spoken words (which mean nothing in themselves), but words can but rarely, in fact I doubt whether they can ever, heighten the effect of musical declamation. To my mind, listening to Wagner's operas may be likened to watching a circus with three rings. That containing the music should have our closest attention, for it offers the most wonderful sounds ever imagined by any man. At the same time it is impossible for any human being not to have his attention often lured away to the other rings, in one of which Fricke's rams vie with the bird and the dragon; or where the phantom ship seems as firmly fixed as the practical rainbow, which so closely betrays the carpenter. In the other ring you can actually hear the dull jokes of Mimi and the Wanderer, or hear Walther explain that he has passed a comfortable night and slept well.

The music to these remarkable scenes, however, does not deign to stoop so low, but soars in wonderful poetry by itself, thus rejecting a union which, to speak in the jargon of our day, is one of the convincing symptoms of decadence; in other words, it springs from the same impulse as that which has produced the circus with three rings.

Summing up, I wish to state what I consider the four elements of music, namely, music that paints, music that suggests, music that actually speaks, and music that almost defies analysis, and is composed of the other three elements.

When we were considering the early works for harpsichord, I said that music could define certain things with quite reasonable exactitude. Just as in the Egyptian hieroglyphics a wavy line stands for water, so it can in music, with the latitude that it can mean anything in nature that we might consider of the same genre. Thus, the figure in Wagner's "Waldweben" means in that instance waves of air, and we know it by the context. His swaying figure of the "Prelude to Rheingold" is as plainly water as is the same figure used by Mendelssohn in his "Lovely Melusina." Not that Wagner plagiarized, but that he and Mendelssohn recognized the definiteness of musical suggestions; which is more than proved by their adopting the same musical ideas to indicate the same things.

More indefinite is the analysis of our second type or element of music. The successful recognition of this depends not only upon the susceptibility of the hearer to delicate shades of sensation, but also upon the receptivity of the hearer and his power to accept freely and unrestrictedly the mood shadowed forth by the composer. Such music cannot be looked upon objectively. To those who would analyze it in such a manner it must remain an unknown language; its potency depends entirely upon a state of willing subjectivity on the part of the hearer.

The third element, as we know, consists of the spoken word or phrase; in other words, declamation. In this, however, the composer cuts loose entirely from what we call language. It is the medium of expression of emotion of every kind. It is not restricted to the voice or to any instrument, or even to our sharps, flats, and naturals. Through stress of emotion the sharps become sharper, with depression the flats become flatter, thus adding poignancy to the declamation. Being unfettered by words, this emotion has free rein. The last element, as I have said, is extremely difficult to define. It is declamation that suggests and paints at the same time. We find hardly a bar of Wagner's music in which this complex form of music is not present. Thus, the music dramas of Wagner, shorn of the fetters of the actual spoken word, emancipated from the materialism of acting, painting, and furniture, may be considered as the greatest achievement in our art, an art that does not include the spoken word called poetry, or painting, or sculpture, and most decidedly not architecture (form), but the essence of all these. What these aim to do through passive exterior influences, music accomplishes by actual living vibration.

XXI

SUGGESTION IN MUSIC

In speaking of the power of suggestion in music I wish at the outset to make certain reservations. In the first place I speak for myself, and what I have to present is merely an expression of my personal opinion; if in any way these should incite to further investigation or discussion, my object will in part have been attained.

In the second place, in speaking of this art, one is seriously hampered by a certain difficulty in making oneself understood. To hear and to enjoy music seems sufficient to many persons, and an investigation as to the causes of this enjoyment seems to them superfluous. And yet, unless the public comes into closer touch with the tone poet than that objective state which accepts with the ears what is intended for the spirit, which hears the sounds and is deaf to their import, unless the public can separate the physical pleasure of music from its ideal significance, our art, in my opinion, cannot stand on a sound basis.

The first step toward an appreciation of music should be taken in our preparatory schools. Were young people taught to distinguish between tones as between colours, to recognize rhythmic values, and were they taught so to use their voices as to temper the nasal tones of speech, in after life they would be better able to appreciate and cherish an art of which mere pleasure-giving sounds are but a very small part.

Much of the lack of independence of opinion about music arises from want of familiarity with its material. Thus, after dinner, our forefathers were accustomed to sing catches which were entirely destitute of anything approaching music.

Music contains certain elements which affect the nerves of the mind and body, and thus possesses the power of direct appeal to the public, — a power to a great extent denied to the other arts. This sensuous influence over the hearer is often mistaken for the aim and end of all music. With this in mind, one may forgive the rather puzzling remarks so often met with; for instance, those of a certain English bishop that "Music did not affect him either intellectually or emotionally, only pleasurably," adding, "Every art should keep within its own realm; and that of music was concerned with pleasing combinations of sound." In declaring that the sensation of hearing music was pleasant to him, and that to produce that sensation was the entire mission of music, the Bishop placed our art on a level with good things to eat and drink. Many colleges and universities of this land consider music as a kind of *boutonnière*.

This estimate of music is, I believe, unfortunately a very general one, and yet, low as it is, there is a possibility of building on such a foundation. Could such persons be made to recognize the existence of decidedly unpleasant music, it would be the first step toward a proper appreciation of the art and its various phases.

Mere beauty of sound is, in itself, purely sensuous. It is the Chinese conception of music that the texture of a sound is to be valued; the long, trembling tone-tint of a bronze gong, or the high, thin streams of sound from the pipes are enjoyed for their ear-filling qualities. In the *Analects* of Confucius and the writings of Mencius there is much mention of music, and "harmony of sound that shall fill the ears " is insisted upon. The Master said, "When the music maker Che first entered on his office, the finish with the Kwan Ts'eu was magnificent. How it filled the ears!" Père Amiot says, "Music must fill the ears to penetrate the soul." Referring to the playing of some pieces by Couperin on a spinet, he says that Chinese hearers thought these pieces barbarous; the movement was too rapid, and did not allow sufficient time for them to enjoy each tone by itself. Now this is colour without form, or sound without music. For it to become music, it must possess some quality which will remove it from the purely sensuous. To my mind, it is in the power of suggestion that the vital spark of music lies.

Before speaking of this, however, I wish to touch upon two things: first, on what is called the science of music; and secondly, on one of the sensuous elements of music which enters into and encroaches upon all suggestion.

If one were called upon to define what is called the intellectual side of music, he would probably speak of "form," contrapuntal design, and the like. Let us take up the matter of form. If by the word "form" our theorists meant the most poignant expression of poetic thought in music, if they meant by this word the art of arranging musical sounds into the most telling presentation of a musical idea, I should have nothing to say: for if this were admitted instead of the recognized forms of modern theorists for the proper utterance, we should possess a study of the power of musical sounds which might truly justify the title of musical intellectuality. As it is, the word "form" stands for what have been called "stoutly built periods," "subsidiary themes," and the like, a happy combination of which in certain prescribed keys was supposed to constitute good form. Such a device, originally based upon the necessities and fashions of the dance, and changing from time to time, is surely not worthy of the strange worship it has received. A form of so doubtful an identity that the first movement of a certain Beethoven sonata can be dubbed by one authority "sonata-form," and by another "free fantasia," certainly cannot lay claim to serious intellectual value.

Form should be a synonym for *coherence*. No idea, whether great or small, can find utterance without form, but that form will be inherent to the idea, and there will be as many forms as there are adequately expressed ideas. In the musical idea, *per se*, analysis will reveal form.

The term "contrapuntal development" is to most tone poets of the present day a synonym for the device of giving expression to a musically poetic idea. *Per se*, counterpoint is a puerile juggling with themes, which may be likened to high-school mathematics. Certainly the entire web and woof of this "science," as it is called, never sprang from the necessities of poetic musical utterance. The entire pre-Palestrina literature of music is a conclusive

The suggestion conveyed by means of pitch is one of the strongest in music. Vibrations increasing beyond two hundred and fifty trillions a second become luminous. It is a curious coincidence that our highest vibrating musical sounds bring with them a well-defined suggestion of light, and that as the pitch is lowered we get the impression of ever increasing obscurity. To illustrate this, I have but to refer you to the Prelude to "Lohengrin." Had we no inkling as to its meaning, we should still receive the suggestion of glittering shapes in the blue ether.

Let us take the opening of the "Im Walde" symphony by Raff as an example; deep shadow is unmistakably suggested. Herbert Spencer's theory of the influence of emotion on pitch is well known and needs no confirmation. This properly comes under the subject of musical speech, a matter not to be considered here. Suffice it to say that the upward tendency of a musical phrase can suggest exaltation, and that a downward trend may suggest depression, the intensity of which will depend upon the intervals used. As an instance we may quote the "Faust" overture of Wagner, in which the pitch is used emotionally as well as descriptively. If the meaning I have found in this phrase seems to you far-fetched, we have but to give a higher pitch to the motive to render the idea absolutely impossible.

The suggestion offered by movement is very obvious, for music admittedly may be stately, deliberate, hasty, or furious, it may march or dance, it may be grave or flippant.

Last of all I wish to speak of the suggestion conveyed by means of tone-tint, the blending of timbre and pitch. It is essentially a modern element in music, and in our delight in this marvellous and potent aid to expression we have carried it to a point of development at which it threatens to dethrone what has hitherto been our musical speech, melody, in favour of what corresponds to the shadow languages of speech, namely, gesture and facial expression. Just as these shadow languages of speech may distort or even absolutely reverse the meaning of the spoken word, so can tone colour and harmony change the meaning of a musical phrase. This is at once the glory and the danger of our modern music. Overwhelmed by the new-found powers of suggestion in tonal tint and the riot of hitherto undreamed of orchestral combinations, we are forgetting that permanence in music depends upon melodic speech.

In my opinion, it is the line, not the colour, that will last. That harmony is a potent factor in suggestion may be seen from the fact that Cornelius was able to write an entire song pitched upon one tone, the accompaniment being so varied in its harmonies that the listener is deceived into attributing to that one tone many shades of emotion.

In all modern music this element is one of the most important. If we refer again to the "Faust" overture of Wagner, we will perceive that although the melodic trend and the pitch of the phrase carry their suggestion, the roll of the drum which accompanies it throws a sinister veil over the phrase, making it impressive in the extreme.

The seed from which our modern wealth of harmony and tone colour sprang was the perfect major triad. The *raison d'être* and development of this combination of tones belong to the history of music. Suffice it to say, that for some psychological reason this chord (with also its minor form) has still the same significance that it had for the monks of the Middle Ages. It is perfect. Every complete phrase must end with it. The attempts made to emancipate music from the tyranny of this combination of sounds have been in vain, showing that the suggestion of finality and repose contained in it is irrefutable.

Now if we depart from this chord a sensation of unrest is occasioned which can only subside by a progression to another triad or a return to the first. With the development of our modern system of tonality we have come to think tonally; and a chord lying outside of the key in which a musical thought is conceived will carry with it a sense of confusion or mystery that our modern art of harmony and tone colour has made its own. Thus, while any simple low chords accompanying the first notes of Raff's "Im Walde" symphony, given by the horns and violins, would suggest gloom pierced by the gleams of light, the remoteness of the chords to the tonality of C major gives a suggestion of mystery; but as the harmony approaches the triad the mystery dissolves, letting in the gleam of sunlight suggested by the horn.

Goldmark's overture to "Sakuntala" owes its subtle suggestion to much the same cause. Weber made use of it in his "Freischütz," Wagner in his "Tarnhelm" motive, Mendelssohn in his "Midsummer Night's Dream," Tchaïkovsky in the opening of one of his symphonies.

In becoming common property, so to speak, this important element of musical utterance has been dragged through the mud; and modern composers, in their efforts to raise it above the commonplace, have gone to the very edge of what is physically bearable in the use of tone colour and combination. While this is but natural, owing to the appropriation of some of the most poetic and suggestive tone colours for ignoble dance tunes and doggerel, it is to my mind a pity, for it is elevating what should be a means of adding power and intensity to musical speech to the importance of musical speech itself. Possibly Strauss's "Thus Spake Zarathustra" may be considered the apotheosis of this power of suggestion in tonal colour, and in it I believe we can see the tendency I allude to. This work stuns by its glorious magnificence of tonal texture; the suggestion, in the opening measures, of the rising sun is a mighty example of the overwhelming power of tone colour. The upward sweep of the music to the highest regions of light has much of splendour about it; and yet I remember once hearing in London, sung in the street at night, a song that seemed to me to contain a truer germ of music.

For want of a better word I will call it ideal suggestion. It has to do with actual musical speech, and is difficult to define. The possession of it makes a man a poet. If we look for analogy, I may quote from Browning and Shakespeare.

> Dearest, three months ago
> When the mesmerizer, Snow,
> With his hand's first sweep
> Put the earth to sleep.
>
> BROWNING, *A Lovers' Quarrel.*

> Daffodils,
> That come before the swallow dares, and takes
> The winds of March with beauty; Violets dim,
> But sweeter than the lids of Juno's eyes.
>
> SHAKESPEARE, *Winter's Tale.*

For me this defies analysis, and so it is with some things in music, the charm of which cannot be ascribed to physical or mental suggestion, and certainly not to any device of counterpoint or form, in the musical acceptance of the word.

INDEX

A.

Accents, 92.
Adagio, 189.
Æolian mode, 83.
Æschylus, 70, 76.
Alberti bass, 197.
Allemande, 182, 189, 195.
Amati, 138.
Ambros, 205.
Ambrose, 98, 99, 102, 104.
Amiot, 50, 57, 61, 263.
Anapæst, 75.
Andaman Islanders, 3, 5, 6.
Animals, 13.
Arabian, 152, 158.
Architecture, 192, 225.
Arion, 76.
Aristides, 74, 84.
Aristophanes, 91, 92.
Aristotle, 49.
Aristoxenus, 73, 81.
Assyrian, 48.
Auber, 216, 217, 219.

B.

Bach, C. P. E., 191, 199, 200, 247, 248, 251.
Bach, J. S., 136, 185, 186, 187, 191, 231, 239; 241, 244, 247, 248, 265.
Bagpipe, 32, 93.
Ballet, 177.

Bamboo, 52.
Banjo, 29.
Basso continuo, 237.
Bassoon, 139.
Bazin, 217.
Beethoven, 14, 16, 17, 22, 185, 189, 190, 196, 197, 199, 200, 201, 202, 203, 234, 247, 250, 267.
Bell, 7, 8, 46.
Bellini, 210.
Berlioz, 14, 65, 219, 266.
Bizet, 144, 151, 197, 217, 219, 222.
Boieldieu, 216, 217.
Bolero, 182.
Borneo, 3, 5.
Bourrée, 179.
Brahma, 36, 37.
Brahminism, 36, 39.
Brahms, 203, 224.
Brevis, 118, 120.
Browning, 198, 272.
Buddha, 36.
Burmah, 23, 64, 65.
Burney, 194.
Byrd, 184.

C.

Caccini, 177, 209.
Cachucha, 182.
Canon, 205.
Cantata, 188.

COMPOSITIONS BY
EDWARD MAC DOWELL

COMPOSITIONS BY
EDWARD MACDOWELL

PIANOFORTE SOLOS

Op. 10. **First Modern Suite.** Praeludium — Presto — Andantino and Allegretto — Intermezzo — Rhapsody — Fugue **$2.00**
Breitkopf & Härtel.

Intermezzo, separately 40
Praeludium, separately 50

Op. 13. **Prelude and Fugue.** New revised edition by the composer 50
Arthur P. Schmidt.

Op. 14. **Second Modern Suite.** Praeludium — Fugato — Rhapsody — Scherzino — March — Fantastic Dance 2.00
Breitkopf & Härtel.

Op. 15. **First Concerto in A-Minor.** Pianoforte Solo with a Second Piano in Score. 3.00
Breitkopf & Härtel.

Orchestra Score and Parts in Manuscript.

Op. 16. **Serenata.** New revised edition by the composer 50
Arthur P. Schmidt.

Op. 17. **Two Fantastic Pieces** for Concert use.
No. 1.   A Legend 50
J. Hainauer.

No. 2.   Witches' Dance.   New fingered edition (4 c) 75
Arthur P. Schmidt.

Op. 18. **Two Compositions:**
No. 1.   Barcarolle in F.   New revised edition by the composer 40
Arthur P. Schmidt.

No. 2.   Humoreske in A. 50
J. Hainauer.

Op. 19. **Forest Idyls.** Forest Stillness — Play of the Nymphs — Revery — Dance of the Dryads. Complete 1.50
C. F. Kahnt.

No. 3.   Revery.   New revised edition by the composer 30
Arthur P. Schmidt.

No. 4.   Dance of the Dryads.   New revised edition by the composer (4 b) 60
Arthur P. Schmidt.

Op. 23. **Second Concerto in D-Minor.** Pianoforte Solo
with a Second Piano in Score $3.00
Breitkopf & Härtel.
Orchestra Score in Manuscript.
Parts (printed) 9.20

Op. 24. **Four Compositions:**
No. 1. Humoresque 65
No. 2. March 75
No. 3. Cradle Song 65
J. Hainauer.
No. 4. Czardas [Friska]. New revised edition
by the composer 50
Arthur P. Schmidt.

Op. 28. **Six Idyls after Goethe:** (Edition Schmidt No. 57)
. . . . net 1.00

No. 1. In the Woods.	No. 4. Silver Clouds.
No. 2. Siesta.	No. 5. Flute Idyl.
No. 3. To the Moonlight.	No. 6. The Blue Bell.

Augmented and Revised Edition. Arthur P. Schmidt.

Op. 31. **Six Poems after Heine:** (Edition Schmidt No. 58)
. . . . net 1.00

No. 1. From a Fisher-	No. 4. The Post Waggon.
man's Hut.	No. 5. The Shepherd
No. 2. Scotch Poem.	Boy.
No. 3. From Long Ago.	No. 6. Monologue.

Augmented and Revised Edition. Arthur P. Schmidt.

Op. 32. **Four Little Poems.** Complete 1.00
No. 1. The Eagle 30
No. 2. The Brook 30
No. 3. Moonshine 30
No. 4. Winter 30
Breitkopf & Härtel.

Op. 36. **Etude de Concert,** in F-sharp 75
Arthur P. Schmidt.

Op. 37. **Les Orientales,** Three Pieces for Piano:
No. 1. Clair de lune 30
No. 2. Dans le hamac 40
No. 3. Danse Andalouse 40
Arthur P. Schmidt.

Op. 38. **Marionettes.** Eight Little Pieces (Edition
Schmidt No. 59) . . . . net 1.00
Prologue — Soubrette — Lover — Witch —
Clown — Villain — Sweetheart — Epilogue.
Augmented and Revised Edition. Arthur P. Schmidt.

Op. 39. **Twelve Studies.**
(Schmidt's Educational Series No. 4)   net **$1.50**
Hunting Song — Alla Tarantella — Romance
— Arabeske — In the Forest — Dance of the
Gnomes — Idyl — Shadow Dance — Inter-
mezzo — Melody — Scherzino — Hungarian.
Also published separately.
Arthur P. Schmidt.

Op. 45. **Sonata Tragica** 2.00
Breitkopf & Härtel.

Op. 46. **Twelve Virtuoso Studies.** Complete 3.00
No. 1. Novelette 30
No. 2. Moto Perpetuo 30
No. 3. Wild Chase 30
No. 4. Improvisation 30
No. 5. Elfin Dance 45
No. 6. Valse triste 30
No. 7. Burleske 30
No. 8. Bluette 30
No. 9. Träumerei 30
No. 10. March Wind 30
No. 11. Impromptu 30
No. 12. Polonaise 45
Breitkopf & Härtel.

Op. 50. **Second Sonata** (Eroica) 2.50
Breitkopf & Härtel.

Op. 51. **Woodland Sketches.**
(Edition Schmidt No. 47) . . . . . . net   1.25
To a Wild-Rose — Will o' the Wisp — At an
Old Trysting Place — In Autumn — From an
Indian Lodge — To a Waterlily — From Uncle
Remus — A Deserted Farm By a Meadow
Brook — Told at Sunset.
Arthur P. Schmidt.

Op. 55. **Sea Pieces:** (Edition Schmidt No. 48) . . net   1.25
To the Sea — From a Wandering Iceberg —
A. D. 1620 — Starlight — Song — From the
Depths — Nautilus — In Mid-Ocean.
Arthur P. Schmidt.

Op. 57. **Third Sonata** (Norse) 2.00
Arthur P. Schmidt.

Op. 59. **Fourth Sonata** (Keltic) 2.00
Arthur P. Schmidt.

Op. 61. **Fireside Tales** (Edition Schmidt No. 67) . . net   1.25
An Old Love Story — Of Br'er Rabbit — From
a German Forest — Of Salamanders — A
Haunted House — By Smouldering Embers.
Arthur P. Schmidt.

Op. 62. New England Idyls. (Edition Schmidt No. 75)
. . . . net $1.25

An Old Garden.	Indian Idyl.
Mid-Summer.	To an Old White Pine.
Mid-Winter.	From Puritan Days.
With Sweet Lavender	From a Log Cabin.
In Deep Woods.	The Joy of Autumn.

Arthur P. Schmidt.

In Passing Moods. Album of Selected Pianoforte Pieces
. . . . net 1.25

Prologue — Alla Tarantella — An Old Love Story — Melody — The Song of the Shepherdess — A Deserted Farm — To the Sea — Danse Andalouse — From a Log Cabin — Epilogue.

Arthur P. Schmidt.

Compositions published under the Pseudonym of Edgar Thorn

Amourette		.50
Forgotten Fairy Tales	net	.75
Sung Outside the Prince's Door — From Dwarf Land — Beauty in the Rose-garden — Of a Tailor and a Bear.		
Six Fancies	net	.75
A Tin Soldier's Love — Summer Song — To a Humming Bird — Across the Fields — Bluette — An Elfin Round.		
In Lilting Rhythm (2 Pianoforte Pieces)	net	.75

Arthur P. Schmidt.

Compositions revised and edited for the Pianoforte by Edward MacDowell

GLINKA–BALAKIREW, The Lark (4 c)	.60
HUBER, Intermezzo (3 b)	.30
LAVIGNAC, Aria from Händel's "Susanna" (3 c)	.40
LISZT, Eclogue (4 b)	.40
MOSZKOWSKI, Air de Ballet (4 a)	.75
PIERNÉ, Cradle Song (3 a)	.50
PIERNÉ, Allegro Scherzando (5 a)	.75
REINHOLD, Impromptu (5 a)	.75
STCHERBATCHEFF, Orientale (4 b)	.40
TEN BRINK, Gavotte in E minor (3 c)	.60
VAN WESTERHOUT, Momento Capriccioso (4 c)	.50
VAN WESTERHOUT, Gavotte in A (3 c)	.60
MOSZKOWSKI, Etincelles (4 b)	.75
RIMSKY–KORSAKOW, Romance in A flat (3 b)	.30
MARTUCCI, Improviso (4 a)	.60
GEISLER, Episode (4 a)	.40
LISZT, Impromptu (6 a)	.50

GEISLER, Pastorale (4 a) . . . . **$** .30
ALKAN–MACDOWELL, Perpetual Motion (6 a) 1.00
LACOMBE, Etude (4 a). 50
DUBOIS, Sketch (4 b) 30
CUI, Cradle Song (3 a) 30
GEISLER, The Princess Ilse (4 a) 40
PIERNÉ, Improvisata (3 b) 50
COUPERIN, F. Le Bavolet Flottant [The Waving Scarf]
    (4 a) 40
COUPERIN, F. L'Ausonienne. Contra Dance (4 c). . . .50
GRAUN, C. H. Jig (4 c) 65
GRAZIOLI, G. B. Tempo di Minuetto (4 c) 60
LOEILLY, J. B. Jig (3 b) 40
MATTHESON, Joh. Jig (3 c) 40
LOEILLY, J. B. Sarabande (5 a) 30
RAMEAU, J. P. Sarabande (4 b) 40
RAMEAU, J. P. The Three Hands (3 c) 50
COUPERIN, F. La Bersan (4 c) 40
BACH, J. S. Six Little Pieces (3 a-3 c). . . . . . net .75
    Courante — Minuet — Jig — Minuet — March —
    Minuet.
                                          Arthur P. Schmidt.

PIANOFORTE DUETS

Op. 20. **Three Poems.**
            Night at Sea. A Tale of the Knights, Ballad 1.50
                                          J. Hainauer.

Op. 21. **Moon Pictures after H. C. Andersen.**
            The Hindoo Maiden — Stork's Story — In
            Tyrol — The Swan — Visit of the Bear . . . 1.90
                                          J. Hainauer.

Op. 22. **Hamlet and Ophelia.** Arranged 2.00
                                          J. Hainauer.

Op. 25. **Lancelot and Elaine.** Arranged 2.00
                                          J. Hainauer.

Op. 29. **Lamia.** Third Symphonic Poem 2.00
                                      Arthur P. Schmidt.

Op. 30. **The Saracens and Lovely Alda.** Arranged . . 1.50
                                      Breitkopf & Härtel.

Op. 42. **1st Suite,** arranged by the composer. 2.50
                                      Arthur P. Schmidt.

VIOLIN AND PIANO

Op. 51, No. 1. To a Wild Rose. Transcription by Arthur
            Hartmann. Original Edition. Simplified
            Edition . . . . each   .50
Op. 37, No. 1. Clair de lune. Transcription by Arthur
            Hartmann. 50
Op. 62, No. 1. With Sweet Lavender. 50
                                      Arthur P. Schmidt.

VIOLONCELLO AND PIANO

Op. 35. Romance for Violoncello with Orchestra Accomp.
Score. $1.00. Parts $1.15.
The same with Piano 90
J. Hainauer.

Op. 51. **Woodland Sketches.** Arr. by Prof. Julius
Klengel.
To a Wild Rose 50
At an Old Trysting Place 50
To a Waterlily 50
A Deserted Farm 50
Told at Sunset 60
Arthur P. Schmidt.

TRANSCRIPTIONS FOR THE ORGAN

First Series 1.00
Idylle (Starlight, Op. 55, No. 4).
Maestoso (A. D. MDCXX, Op. 55, No. 3).
Pastorale (To a Wild Rose, Op. 51, No. 1).
Romance (At an Old Trysting Place).
Legend (A Deserted Farm, Op. 51, No. 8).
Reverie (With Sweet Lavender).

Second Series 1.00
Nautilus (Op. 55, No. 7).
Andantino (Romance, Op. 39, No. 3).
Sea Song (Op. 55, No. 5).
Meditation (By Smouldering Embers, Op. 61,
No. 6).
Melodie (To a Waterlily, Op. 51, No. 6).
In Nomine Domini (Op. 62, No. 8).
Arthur P. Schmidt.

ORCHESTRA

Op. 22. **Hamlet and Ophelia.** Two Poems for Full Orchestra. Score n. $3.00. Parts $6.00
J. Hainauer.

Op. 25. **Lancelot and Elaine.** 2nd Symphonic Poem
for Full Orchestra
Score n. $4.00. Parts $5.50
J. Hainauer.

Op. 29. **Lamia.** Third Symphonic Poem for Full Or-
chestra.
Score n. $3.00. Parts n. $6.00.
Arthur P. Schmidt.

Op. 30. **The Saracens and Lovely Alda.** Two fragments
from the Song of Roland for Full Orchestra.
Score $2.00. Parts $4.00.
Breitkopf & Härtel.

Op. 42. **First Suite for Full Orchestra.**
Score $4.00.   Parts $12.00.

Arthur P. Schmidt.

Op. 48. **Second (Indian) Suite for Full Orchestra.**
Score $7.50.   Parts $10.40.

Breitkopf & Härtel.

SONGS

Op. 9. **Two Old Songs** . . . . $ .50
No. 1.   Deserted.   No. 2.   Slumber Song.
Arthur P. Schmidt.

Op. 11 and Op. 12. **An Album of Five Songs.** English
and German words 1.00
My Love and I — You love me not — In the
Skies. — Night Song — Bands of Roses.
C. F. Kahnt.

Op. 26. **From an Old Garden, Six Songs** . . . . . n.   .75
The Pansy — The Myrtle — The Clover —
The Yellow Daisy — The Blue Bell — The
Mignonette.
G. Schirmer.

Op. 33. **Three Songs for Soprano or Tenor.** German
and English words 75
No. 1.   Prayer 25
J. Hainauer.
No. 2.   Cradle Hymn.   New revised edition by
the composer 30
Arthur P. Schmidt.
No. 3.   Idyl.   New revised edition by the com-
poser 40
Arthur P. Schmidt.

Op. 34. **Two Songs with Piano Accompaniment.**
No. 1.   Menie.   D min. (d-f) 30
No. 2.   My Jean.   A (e-e) 40
Arthur P. Schmidt.

Op. 40. **Six Love Songs with Piano Accompaniment**
(Edition Schmidt No. 19) . . . . net   .75
(Sweet Blue-eyed Maid — Sweetheart tell me
— Thy beaming eyes — For sweet love's sake
— O Lovely Rose — I ask but this.)
Arthur P. Schmidt.
Thy Beaming Eyes.   Separately F (c-f)
Eb (bb-cb) 30
Arthur P. Schmidt.

Op. 47. **Eight Songs with Piano Accompaniment** 1.00
No. 1.   The Robin Sings in the Apple Tree.
No. 2.   Midsummer Lullaby.   No. 3.   Folk
Song.   No. 4.   Confidence.   No. 5.   The
West Wind Croons in the Cedar Trees.   No.
6.   In the Woods.   No. 7.   The Sea.   No. 8.
Through the Meadow.
Breitkopf & Härtel.

Op. 56. **Four Songs, High or Low Voice**
(Edition Schmidt 49 a b) . . . . . . net $ .75
(Long ago, Sweetheart mine — The Swan bent
low to the Lily — A Maid sings light and a
Maid sings low — As the gloaming Shadows
creep).

Arthur P. Schmidt.

A Maid sings light and·a Maid sings low.
F (d-g). D (b-e) separately 40

Arthur P. Schmidt.

Op. 58. **Three Songs** (Edition Schmidt No. 50) . . net .75
(Constancy — Sunrise — Merry Maiden Spring.)

Arthur P. Schmidt.

Op. 60. **Three Songs** (Edition Schmidt No. 65) . . net .75
(Tyrant Love — Fair Springtide — To the
Golden Rod.)

PART SONGS

Mixed Voices

Op. 43. **Two Northern Songs:**
No. 1. Slumber Song 10
No. 2. The Brook 10

Op. 44. **Barcarolle.** Four Hand Piano Accompaniment. .75
The same. Voice Parts only 25

Arthur P. Schmidt.

Women's Voices

Summer Wind 10
Two College Songs: { Alma Mater.
{ At Parting.   each   .10

Arthur P. Schmidt.

Men's Voices

Op. 27. **Three Songs.** German and English words.
No. 1. In the Starry Sky Above Us 12
No. 2. Springtime 10
No. 3. The Fisherboy 12

Op. 41. **Two Songs:**
No. 1. Cradle Song 10
No. 2. Dance of the Gnomes 12

Op. 52. **Three Choruses:**
No. 1. Hush, Hush! 10
No. 2. From the Sea 10
No. 3. The Crusaders. English or German text. .15

Op. 53. **Two Choruses:**
No. 1. Bonnie Ann 10
No. 2. The Collier Lassie 12